WOMEN'S EMPOWERMENT IN INDIA

About the Authors

Sarojini Nayak (M.A). is a journalist by choice and has been a student of two diverse subjects—English Literature and Management. It was the love for writing that prevailed. After a short stint in teaching, she took up journalism as a full-time occupation. Women and development is a recurring theme in her articles and columns. Her association with several organisations working for the development of women provides her an insight into the present problems and trends in the movement for empowerment. Other areas of interest include children, education and culture.

Jeevan Nair, who holds a Ph.D. in English from Delhi University, has been a journalist for nearly four decades and worked in one of the leading English newspapers of the country. He now advises several magazines in regard to their editorial content. He has 20 books to his credit.

WOMEN'S EMPOWERMENT IN INDIA

SAROJINI NAYAK
JEEVAN NAIR

Pointer Publishers
Jaipur 302 003 (Raj.) India

Distributed by
Prem C. Bakliwal for
Aavishkar Publishers, Distributors
807, Vyas Building, Chaura Rasta
Jaipur 302 003 (Raj.) India
Phone : 0141-2578159
e-mail : aavishkarbooks@hotmail.com

2017

ISBN 81-7132-410-X

Published by
Mrs. Shashi Jain for
Pointer Publishers
807, Vyas Building, Chaura Rasta
Jaipur 302 003 (Raj.) India
Phones : 0141-2578159, 2708286
e-mail : pointerpub@hotmail.com
Visit us at : www.pointerpublishers.com

Price : ₹ 1350.00

Printed at
Sheetal Printers
Jaipur (Raj.)

PREFACE

A few years ago, a major controversy arose when the Shankaracharya of Puri prevented a lady from reciting Vedic verses at a public function. The Shankaracharya's stand that religious scriptures barred women from reading the Vedas was vehemently opposed by many women who perceived this discrimination as an affront on women's rights. Interestingly, the occasion where this controversy erupted was the centenary celebrations of Saradeshwari Ashram in Kolkata. This ashram was founded by a disciple of Ramakrishna Paramhansa, a saint who had accorded women an elevated status.

The greatness of women has been acknowledged in the Vedas. Long ago, our ancient law-giver, Manu, who is often attacked for his anti-feminist disposition, descending from the high level of the law, accorded a high position to women: "where women are worshipped, there the gods live, and where they are dishonoured, everything fails" (Manu, 3/56). He even advised as to what the names of women should be. He said: "Let the names of women be good to pronounce—sweet, simple, pleasant and appropriate. Let them terminate in long vowels and resemble words of benediction." Today when society has reached a stage where we have women priests, isn't it paradoxical to prevent them from chanting hymns?

This book is an attempt to trace the journey of the status of the Indian woman in society from the Vedic period to the 21st century. Twenty five years after the observation of the International Women's Year in 1975, another thrust on women's development came in the form of declaring the year 2001 as Women's Empowerment Year. In between, there was the United Nations Decade for Women and the Year of the Girl Child. This may lead us to wonder if we have to wait for a quarter century before we see a perceptible change in the status of women.

Moreover, during the last 30 years, we have witnessed the emergence of hundreds of women's organisations across the country with one common goal of empowerment. The ways and methods may be different, such as enabling women to be financially independent, developing a consciousness among them to fight for their rights, to demand better health care, be educated and demolish the walls of inequality that segregates them as weak and inferior. The outcome of such collective endeavour has been amazing. Working in groups they have not only managed to secure a number of rights, but have also improved the quality of life for themselves as well as their families.

Unfortunately, most of the activities of these women's organisations have remained confined to the urban middle class. Thus a vast majority of the women in the rural areas and those belonging to the poor classes in the urban areas are completely deprived of the benefit of their activities. This indicates a lack of consciousness of the actual problems of Indian women.

While examining the status of Indian women, one is perplexed by the contrasts—examples of highly educated, independent and empowered women co-exist with their illiterate, voiceless and exploited sisters. Even the so-called modern and broad-minded families have a different set of rules for boys and girls. And, many atrocities and discrimination are still perpetuated in the name of religion and social norms.

Despite women being bracketed as the weaker sex, past experiences and recent studies indicate that women are stronger, have more capability for endurance and even live longer. Hence, there is no reason not to be optimistic about the future of the Indian woman. An oft-repeated inequality pointed out in political circles is that the country has not had a woman as President or even occupied the chair of Vice-President. But the search for the 12th President of India witnessed a woman contesting for this high office. Whatever political reasons may be attributed to this development, or the fact that she lost the election, will not cease to deter women from trying again.

Women in other countries have envied the status of counterparts in India. We have had a woman prime minister and a number of women members of Parliament. The number of women ministers that this country has had is probably the highest in the world; no other democracy has had such a large number of them. However, it would not be fair to be content with the presentation of the bright side of the picture. Evidently the legal system safeguarding the interests of women is hardly sufficient without the support of an equally favourable system of values and behaviour based on the socio-religio-historical traditions. The concept of a social revolution must encompass the emancipation of women from the drudgery of existence in rural areas as also in urban slums.

What sets apart Indian women is that they draw their strength from tradition and cultural values of our great civilisation. In their quest for development, they have not forgotten their familiar duties and responsibilities. Neither have they discarded the essence of womanhood. The long years of suffering and discrimination have not cowed down their indomitable spirit; rather, it has strengthened their resolve to relentlessly pursue and achieve their rightful place and be masters of their own destiny.

Over the years, there has been a shift in India in the perspective on women, from treating them as welfare targets to recognising them as a critical group in the national development process. Recognising that women need to be empowered if they are to play their expected role in national advancement, a number of policies and programmes have been initiated to equip them to reach the desired goal.

While lauding the emergence of a national machinery for the overall well-being of women, it has to be conceded that women remain the poorest of the poor. The reconstruction of the economy in the past decade has marginalised them within the work force. In the new economic order, women who have lower skills will either get low-paid peripheral jobs or be declared surplus labour. Almost 90 per cent of women in employment are marginal workers and thus outside the purview of progressive labour laws. In some areas, women have made small gains, but the improvement in their financial status is nothing spectacular.

Periodically there is talk of persuading the private sector, especially those enterprises that seek government support, to ensure a minimum percentage of women among their workers. One wonders if the idea has been put into practice. And what sort of positions women, those who do manage to enter the organised sector, hold? About 57 per cent of them are in community, social and personal services, and 16 per cent in transport, storage, etc. It is not that employable women are not available, but they fail to secure jobs. The number of unemployed women workers is reported to have gone up in recent years.

The Government has a number of employment and income generating schemes aimed at providing additional work to the under-employed, to help marginal and poor farmers, loan schemes for women, etc. But these bring only small benefits to a limited number and have not changed the poverty profile of women. In rural areas, 30 to 35 per cent of households are headed by women—deserted and abandoned wives and widows. They are the sole breadwinners with responsibility to bring up the children. Their hopeless financial situation coupled with intra-family prejudices make their chances of rising above the poverty line extremely slender.

With improved agricultural practices, government price support systems, subsidies, etc., the benefits accruing through farming operations have brought affluence to cultivators, but women, a majority of whom are landless labourers, have not benefited. In fact, they continue to be paid wages that are lower than that of men.

There is unending talk of changing social attitudes towards women. Reports like that of the Committee on Status of Women in India (CSWI), the Bhor Committee report on health and the Durgabai Deshmukh Committee on women's education will remain relevant for many decades to come. They had stressed the need for the eradication of polygamy and changes in Muslim law to put all women on an equal footing before the law. That would have been the first step towards social justice and equality for all women.

Yet another vital recommendation was the setting up of family courts to provide quick justice to women in family, especially, marital, disputes. Some States set up such courts after a lapse of 10 to 15 years, but the implementation of the measure remains half-hearted and thus has not fully served its purpose.

The two major events of the past two decades concerning women have been the setting up of the National Commission for Women in India (NCWI) and the constitutional amendments reserving 30 per cent of seats for women in all elected local bodies. With this reservation thousands of women have been put into positions of leadership and decision-making and many of them are chairpersons at village, block and district levels taking vital decisions affecting millions of people.

Many years ago, the CSWI had recommended the establishment of statutory autonomous panchayats with resources to put through programmes for women and children. This was to be a transitional measure; a training opportunity enabling women to overcome inhibitions and prejudices before entering panchayats and zila parishads. This was not acted upon. The short-term training given to them has not proved adequate for the role they have been called upon to play.

A few noteworthy attempts in the empowerment of women have been made by voluntary organisations, not necessarily the high profile all-India types but little groups fighting for issues concerning their community. Examples of SEWA, which began as a modest attempt in Ahmedabad, Chipko in Chamoli and the anti-arrack movement in Nellore may be cited in this context. But there is a lot more to be done.

We are grievously conscious of the fact that this book presents only a vague survey of the women in India, especially in view of the fact that their status has changed greatly during the post-Independence period, which is in conformity with the radical change in the status of women throughout the world since World War II. However, we have tried to present as comprehensive an image as possible of the position of the Indian woman as the diversities and inequalities prevailing in our society for millennia of years render the assigning of any precise role to the women well-nigh impossible.

We present this modest attempt with the firm faith in a bright future by means of a progressively increasing liberation of women replacing the traditional role of an ungrudging victim of exploitation by a new dynamic role of fully liberated partners in the reconstruction of society and the development of culture.

Bhubaneshwar

Sarojini Nayak
Jeevan Nair

CONTENTS

Section IV
THE NEW MILLENNIUM: STARK CONTRASTS

Section V
EMPOWERMENT AT WORK

ABBREVIATIONS

ANM	Auxiliary Nurse-Midwife
BDO	Block Development Officer
CILAS	Committee for the Implementation of Legal Aid Schemes
CSIR	Council of Scientific and Industrial Research
CSO	Central Statistical Organisation
CSWB	Central Social Welfare Board
CSWI	Committee on Status of Women in India
DGSS	Dashoti Gram Swaraj Sangh
DST	Department of Science and Technology
DWCRA	Development of Women and Children in Rural Areas
EIWIG	Economists Interested in Women's Issue Groups
FLAW	Functional Literacy for Adult Women
ICCSR	Indian Council of Social Science Research
ICDS	Integrated Child Development Services
ILO	International Labour Organisation
IRDP	Integrated Rural Development Programme
KVIC	Khadi and Village Industries Commission
LDC	Less Developed Countries

MCH	Maternity and Child Health
MEGS	Maharashtra Employment Guarantee Scheme
MNP	Minimum Needs Programme
MPR	Male Participation Rate
NAEP	National Adult Education Programme
NCAER	National Council of Applied Economic Research
NCERT	National Council of Education Research and Training
NCLA	National Committee of Legal Aid
NDDB	National Dairy Development Board
NFE	Non-Formal Education
NGO	Non-Governmental Organisation
NLM	National Literacy Mission
NPA	National Plan of Action
NRDA	National Research Development Agency
NREP	National Rural Employment Programme
NSS	National Sample Survey
PADI	People's Action for Development, India
PHC	Primary Health Centre
RTDCT	Rural Technology Demonstration-cum-Training
SEWA	Self-Employed Women's Association
SFDA	Small Farmers Development Agency
SIDA	Swedish International Development Agency
TPIC	Technology Policy Implementation Cell
TRYSEM	Training of Rural Youth for Self-Employment
UGC	University Grants Commission
WPR	Work Participation Rate

1

INTRODUCTION

THERE has been a tremendous change in the status of the Indian woman during the last century, especially after India gained independence. Rapid industrialisation and urbanisation, and the increasing number of Indian women going in for higher education and professional courses has led to far reaching changes in the criteria of values and standard of behaviour. At the same time, however, we have not altogether lost the deep feeling of respect for traditions involving Indian women, as these stretch into antiquity and are too ingrained in the Indian psyche to disappear altogether.

The achievements of the Indian women from pre-*Vedic* times to the present indicate that they have been equal partners with men in all walks of life. Their involvement in the struggle for independence especially highlighted their contribution to the national effort and showed that they are endowed with certain unique qualities which has led to their participation in different fields of social activity at the highest leadership and decision-making levels.

Indian civilisation has given woman a place in society where she can make her best contribution in conformity with her potential and ability without losing her fundamental feminity. Analysis of the various institutions and practices in a society reveals that even obstacles to the development of a particular section of society may prove to be a blessing in disguise. Thus, girls brought up in an atmosphere which gives preference to male offspring were indirectly made more conscious of their responsibilities, ranging from looking after themselves as well as others and managing the household. Paradoxically, preferential treatment of the male child in Indian society resulted in making the female child a stronger personality capable of facing its destiny as a wife and a mother. On the other hand, the male child could not develop corresponding emotional strength and remained dependent on women—first the mother, then sisters and, later, wives.

It has to be said that some ancient traditions pertaining to women in society were sought to be forcefully justified instead of simply presenting them as facts. Thus, where child marriage was concerned, it came to be argued that this practice helped a girl know whom she had to spend her life with before any sexual consciousness awakened in her. Similarly, the economic dependence of women on men from childhood till death was justified on the ground that she would make herself ridiculous if she claimed identity of temperament and functions with men. According to H. C Chakladar:

> "Evidently Indian society presents an ethnic museum containing a vast range of marital mores. Almost all forms of marriage known in the world had their vogue in India at different periods of history."

Many of the age old practices such as *sati,* lifelong widowhood, child marriage, caste endogamy, etc., continued even in the last century, although their occurrence has largely diminished. These unfortunate practices were presented as if deriving sanction from the *Dharma Shastras* and enlightened sections saw the need to establish that these were traditions which had been deformed in the course of time and that, in their present form, they could not claim any sanction from the *Dharma Shastras.* To this end, a reform movement was started in 1818 by the Ramakrishna Mission with the publication of a small tract against the practice of *sati*, explaining that, according to the *Dharma Shastras, sati* was not the best way for the salvation of women. Another social reformer, Ishwar Chandra Vidyasagar, ransacked Smriti literature in order to make out a case for widow remarriage.

In the 1870s, Swami Dayananda, the founder of the Arya Samaj, brought out a revolutionary book *Satyartha-Prakash* containing references from the *Dharma Shastras* in support of widow remarriage as also the Shudras' right to Vedic education and the rejection of caste based on birth.

During certain periods of Indian history, there have been attempts to overshadow the position of Indian women, but with the dawn of the 20th century, and especially with the involvement of women in the Indian struggle for independence under the leadership of Mahatma Gandhi, most of the disabilities attributed to women were removed in a single sweep by the political and legal provisions of the Constitution of India.

Progressively increasing education among women preparing them for all types of jobs and positions, coupled with industrialisation and urbanisation which resulted in the disintegration of the traditional joint family and the abolition of the distinction between men's and women's work, accelerated the liberation of women. Of course, this strange, new status of women was not accepted overnight or all of a sudden. As Ram Mohun Roy commented: "Indian women have all rights, except the right to assert them."

Today, however, the position of Indian women is not inferior to her sisters anywhere in the world. India has had a woman Prime Minister and a number of women Ministers and Members of Parliament—perhaps more than any other democracy in the world. However, in all fairness, it has to be said that much still needs to be done. The present legal system safeguarding the interests of women is hardly adequate without the support of an equally favourable system of values and behaviour based on socio-religio-historical traditions. The concept of a social revolution still has to encompass the emancipation of women from the drudgery of existence in rural areas and urban slums.

The subject demands dispassionate and detailed treatment given the great social, economic and political, religious and cultural diversity of India. Almost every State has a distinct cultural tradition. India has 15 major languages and over 400 dialects and among its people are followers of almost all the major religions of the world—Hinduism, Islam, Christianity, Jainism, Buddhism and Sikhism. The economic division of society mainly in two classes, namely, the disproportionately rich and the unjustifiably poor with a relatively very limited middle class manifests itself not only in the pattern of living but in moral behaviour as well.

In the villages, where women work in the fields along with men, the women are comparatively independent and outspoken as they contribute almost equally in the earnings of the family. Against this, women in small towns have less economic opportunity and, hence, are suppressed, inhibited, self-effacing, non-assertive personalities and their behaviour and values are virtually determined by their husbands or mothers-in law. In the big cities, the women of the poor classes behave identically with their counterparts in the villages or small towns. However, middle class women and those belonging to the upper classes have much leisure and enough opportunities of education and enjoy more freedom either due to their economic stability or on account of their earning potential. The fourth category, quite unique from the other three, comprises the tribal and hill women, who have remained secluded in the mountains and tribal areas and, thus, evolved a different standard of behaviour towards sex and children.

In regard to the position of women in Indian society at large, R. C. Dutt has remarked that no nation or community has held their women in higher esteem than the Hindus. Perhaps no other literature has presented a more admirable type of character in women than that of Sita. It is a great pity that the Hindus have been misjudged and wronged by writers who, without acquainting themselves with ancient Indian literature and other sources of information, based their opinion on the position of women in the East on certain Turkish and Arab customs.

In this connection, J. J. Meyer has stated that no literature could claim more enchanting songs of a faithful wife's love for her husband than those of Damayanti and Savitri. He added further that Indian literature testifies to a deep ethical spirit and wholesomeness towards women in contrast to the often empty frivolity—the nauseating filthiness and vulgarity—that marks most of the literature of the Middle Ages, Old and Modern French and Italian literature and even many highly praised later Western writings.

Historically speaking, the status of women in India in the pre-Vedic and Vedic periods was equal to that of men in religious and social duties. But in the later period, a steady deterioration took place when persons like Manu, the great Hindu lawgiver, made the following observation:

> It is the nature of woman to seduce man in this world, and hence the wise are never unguarded in their company of females.

In the course of time, a formidable list of vices came to be attributed to women who were later debarred from the performance of sacramental rites and even the study of the sacred texts. Thus, woman was deprived of her social and educational rights and her role came to be restricted to the domestic sphere which ultimately led to her economic slavery to man. However, there finally emerged an ideal of Indian womanhood which, instead of debasing the woman, exalted her to an impassable pedestal: the chaste and puritanical image of the self-effacing Sita and Savitri and innumerable similar characters introduced in the two great Hindu epics, namely, the *Ramayana* and the *Mahabharata*. The virtues attributed to Sita and Savitri elicited reverential awe from old women and provided role models for instruction to the young.

This state of affairs provided men with the criteria expected of a woman, which were mostly favourable to the men themselves. Thus, a woman came to be expected to be faithful, submissive, unquestioning, completely in accord with her husband's interests and authority in keeping with the ideal characters of Sita and Savitri.

Sita stood for the comparatively negative virtues of passivity and fortitude. When, despite her innocence, her husband, Ram, forsook her in the interest of public confidence she, as the perfect wife, went through the ordeal of fire to prove that she had remained unsullied by Ravana's temptations. Another step further, she left home without a murmur and without any hesitation when her lord, Ram, decreed it.

As against the submissive and unquestioning character of Sita, Savitri's story presents a woman's struggle and triumph to win back her rights (husband) from the jaws of Yama, the lord of death, through her obsessive pleadings and her defiance of all the obstacles in her way.

This concept of womanhood has greatly influenced shaping the behaviour and the standard of values among women of all classes and regions. So much so, that even after the revolutionary changes in the social structure in India, one often comes across traditional behaviour even among women of the upper classes.

It is often argued that the roles assigned to men and women under the traditional concept of *Dharma* grant a dignified position to the woman which is highly valuable. But with the rapid changes in society, especially in the behavioural pattern, the whole harmony of relationships has broken down. It is evidently necessary to keep in mind the difference between the so-called traditional and modern values in so far as they affect the position of women. Evidently, traditional values have continually evolved from generation to generation on the ideal behaviour pattern of the upper classes of a society.

The assertion of individuality is supported by the argument that role-playing thwarts personality development. The disintegration of the family among the advanced Western societies, the growing disharmony in husband-wife relations and the alienation of the child from the parents are often attributed to the development of the ideology of individualism. This state of affairs seems to have resulted in a chaotic situation for society. However, it is an admitted fact that often chaos precedes the emergence of a new order.

Since the attainment of independence, education has been gaining increasing importance, particularly among women, and the government aims at ensuring hundred per cent education of women so that they can make their best contribution in the nation's struggle against hunger, poverty, ignorance and social injustice.

In conformity with the Constitutional guarantees in the sphere of social life, certain reforms have been introduced in the personal laws applicable to different communities governing marriage, inheritance, etc. and by the framing of social laws for the protection of women and children against exploitation and immoral traffic and by the legislative measures taken for ensuring human conditions of work and welfare of women employed in industry.

Besides the various welfare and development programmes undertaken by the Government for expanding education, family planning, health services, etc. there has been a continuous effort by individuals as well as social organisations for transforming social attitudes and standards of behaviour in conformity with modern social conditions. These efforts trace their origin from the various movements for social and religious reforms that developed in the 19th century.

Another point for consideration in the present context is whether educated Indian women, evidently forming the leadership in their community, have actually got to a point from where their leadership could start generating a programme aimed at ensuring their due contribution to social and national development as well as accelerate the pace of social change which the nation undergoes through various social, legal and administrative measures which the nation takes in the course of its struggle for economic progress and social justice for all its people.

The political elite of both the sexes seem to have assumed that the problem of women had practically been solved with the legal and administrative measures adopted by the Government in the post-independence period. This is evidently due to the lack of an active women's movement for taking up their specific problems. Despite the various legislative steps of the Government, there is no denying the fact that large masses of women are still exposed to exploitation and injustice. Thus the social and political parity of women guaranteed by the Constitution seems to be still distant.

In the recent decades, a number of women's organisations have emerged and they have been struggling for the redressal of their grievances. However, their activities have obviously remained confined to the urban middle classes. Thus, a vast majority of the women in the rural areas and those belonging to the poor classes in urban areas are completely deprived of the benefit of these movements. This indicates a lack of consciousness of the actual problems of Indian women.

The programmes generated during the International Women's Year included higher literacy, extension of vocational training in basic skills, establishment of infrastructural services in rural areas and an increased participation of women in policy-making decisions at the local, regional and national levels. The canalisation of the women's force for the progress of the nation, thereby eradicating poverty and ensuring social justice, as initiated under the leadership of Mahatma Gandhi needs to be continued and increased progressively.

The changes in the position of women can be summed up as under: throughout the world, women have moved towards greater freedom and equality at home and outside in the society at large. Among the women in the West, where they have achieved full emancipation and equality, a growing tendency has been observed for home and motherhood as against careers. Admittedly, the purpose of all human activity is the achievement of happiness which, in turn, is realised through the development of harmony and cooperative effort and not by conflict with the other entity which is indispensable to make a united whole. Thus, present-day conflict between new principles of equality and traditional culture brings forth a pertinent question: "What direction is the ambivalence of women's situation today going to take in the future?"

It would, perhaps, be justified to extend our hopes for the future direction of women beyond their increasing liberation, replacing their traditional role of ungrudging victims by a new dynamic role of fully-liberated partners in the reconstruction of society. Women in the West are evidently facing a psychological problem in attempting to reconcile their role as wife/mother to their new role of breadwinner. Along with their achievements and emancipation, they have taken a pause to review their past struggle and to chalk out a more realistic programme for the future years to come.

The complexity of the task before India today is unprecedented. The tremendous task of transforming society can be accomplished only through a conscious and realistic effort directed to the development of the people's capacity to change. The capacity for change depends mainly on the motivation structure of a society coupled with its distinct culture. Evidently, traditional forces strongly influence, even if they do not wholly determine, human character. Thus an analysis of the interaction between tradition and modernity is indispensable to attain a clear vision of the future direction.

It is undeniable that social transformation in India is on a pattern distinct from that of the West. The policy of our leaders has long been to eradicate evil traditions with a view to attain more humane goals and to ensure social justice, abolishing all forms of exploitation. Obviously, for ensuring success and happiness in conjugal life, preparation for marriage is necessary which, in turn, actually involves preparation for life itself, that is, a simultaneous intellectual and emotional development so that both the parties to marriage may assume adult responsibilities not with a negative attitude of merely pursuing a tradition, but with a positive attitude of spiritual devotion.

The institution of marriage offers a situation to be taken up with the courage of a realist and not to be evaded like an escapist. Escapism is evidently no solution to a problem and especially in regard to marital relations. The most important human institutions of marriage and family are facing a grave challenge today. Their future would depend on the cultural characteristics of different societies.

It is not claimed to present a comprehensive image of the position of Indian women because the diversities and inequalities prevailing in our society since ancient times make it well nigh to assign a precise role to women in Indian society. On the other hand it is felt that an honest attempt has been made to present convictions. How far they go in meeting the aspirations of the Indian woman or answering the apprehensions of the Indian male are best left to the wisdom of the discerning reader.

—oo(O)oo—

SECTION I

Marriage in India

2

CONCEPT OF MARRIAGE

ACCORDING to Hindu belief, humanity comprises two inseparable entities, *Purusha* and *Prakriti,* signifying Self and Not-Self or, in common parlance, the Male and Female sexes. The two entities have various qualities which, seemingly opposed to each other, on being united make a perfect whole. *Purusha* is endowed with courage, strength, authority, etc., whereas *Prakriti* is vested with the qualities of inspiration, delicacy and surrender to the Self. Evidently, for a harmonious development of the human personality, both these sets of seemingly opposite qualities are indispensable and inseparable.

These two entities have an inherent attraction towards each other which is manifest in the form of physical or sexual attraction between the male and the female. In course of time, this attraction led to the institution of marriage, varying in form according to the geographical, social and cultural conditions of the different regions.

Primitive man was content with any partner of the opposite sex. Due to lack of spiritual consciousness, he had no consideration for a spiritual inner union. But with the development of human consciousness, physical consideration alone proved to be insufficient for holding together two persons of opposite sexes. Evidently, a person with a developed state of consciousness can experience the physical and spiritual blessings of conjugal life only with a partner of a corresponding state of consciousness.

In India, this institution of marriage developed on the basis of the cited concept of life, which stands more for cooperation than for competition, more giving than demanding.

WEDDING HYMNS IN THE VEDAS

The wedding hymns in the Vedas relates, first, the symbolic wedding of the moon and the sun as a prototype and ideal of all human marriages complementing each other in perfect harmony. The two Asvins present the suit of Soma to Savitar for the hand of his daughter, who agrees to be led to her husband's house. The wedding of the moon and the sun is pointed to as the pattern of the married union to be followed. As the sun and moon ever support each other and alternate in their office on the constant fulfilment of which depends not only the prosperity of all animate and inanimate nature, but also the whole cosmic order, even so man and wife must work together in harmony and with united powers, enduringly fulfil the duties laid upon them in their vocation for the advancement of the family.

The traditional marriage ceremony performed even today upholds the same lofty view of marriage. However, some people assumed that Indians are amoral in their sex life, like those of certain other tropical countries, or that Indians have a somewhat different code of morals regulating their sexual behaviour. The erotic sculptures in certain Hindu temples and the phallus-worship prevalent among devotees of Shiva (the lofty symbol of spiritual *Yoga*) are quoted in support of their assumptions. During the period of foreign dominance, the original concept of woman as *Shakti,* the female principle of life synonymous with energy and power, was obscured. She was no more considered good enough to be initiated to the religious (priestly) order to lead congregational prayers, even though the objects of worship were in female form, namely, Durga, Kali, Saraswati, etc.

In this connection, it may be stated that the transformation of sex into a mystical experience or the sublimation of sex has been the fundamental motive in ancient India. To Indians, contact of male and female did not cause excitement. Rather, it indicated the polarity of existences supplementary to each other. Thus, these sculptures and paintings which appear, *prima facie,* to be pornographic, have a symbolic significance for Indians and are not meant to arouse their sexual desires. In this way, the science of love, apart from being erotic, was given an element of sanctity. The most outstanding book on the subject is the *Kama Sutra* (compiled by Vatsyayana in the third century A.D.) which is not the first book of its kind and contains mostly a compilation of the various contemporary ideas about sex together with many suggestions on contemporary customs and the social order.

The sexual frankness in ancient Indian art was permitted in a religio-philosophical aspect. This represented a symbolism of creation and the sacredness of love. It is an admitted fact that, despite this erotic representation in various forms of art—sculpture, painting, literature, etc.—Indians have a highly developed level of modesty in personal morality. Strangely enough, as opposed to the sexual frankness in ancient Indian art, sexual suppression is at the root of modern society in India. The large number of *sanyasis* leading an ascetic life coupled with the vow of celibacy substantiates this. Another glaring example in this regard is that of Mahatma Gandhi, who took the vow of celibacy even before the age of forty. If one makes a comparative study of the history of sex-morality in the East and the West, one finds a contrasting view. In religious representations, frankness was never permitted in the West whereas a positive attitude towards sex is observed in personal life. Thus, in this regard, India and the West seem to be oriented in opposite directions. India, starting with sexual display, is going towards sexual modesty and discipline whereas the West, starting with sexual modesty, seems to be going towards a positive attitude towards sex.

In regard to Indian morality, it may be mentioned that right from ancient times, the male-female distinction was not seen as in opposition causing the sexual drive, but as polarities which are bound to supplement each other to attain the entirety of human existence. What man seeks for is neither flesh nor divinity, but realities of human life interwoven of flesh and spirit, joy and sorrow. Anthropological evidence vouchsafes the validity of the approach that life can be found only in a complex of philosophical, psychological and biological realities, none of which could independently help the individual in attaining happiness.

In the *Grihyasutras,* or precepts for the religious aspect of domestic life of the Hindus, one finds, besides the various old traditions, two ardently sought-for goals. The first was the blessing of many children, especially sons. It would seem strange to a foreigner that earlier the traditional Hindu married principally to have children and the more they had the happier they were. No Hindu could ever dream of complaining that his family was too large, however poor he might be or however numerous his children. The second objective was cordial relations between husband and wife based on mutual love. At the wedding itself, many ceremonies and rituals were observed for bringing about a true bond between two hearts, when Kamdeva, the god of love, was called upon in the wedding ritual to bless the couple with an everlasting bond of love.

Ancient Indian literature is replete with innumerable episodes of highly developed matrimonial harmony based on mutual love. The well-known songs of Nala-Damayanti and the tale of Satyavana-Savitri indicate that the basis of an ideal wedding in India was absolute love. Further, from a discussion of the various types of marriage and the moral behaviour enjoined by the different Hindu lawgivers, it is clear that the concept of chastity has undergone progressive evolution.

The Brahmachari (a celibate who engages in studies pursuing the life of an ascetic) and the widows were urged to lead a strict life of celibacy. Thus, out of diverse forms of marriage and sexual practices, there emerged a standard pattern of sex-relations in Hindu society:

1. The marriage must be performed by recitation of the rituals to the accompaniment of the *Yajna* (sacrificial fire) and the pacing of seven steps round the sacrificial fire, which signify seven vows for leading a harmonious married life.

2. The marriage must be performed within the same caste (an endogamous group), but outside one's *gotra* (an exogamous group).

3. The marriage must be accepted as an indissoluble union not only in this world but in the world beyond as well.

Evidently, a person with a developed state of consciousness can experience the physical and spiritual blessings of conjugal life only with a partner in a corresponding state of consciousness. Hence, for ensuring harmony in conjugal relations, it is the spirit of cooperation that can be of real help rather than that of competition. For this, it will be necessary to develop a sense of giving and not demanding. The wedding of the moon and the sun which support each other and alternate in their office in perfect harmony, on the constant fulfilment of which depends the whole cosmic order, has been referred to as the pattern of the marriage union to be followed in general.

What man seeks for is neither flesh nor divinity, but the reality of human life interwoven of flesh and spirit, joy and sorrow. Hence, the science of love was given an element of sanctity with its religio-philosophical aspect as against the accidental association of sin with sex. This background explains the highly disciplined sex-morality in India and the highly positive attitude towards sex in the West.

Right from the earliest times, Indians have aspired to cordial relations between husband and wife, based on mutual love and the various rituals observed at the wedding ceremony for bringing about an everlasting and true bond between the two through the invocation of Kamdeva (the god of love). This is not merely an ideal but an accomplished fact. An observer of Indian life would immediately discern that the poorest villager loves his wife as tenderly as the most refined man on earth.

One of the principal pursuits of a social scientist is a living concern for the shape of the future. It would be highly unrealistic to think of a society or a country in isolation from certain global trends. There is no gainsaying the fact that a beginning has already been made, at least ideologically, to give progressively increasing stress to equality and social justice in shaping the society to come.

—oo(O)oo—

3

IDEAL OF WOMANHOOD

THE ideal of womanhood can be classified under three heads—sacramental, sociological and individualistic or hedonistic. The sacramental ideal is overwhelmingly influenced by the dictates of religion, while the sociological ideal is governed by motives in the interest of society and the individualistic ideal has always been looked at mainly from the point of view of the happiness of the individual concerned. For example, in the sacramental ideal of womanhood, divorce has no place; the sociological ideal does not preclude divorce whereas it recognises the limitations on divorce based on the interest, not of the individual concerned, but of society at large. In the individualistic ideal, it is for the parties concerned to consider the question and society has no voice in any matter. The same principle applies to the institution of marriage.

These three ideals of womanhood can be traced in the history of all nations, in the West as well as in the East. Before the advent of the Industrial Revolution, the sacramental and sociological ideals were predominant throughout the world. But in the wake of technological progress, coupled with the expansion of education and the creation of possibilities of economic self sufficiency for women, the individualistic ideal has been gaining increasing importance in Western societies.

The ideal of Indian womanhood is, strictly speaking, a happy blending of all the three ideals. Right from the Vedic period, Indian women have participated equally in religious, philosophical and social activities, and their contribution to the and Brahmanic literature as also to the *Upanishadic* thought has been admittedly commendable. There are abundant references to women seers and thinkers in Vedic and post-Vedic literature.

In regard to their sociological ideal, the position of honour held by Indian women would be substantiated by a single reference that, during his campaign for religious propagation, Jagatguru Adi Shankaracharya had to stand for a competitive discussion on religion with the most outstanding scholar of the time, Mandan Mishra, with the condition that if the Shankaracharya could not establish the superiority of his school of thought, he would give up his campaign then and there. Strangely enough, the jury for the decision in this discussion between the most outstanding scholars of the time comprised of Mandan Mishra's wife who, by pronouncing her decision in regard to the superiority of the Shankaracharya's thought, established beyond doubt the sociological considerations weighing upon the behaviour of the Indian woman. Further, this episode goes to prove that Indian women have not lagged behind in respect of academic achievements.

It will be worthwhile to mention here certain Indian women calling for our special attention and respect for womanhood in the past. The lack of historical details has, in no way, hindered their assuming the role of an ideal of Indian women throughout the ages. One of them is Savitri, the symbol of an ideal wife.

As the story goes, Princess Savitri was the daughter of goddess Saraswati (the goddess of learning and fine arts) brought up by Aswapati, the King of Madras and his Queen. Being bestowed with enchanting beauty and cultural and spiritual attainments, she attracted many mighty kings who came to woo and win her as their bride, but left to worship her memory as a goddess. However, the royal courts of the mighty kings had no attraction for her. Later on, King Aswapati sent his daughter on a long journey to the religious centre of Varanasi, escorted by counsellors and attendants.

On the way, they happened to pass through a forest where ascetics and sages spent their lives in hermitages in peaceful surroundings. There she saw a young man dressed as an ascetic. On seeing him, Savitri, the dignified and self-possessed princess, felt the chords of her heart touched by this unknown hermit. It was he for whom she had waited so long. It was he who had been her lord for cycles of existence and none but he could be her life's lord in this existence too. However, her modesty did not permit her to speak to him directly. Her royal escorts, having understood her feelings, made enquiries about the young man who was named Satyavan. They also asked about his horoscope, etc. and came to know that he was predestined to die within a period of just one year.

The sage's prediction about the future of Satyavan struck the princess like a bolt of lightning. She felt as if she had ended the phase of girlhood and had become a woman. She had to live up to her womanhood and choose the path of virtue and true love although it meant walking barefoot over thorns. The following reply of Savitri rang through the court of her royal father and still rings in the heart of every Hindu woman:

> The die is cast. It is only once that one can say, 'I give away'. Whether he has a short or long life, I have selected my husband once and for all and I will not select a second one.

She knew a dreadful fate lay before her, but she did not falter. By virtue of her strength of will she succeeded in creating compassion in the heart of Yama, the god of death, who came to rob her husband of his soul and offered the pleading princess a boon. But Savitri would not yield and followed Yama to the other world. Yama offered many boons to Savitri but the princess was inflexible. Accepting defeat with grace, Yama spared the life of Satyavan.

Another Indian ideal of a woman is Sita, the heroine of the epic *Ramayana*: tender and soft, dream-filled with moonlight, unselfish, filled with love, devotion, sincerity, faithfulness and yet, when it came to defending womanly virtue displayed nobility of the soul and purity of body, patient in her long suffering but unyielding in her pride.

Despite millennia that have passed since the age of the *Ramayana,* its undying fountainhead of inspiration continues to direct the course of life of Indian society. The wife's cooperation with her husband, an active participation in his major activities, is depicted by the fact that Kaikeyi extended her active support to Dashrath in the battlefield when he was hard-pressed in the fight with Champasura.

The capacity of women in that age is highlighted when Vashishtha proclaimed, on the eve of Rama's departure on exile, that Sita would reign in the place of Rama, till Rama came back on the expiry of the term of exile.

The beauty of soul and body go hand in hand; where one is, there the other is too. In *Puranic* literature, as also in classical Sanskrit literature, popular sayings, poetry and even the philosophical literature present certain specific comments as to the Indian ideal of womanly beauty as garnered from the description of various women. Draupadi has black curly hair, long eyes like the leaf of the autumn lotus, face like the jasmine flower when it is covered by delicate moisture, slender waist, long hair and red lips. She is neither too tall nor too short; she has beautiful hips; she is the embodiment of beauty. Whoever sees her folds his hands in reverence. Queen Sudeshna sees her from her palace, and wondering greatly, describes her beauty in the following words:

> Her ankles do not stand out (but are embedded in the flesh, something which the epic often states about the fair), and her thighs are firm and hard. Three things in her are deep, namely, voice, understanding and navel; six high-arched (nose, eyes, ears, nails, breasts, the joint of the neck); five red (the palms of the hands, the soles of the feet, the corners of the eyes, the tongue and the nails). She speaks as clearly as the swan, her brows and eyes are round-arched, red as the bimba-fruit are her lips, her neck is like a shell, her veins are hidden, face is like the full moon...

It is clear that the figure, build and beauty of women are important to their destiny, quite apart from conquests over the hearts of men. Shree or Lakshmi is, at the same time, both the goddess of beauty and of happiness.

—oo(O)oo—

4

MARRIAGE IN EARLY INDIA

TO know of the sexual mores and marital pattern of the Aryans, we have to refer to the earliest Vedic literature, of which the *Rig Veda* is believed to be the oldest composition. The *Rig Veda* provides an insight into the social life of the Aryans among whom the unit of social organisation was the family. The Aryan family of the Vedic period was patrilineal and patrilocal, headed by the eldest male member. However, the women played an important role in Vedic society and had well-defined duties in regard to the management of household affairs, etc. Apart from their equal right of participation in the rituals, religious and intellectual activities, they were, above all, required to provide the husband with a son. The importance of the birth of a son in Vedic society has been discussed elsewhere. Further, there is no reference indicating the prevalence of child marriage in Vedic society. Although monogamy was *de rigeur,* polygamy is also indicated by the existence of certain terms like *sapatni* (co-wife), etc.

There evidently is a close relationship between racial elements and marital mores in every society. The same thing happened in India as well. For example, in northern India, with the majority of population Aryan, the marital mores have been more influenced by the law of consanguinity, under which one is not allowed to marry kin in the upward line of seven generations from the ego on the male side, and of five generations from the female side. Against this, in south India, with its Dravidian racial elements, the wife is preferably chosen from some specified kinship either on the father's side or the mother's side, for example, father's sister's daughter, mother's brother's daughter or the mother's sister's daughter; in certain parts one finds polyandry, polygamy as also the strange practice of marrying the widow of the father by the son of a different mother in certain tribal hill areas, and the prevalence of premarital sex accompanied by the strictest rules of chastity after marriage among tribals of Central India (Madhya Pradesh). However, in modern India, this diversity of marital mores is giving way to a uniform monogamous marriage widely prevalent throughout the country.

DIFFERENT FORMS OF MARRIAGE

As stated, the sociological scene in India presents a wide diversity of marriage customs and practices which is evidently an outcome of the wide cultural and racial diversity of the people. It may be safely said that almost all the forms of marriage known in the world, have had their place in India. In the Vedic period, monogamy was predominant.

Later on, in the Epic period, polygamy became the fashion of the day. Simultaneously, there developed certain strange traditions, for example, *Niyoga* (begetting children by a widow) and leviration (taking in the widow of the elder brother as wife by the younger brother of the deceased husband) which will be discussed in detail later. This state of affairs presents India as an ethnic museum of marital forms and patterns.

The marriage hymns of the *Rig Veda* suggest that the bride and the bridegroom belonged to different localities, their union being effected through a middleman called *Sambhala.* During the Vedic period, normally the girl was allowed to mix freely with young men and choose her husband. This is evident from the custom of the girl's participation in the Samana festival, comparable to the popular fairs of modern times.

The use of this Samana festival by the girls to find a husband was not a contradiction of the custom of arranging marriages through a mediator, called *Didishu* (*Rig Veda* X. 18.6 and VI .55.5). It seemed that the youth who found a girl attractive had to go to the parents of the girl with a proposal of marriage. Later on, the Samana festival fading away, the services of a mediator might have become necessary and the same term, which earlier meant a wooer or husband, assumed reference to a mediator.

In regard to the later Vedic period extending from 900 B.C. to 600 B.C., some light is thrown by the *Griha Sutras* laying down detailed rules pertaining to various religious and domestic ceremonies. The *Griha Sutras* were composed during the earlier half of the first millennium B.C. From contemporary literature, it becomes evident that by this time the girl had lost the freedom enjoyed during the Rig Vedic period. Her freedom in regard to the choice of a husband gave way to the custom of settling marriages through the mediation of friends or relatives. During this period, the marriage ceremony became an elaborate celebration comprising rituals. Another change that we observe during this period is that while during the Rig Vedic period, monogamy was the marriage *de rigeur,* polygamy was fast becoming prevalent. There are also references to widow remarriage (*Atharva Veda* IX. 5.17-28) with some magical rites for disrupting her ties with the first husband.

By the beginning of the Brahmaṇical period, polygamy became widely prevalent. Obviously, in a polygamous society, different wives had to be designated differently, indicating their order of precedence in regard to inheritance and various other rights. In the Brahmanic literature, we often come across such designations as *Mahishi, Patni, Parivirkti* and *Vivata* referring to different wives. In case a man had only one wife, she was called *Patni. Parivirkti* referred to a wife who bore no children. The chief queen of a king was called *Mahishi.* In the case of others, the favourite wife was called *Vivata.*

Up to this time, the rigidities of the hereditary caste system did not enter matrimonial relations. However, this was a period of transition in the history of Hindu society.

With the advent of the Epic period, the institution of marriage underwent a fundamental change. As against the single form of marriage in the earlier periods, in the Epic period we find different forms of marriage. The great epic, the *Mahabharata,* mentions four forms of marriage, namely, *Brahma, Gandharva, Asura* and *Rakshasa,* whereas Gautama and Asvalayana (ancient Hindu lawgiver) refer to eight forms of marriage, which is also confirmed by the *Manusmriti,* another ancient Hindu law book: These eight forms of marriage were:

1. *Brahma* in which the parents of the bride invited a virtuous and learned young man and married their daughter to him giving him presents of clothes and ornaments.

2. *Daiva* in which the father of the bride performed a sacrificial ceremony, and the learned bridegroom (evidently one of about 25 years of age having just concluded his studies in an ashram) was offered the bride along with some dowry (normally a cow).

   These two forms of marriage were called *Daiva* (divine) and were valued very highly.

3. *Arsha* in which the father of the bride received from the bridegroom a pair of cattle in exchange for his daughter.

4. *Prajapatya* in which the bride was given to a young man of choice, extolling the virtue of the married state with the blessing that the union may turn out to be happy and prosperous.

5. *Asura* which was prevalent among aborigine tribes and which is ritually observed even today among certain backward communities. It was almost the same as marriage by purchase, and has been regarded by Westermark as of universal character in ancient India (Westermark. *History of Marriage*. London: 1926). In this form of marriage, the relatives of the bride received some money from the bridegroom. There was, however, no limit on the amount to be paid. The main difference between the *Arsha* and *Asura* forms of marriage was that in the former the bride received a pair or two of cattle and in the *Asura* form the bride-price was settled by the parties and there was no custom controlling such an exchange. This form of marriage was, however, condemned by the *Dharma Shastras*. On account of its association with wealth, this form of marriage was prescribed for the Vaisyas or the commercial community. Manu refers to the opinion of a sage that *Asura* marriage was permissible only for Vaisyas and Shudras.

6. *Gandharva* in which marriage was concluded by mutual choice, without any consideration of the wish of the parents. In this form of marriage, the couple took the decision often

without consulting their parents. According to Jolly, the *Gandharva* marriage was a privilege of the nobles (Jolly. *Hindu Law and Custom*. Calcutta: 1928), and was practically confined to the Kshatriyas and ruling classes and actually the law books permitted *Gandharva* marriage only for the Kshatriyas (*Manusmriti*, III, 26). Baudhayana supported the general opinion that it could be performed by all. According to Vatsayana (third century, A.D.), the *Gandharva* marriage was determined mainly by mutual love and the considerations of birth and money, etc. played no role, which made the *Gandharva* marriage quite plebian.

As the Indian social system did not undergo drastic changes till the middle of the 19th century, certain latter-day social practices clearly indicate the social conditions of the earlier times, for example, among certain lower classes the term *Gandharva* denotes remarriage. It seems that this form of marriage was earlier prevalent among the lower classes, but later the princes and nobles used it as a camouflage for their licentious love affairs, ultimately leading to polygamy. This is corroborated by the fact that there is virtually no example of a Kshatriya princess going in for a *Gandharva* marriage with persons of other castes.

7. *Rakshasa* in which marriage was concluded by capture or seduction, sometimes with a careful plan, the execution of which had legal sanction. This form of marriage was introduced to solemnise the union of the women of a conquered people who were taken away by the men of the victorious group. Among certain Adivasi tribes, this form of marriage has been observed until recent times. Certain surviving rituals reminiscent of the *Rakshasa* form of marriage are found among some of the high-caste Hindus even today. A mock fight between the bridegroom's and the bride's parties is also a regular feature of many low-caste Hindu marriages.

8. *Paisacha* in which even raped women were given social status of lawful brides. The Brahmanical law books describe this form of marriage as one in a state of

intoxication, carelessness or sleep and, therefore, the basest of all forms of marriage.

According to Manu, the performance of *Yajna* (ceremonial offering to god) was necessary only in the case of the *Arsha* form of marriage, whereas the others could be performed without any form of ritual. During the age of the *Mahabharata,* we find the prevalence of the *Brahma* and *Gandharva* forms of marriage. Many heroes of the *Mahabharata* contracted the *Gandharva* form of marriage; for example, Shantanu married Ganga (a fisherwoman), Bhima married Hirimba, Arjuna married Ulupi and Chitrangada, Dushyanta married Shakuntala, Parikshit (of the *Ikshvaku* race) married Susobhana, all in the *Gandharva* form of marriage.

Apart from these forms of marriage, there prevailed another variant of *Rakshasa* marriage called *svayamvara,* which is often presented as free choice by the bride. This becomes clear from a reference to the *svayamvara* meeting of Amba, Ambika and Ambalika (daughters of the king of Kashi), in which Bhima says to the assembly:

> "The lawgivers approve of the winning of the girl by vanquishing the rivals in a *svayamvara* meeting."

The prevalence of the *Rakshasa* form of marriage (marriage by capture) is confirmed by innumerable references in the *Mahabharata;* for example, Rukmini was captured by Krishna and Karna captured Chitrangada for marrying her to Duryodhana.

There is another reference worth mentioning in this connection. During his stay at Rajvatika, Arjuna was enamoured of Subhadra, the sister of Krishna. With the tacit approval of Krishna, Arjuna carried Subhadra off by force. When the Yadavas became infuriated at Arjuna's conduct, Krishna consoled them saying: "It is not conceivable to Arjuna that we sell our daughters for money. Further, the *Svayamvara* was not acceptable to him. So he decided to capture her by force." This clearly indicates the prevalence of the *Asura* form of marriage among the Yadava community.

In the *Mahabharata*, there are numerous references to the *Asura* form of marriage by payment of bride-price. When Richika, the son of Bhrigu, pleaded for the hand of the daughter of Godhi, he was told:

"According to our family tradition, one thousand speedy horses must be paid as bride-price for her hand."

Further, the attitude of tolerance for the marriage of an Aryan to a non-Aryan during the age of the *Mahabharata* becomes evident from various passages in the epic, when the non-Aryan king, Nala, married Damayanti, the daughter of the King of Vidarbha (an Aryan) in a *svayamvara* meeting. Even some Aryan kings and princes married non-Aryan girls, for example, King Shantanu married the daughter of a non-Aryan fisherman, King Devaka married a Shudra woman.

The first four approved forms of marriage were recommended for the Brahmins, which implies that the other three *Varnas* could go in for the unapproved form of marriage as well, of course with varying degrees of approval or disapproval. According to Baudhayana, this prescription of different forms of marriage for different castes was based on economic reasons.

He has made the observation that due to their preoccupation with agriculture and service, the wives of the Vaisyas and Shudras cannot be kept under control. The participation of women among the lower castes in the task of production as also their economic independence necessitated the slackening of the bonds on them, whereas the women of the upper castes were comparatively more dependent upon the male members.

These different forms of marriage seem to have some parallel in early Roman history where, under the Republic there were three forms of marriage, namely, *Usus, Confarreatio* and *Coemptio.* The *Usus* form of marriage required no ceremony and could be dissolved at will and was an old, plebian form of marriage. *Confarreatio* involved a deed of transfer placing the bride under the husband's authority and was a patrician form of marriage. *Coemptio* involved a deed of purchase giving the husband a contractual right to the possessions of the wife and it was a later plebeian form of marriage (George Thomson. *Studies in Ancient Greek Society.* New York: 1949).

It is clear that the lower castes also enjoyed certain advantages. The *Asura* form of marriage was widely prevalent and this form of marriage in which the position of women was somewhat better, was recommended only for the lower classes.

During foreign domination, these forms of marriage could not retain their original character and, with increasing faith in the religious duty of every parent to give the daughter in marriage, there emerged a new form of arranged marriage, accompanied by dowry. In this form, the parents of the bride and the bridegroom settled the amount of dowry by mutual consent. These marriages were normally arranged between the members of the same caste residing close to each other. The traditional caste panchayats, exercising an overwhelming influence on the members of the particular caste, guarded against all unfair practices on the part of the two families in regard to dowry as well as treatment of the bride after marriage.

In the post-independence period, these caste panchayats have been replaced by the institution of gram panchayats which have certain administrative and legal authority. But they have no influence on the village community in regard to caste traditions. In this state of affairs, the tradition of dowry assumed a criminal form and huge amounts of money came to be given as dowry which made the lot of the girls' parents miserable. This matter is discussed at length separately.

POLYGAMY AND POLYANDRY

POLYGAMY

Though monogamy has been the only legal form of marriage in India throughout the ages, bigamy in both forms, namely, polygamy (more than one wife) and polyandry (more than one husband) also had sanction and prevailed among the Hindus. In the *Mahabharata,* we find a number of characters with more than one wife, for example, Yajati married Sarmishtha and Devayani. Dushyanta married Shakuntala and Lakshana. Shantanu married Satyavati and Ganga. Vichitravirya married Ambika and Ambalika, Dhritrashtra married Gandhari and Vaishya and Pandu married Kunti and Madri. In addition to having Draupadi in common with his brothers, Arjuna married Ulupi, Chitrangada and Subhadra and Bhima married Hirimba. Vrihadaratha, the king of Magadh, married the twin daughters of the king of Kashi. Krishna, the most important character of the *Mahabharata,* is stated to have had many wives.

The provisions in the *Dharma Shastras* in respect of monogamy and polygamy indicates that polygamy, a characteristic of a patriarchal society, was prevalent among the upper castes. The caste determined the number of wives a person could have. Generally, a Brahmin could take up to four wives, a Kshatriya three and a Shudra one. According to Vasishth, a Brahmin could marry three wives, a Kshatriya two and a Vaishya and Shudra one each (Vashishtha, I.24).

There are numerous instances showing that priests and princes often maintained a large number of wives. Later on, this tradition continued throughout the period of Muslim reign in India, with the slight difference that among the Muslims, caste did not determine the number of wives permitted to a person. This evidently depended on one's economic status. Certain nawabs and maharajas are believed to have maintained more than a hundred wives in their harems. Strictly speaking, the concept of marriage during the Middle Ages seems to have been a bit different in the sense that an emperor or maharaja maintained more wives to show his superiority over others.

Polygamy was considered the right of men but polyandry was dubbed an evil. Thus, no blame is laid on men who marry many wives, but women offending their first husband through a new marriage have been condemned.

The 19th century reform movement generated social reaction against polygamy as it constituted an indignity to the status of women. Apart from a general stir among the elite against this evil custom, certain contemporary leaders like Ishwar Chandra Vidyasagar, organisations like the Brahmo Samaj and Christian missionaries pleaded for legislative measures to prohibit this practice. Later, under the leadership of Mahatma Gandhi, this demand for legislative measures gained momentum. Consequently, the Baroda Government passed an Act in 1942, followed by the Governments of Bombay, Madras and Saurashtra in 1946, 1947 and 1954, respectively.

Later still, the Hindu Marriage Act of 1955 introduced the principle of monogamy, prohibiting all forms of polygamy and polyandry.

POLYANDRY

Although monogamy prevailed in Vedic society, there are certain stray references indicating the prevalence of polyandry whereby the bride was given to a family of brothers. *Apastambha Dharmasutra* (a work of the post-Vedic period) asserts that a bride is given to a family of brothers and not to one individual only (*Apastambha Dharmasutra*, II, 10-27, 2-4). This implies that in such cases, the marriage of a girl was ritually performed with the eldest brother and the younger brothers were tacitly vested with the right of sex with the wife of the eldest brother. The term *Devri* or *Devra,* referring to the younger brother of the husband (in relation to the wife) has often been interpreted to indicate the sexual right of the younger brother over his elder brother's wife.

The renowned Hindu lawgiver, Manu, also laid down that in the *Kali* age "one must not give away a girl to a family." The chief heroes of the *Mahabharata*, namely, the five Pandav brothers, had one wife or head-wife in common, namely, Draupadi. Apart from the episode of Draupadi, there is another reference that Jatila (of the race of Gautama) married seven sages and that Varksi (the daughter of another sage) had ten husbands.

It is often held that polyandry was prevalent among the non-Aryans living in India and that the five Pandav brothers, too, were non-Aryans. They might have belonged to one of the many aboriginal peoples or tribes that dwelt and still dwell in India and on its boundaries among whom polyandry is restrictively observed even today (J. Jolly. *Recht and Sitte*. 1896).

It has been extremely difficult to justify this act of the heroes of the *Mahabharata.* One of the chief explanations given in this connection is this: when the five Pandav brothers, who were going about in the garb of Brahmin ascetics, sought to surprise their mother with Draupadi, the mother thinking that her sons had brought some eatables home from the journey said: "Enjoy it together." The mistake had been made and both she and her sons felt that the words of a mother, being holy, must be held sacred absolutely and to the letter. Moreover, the brothers were all struck by the wonderful beauty of Draupadi, and Yudhisthar decided that they would possess her together rather than come to strife on her account. When they told Draupadi's father about their intention, he was deeply wounded as he felt that Arjuna, having won her, should alone marry her. He strongly protested against this unheard of *Adharma* (moral wrong), conflicting both with worldly and Vedic traditions.

The tradition of polyandry has existed till quite recently among many tribes in the hill areas of the North East, Madhya Pradesh and Himachal Pradesh and this indicates that the references to polyandry in the epics might be the result of the fusion of certain non-Aryan tribal traditions with Aryan society.

Among the tribals assimilated in or remaining outside the Hindu caste hierarchy, polyandry has been prevalent among the Todas and Notas of south India and Khasas of Jaunsar Bewar in Dehra Dun and a few other castes in the north.

The polyandry prevalent in India was of two types, namely, fraternal and non-fraternal. In the fraternal type, the husbands were all brothers or cousins on the father's side. In the non-fraternal type, the husbands were not so related, as evidenced by the practice of polyandry prevalent till quite recently among the Nairs of Kerala.

Among the Nair women, polyandry has been a recognised institution and there was no limit to the number of husbands a woman could have at the same time. The polyandry prevalent among the Nairs was of the non-fraternal type, that is, they could be from different families and castes living in different houses. Hence, it was not practical for the Nair woman to stay with all her husbands. The wife, therefore, stayed in her own house and the husbands visited her by night in rotation on mutual understanding and adjustment. This system has been discussed in detail later.

MARRIAGE AMONG THE KULINS OF BENGAL

The Kulin (meaning high-born) Brahmins of Bengal claim to form the purest caste, their ancestors having come from Kannauj and settled in Bengal on the invitation of King Bellala Sen (11th century A.D.), who made a rigorous selection on the basis of certain noble qualities, namely, observance of the Brahmanical code of conduct as enjoined by the scriptures, meekness, devotion to learning, asceticism, liberal disposition and a strict adherence to the concept of ritual purity in regard to marriage and community meals. It may, however, be stated in this connection that in no region of India are the Brahmins numerically preponderant, for example, Kulin Brahmins of Bengal, the Nambudiris of Kerala, the Nandis of Gujarat, etc.

It would be observed from the previous chapters that women were literally considered as points of entrance to the caste group. It was believed that if women were married to men of higher castes, the children born of such alliances would have a ritual status higher than that of their mothers. But if men of lower ritual status married women of higher ritual status, then their descendants would have a lower ritual status than that of the mother. Thus, for the protection of the ritual purity of the group, it became necessary to guard the sexuality of the women and to marry them to men of ritually correct status.

There existed among the Hindus a system of *Anuloma* marriages, whereby the marriage of a man of higher caste with a woman of a lower caste was given high social approval. This provision went on well till it was applied to marriages based on mutual love between two persons of different castes. However, as is usual with all social customs, the provision of *Anuloma* marriage came to be applied to economic and other forms of exploitation and, ultimately, it led to one of the social abuses of Hindu society. The Brahmins of the other sub-castes wanted to marry their daughters to the Kulin Brahmins. Evidently, in such a marriage, the men of the Kulin sub-caste had to accept the lowering of status in the caste hierarchy, for which they could be expected to agree when compensated financially or otherwise. This state of affairs led to a mad race among the non-Kulin Brahmins to improve their status in the caste hierarchy by giving their daughters in marriage to the Kulins.

Further, the Hindu traditions pertaining to marriage did not permit a woman being married in a caste lower than her parents. Hence, all the Kulin women had to be married to Kulin husbands only. This gave rise to polygamy with a vengeance (P. Thomas. *The Hindu Religion, Customs and Manners*. D. B. Taraporewala, 1971). The Kulins commercialised marriage by offering themselves for marriage with Brahmin women of any other sub-caste on payment of dowry. The Kulin Brahmins were in such great demand as grooms by non-Kulin Brahmin girls that a Kulin Brahmin was married to a number of girls spread over various villages. He had no obligation to his wife or children. A girl married to a Kulin Brahmin might see her husband only once, but if such a husband died she was expected to follow the strict ritual routine of a widow. The situation degenerated to such an extent that in many cases, the Kulin Brahmin, having contracted such a marriage on the payment of a huge dowry, went away leaving the wife at her parents' house which he rarely, and in some cases, never visited. Some Kulins are said to have contracted a few hundred such marriages. Whenever they needed money, they simply visited the father-in-law's house where they were invariably provided with money and treated with extreme hospitality.

This concept of the purity of the Kulin Brahmins defeated the significance of the institution of marriage. Cases were not rare where a Kulin boy of 16 to 18 years got married to women much older than himself and, similarly, old men contracted marriages with very young girls. In some cases it is said a Kulin husband did not even remember the number of his wives and hence a record of such marriages was maintained by a particular class with the responsibility of keeping genealogical records of the Kulins. Needless to say, in such circumstances, there was hardly any sentimental or psychological unity between the different members of the family, who mostly did not even recognise each other. The children were brought up in an atmosphere of extreme neglect. The misery of the neglected Kulin wife can be imagined. The expansion of education and increasing industrialisation have changed the situation in that the Brahmins of the so-called inferior sub-castes no longer consider it a privilege to form matrimonial relations with the Kulins of Bengal.

Apart from this, there are certain social reasons for the tradition of polygamy, for example, barrenness of the wife, her prolonged illness, the absence of a male child or the custom of marrying the elder brother's widow, etc. In some cases, another social reason was the irreconcilable disparity between the two partners in a marriage arranged by the parents or elders at an early age, in some of which the wife remained illiterate and the husband went in for advanced education.

This is the outcome of child marriage. In such cases, the husband goes in for a second marriage without any serious misgivings. Even if the first wife is offered a divorce, she prefers to continue living as a neglected member of the husband's family because the status of a deserted wife is considered to be better than that of a divorcee.

Another motivation for polygamy is the economic gain among the communities in which the women contribute substantially to productive activity like agriculture and handicrafts. This was noticed among artisans also.

It is unfortunate that even more than several decades after the enactment of the law banning polygamy, the evil tradition has not been totally eradicated, partly on account of the flexibility permitted for the customary forms of marriage, for example, *Natra* in Uttar Pradesh, Rajasthan and parts of Madhya Pradesh and Gujarat and *Reet* in Himachal Pradesh and partly on account of certain communities not coming within the purview of the Act.

MARRIAGE AMONG THE NAMBUDIRIS OF MALABAR

Apart from the Kulin Brahmins of Bengal, the Nambudiri Brahmins of Malabar have also been victims of a similar tradition comparable to polygamy. According to a legend, the Nambudiri Brahmins are believed to be descendants of pure Aryan stock, brought from the north by the warrior priest Parasuram who is said to have reclaimed the Malabar coast from the sea and presented it to those Brahmins in atonement of the sins committed in destroying the Kshatriyas and the Brahmins. These Nambudiris had an entirely privileged position in all social, religious and political spheres of the Malabar area.

Traditionally, the Nambudiris have been polygnists. According to their custom, only the eldest son is allowed to marry and bring his wife into his house. The other brothers who lived in the same house along with him were deprived of the right of marriage but could form sexual relationships with the women of other castes.

This state of affairs gave rise to the development of a peculiar custom among the Nair community, known as *Sambandham,* which signified the conjugal relations of the Nair women with Nambudiri Brahmins without going in for the ritual formality of marriage. As the Nambudiri Brahmins were considered to be direct representatives of god, this institution of *Sambandham* came to be considered a sacred and divine privilege. It was believed that by pleasing a Nambudiri, one could attain divine favour and be blessed with eternal affluence and happiness. Thus, the Nair women longed for their *Sambandham* with the men of higher Nair sub-castes, preferably the Nambudiris. Till recently, one could find the custom prevalent among some orthodox

Nair families that if a Nambudiri visited them and expressed his wish for *Sambandham,* he could not be refused by the parents.

As stated, the institution of *Sambandham* had social, economic and religious approval. This relationship between the Nambudiri man and Nair woman emanated from the concept of high value given to the good seed or to the men of higher status in the caste hierarchy. In this connection, it would be worthwhile to state that the Nambudiri Brahmins and Nairs, though separated by a gulf in religious and most social matters, were yet united by their tie of sex, which can be called marriage, but was considered more respectable than concubinage. It may also be mentioned that the Nambudiris have been a strictly patrilineal society. If all the male members married and produced children, the family would be divided leading to the disintegration of their patriarchal structure. But if only the eldest son married, there would be fewer heirs and the family would continue to remain an ideal and harmonious unit. This arrangement worked well for the male members of the Nambudiri community, who could have *Sambandham* with any number of Nair women, whereas the Nambudiri women became the worst affected by this unjust institution. They were not allowed to marry men of any other caste. As stated earlier, only the eldest male member in a Nambudiri family was allowed to marry, hence all the women of the community had to be shared by these eldest male members of different families, leading ultimately to the development of the custom of polygamy and trading in marriage, that is, every Nambudiri demanded an exorbitant dowry for getting married.

The miserable lot of the Nambudiri women can be imagined from the fact that they were not allowed to go out alone or to talk to any men except their husbands. In case they had to go out, they travelled in groups escorted by Nair women. After attaining puberty, the Nambudiri girls were not allowed to speak even to their own fathers or brothers.

Strictly speaking, the Nair women who entered into *Sambandham* with the Nambudiris had no legal status of wives, but lived with their brothers and sisters, who looked after the children born of the *Sambandham.* This term has often been confused with marriage. Therefore, it seems to be necessary to elucidate. In *Sambandham,* the conjugal relations between the Nambudiri man and Nair woman did not grant them the status of husband and wife. No religious formalities were observed while entering into *Sambandham.* Except for sexual intimacy, both the parties strictly observed their respective caste rules. The Nambudiri never took his Nair *Sambandham* partner and children to his house. If they happened to go there, they were kept at a distance. The Nambudiri did not eat anything prepared or touched by his Nair wife or her children. It may be mentioned in this connection that under the concept of ritual purity, the acceptance of food from a woman of a lower caste involved highly undesirable consequences, and the man having accepted such food was treated as having been polluted internally. But cohabitation with a woman of lower ritual status resulted only in external pollution which could be cleansed by a body bath.

It is strange that the concept of caste purity which, on the one hand, laid the strictest sex-taboos on the Nambudiri women, on the other gave practically a free hand to the sexuality of the Nambudiri men. The *Sambandham* relationship comprised mainly of nocturnal visits of the Nambudiri husband who could have *Sambandhams* with as many Nair women as he wanted. On getting bored with one, he could simply leave her and, under the customary law, his Nair partner and her children could not lay any claims on him. In these circumstances, there developed a tendency among the Nair women to engage as many husbands as possible, so that there was no difficulty in finding substitutes for the dropouts. In this way, both polyandry and polygamy may be said to have existed simultaneously and in many cases the paternity of children could not be ascertained. Even if paternity was ascertained, the fathers of the different children being of different castes, the children would be required to follow different professions assigned to the particular caste of their respective fathers.

The husband-wife relation in *Sambandham* being restricted to nocturnal visits only, in many cases the children did not see the father for years together The husband's interest in the wife was thus temporary and, strictly speaking, just a partnership. It was, therefore, quite natural for him not to have much feelings for his children.

MATRILINY

In a polygamous society, the patrilineal family in which the husband, wife and their children lived together could not develop. The alternative was to dispense with the doubtful and heterogeneous factor (the father) and adopt the uniform and indubitable factor (the mother). Hence, there developed the institution of matriliny in which the father had no responsibility towards his own children. Instead, the maternal uncle became the head of the family and performed the functions of a father for his sister's children. The burden of the children had naturally to fall on the shoulders of the maternal uncle, who was the eldest male member in the mother's family. In turn, his own children were looked after by their maternal uncles.

The term 'matriliny' means the recognition of kinship and inheritance through the maternal line. In the matrilineal system, a family unit is based on the female members and continues through female children born to female members, that is, sisters and sister's daughters. Thus, in a matrilineal family the women had pride of place from the point of view of inheritance as well as continuance of the family unit. Under this system, the husband and wife do not live together but with their own respective families. Husband-wife relations are generally restricted to the husband's visits to his wife's house at night.

ORIGIN OF MATRILINY

In order to avoid confusion between 'matriliny' and 'matriarchy', it may be stated that the Nairs were not matriarchal but matrilineal, that is, they followed the maternal line only in regard to inheritance and kinship, which fact did not confer the rights and powers of the head of the family on the mother. For all practical purposes, the uncle was the supreme head of the family.

While tracing the origin of this system, it becomes clear that with the dawn of civilisation, the primitive matrilineal system had vanished and whatever matrilineal customs had survived among the Nairs or elsewhere are fast dying out.

There are different theories in regard to the origin of this system among the Nair community. One is that they adopted matriliny out of sheer respect for women, perhaps inspired by their devotion to the Hindu goddesses Kali, Durga, Lakshmi, Saraswati, etc. However, this theory is hardly convincing on account of the matrilineal system being restricted to the Nair community forming a very small section of Hindu society which is fundamentally patrilineal as the whole body of Vedic literature, *Smritis* and Hindu codes of law trace kinship along the male line.

Another theory in this regard is that the Nairs, being a martial race, were generally away from their homes and the assumption of all domestic responsibilities by the women in the absence of their husbands paved the way for the development of matriliny. This is, however, hardly convincing as the influential position of women should not have necessitated the customs of polyandry and *Sambandham*. Further, this theory seems to be based on the assumption that there existed matriarchy among the Nairs, that is, the women were the rulers in the family, whereas the rights and responsibilities of the head of a Nair family were actually vested in the maternal uncle.

But these theories fail as one finds the strongest form of patriliny among the martial races. Once a German was asked why they called their country 'fatherland' instead of 'motherland'. He replied that while the mother looked after the family, it was the father who fought for the country.

HYPERGAMY (*ANULOMA* MARRIAGES)

Hypergamy is a social institution in regard to conjugal relations, which allows a man but forbids a woman to marry a person of lower social standing. Underlying this rule was the high value attached to the purity of women which was jealously protected among the higher castes.

When the castes were divided into several groups with different ritual and social status on account of their having different origins, the parents were required to get their daughters married to men belonging to a group equal to or higher than their own. The marriage of a daughter of a man into a higher group (or caste) came to be regarded as a symbol of honour. This resulted in a great demand for bridegrooms in the higher castes and ultimately led to the atrocious tradition of murdering female infants.

During the last two centuries, certain castes and communities, in an attempt to improve their social status and desiring upward social movement in the caste hierarchy, adopted a system of marrying their daughters into higher castes. This has been explained in detail earlier in the section on marriage among the Kulins of Bengal. It may, however, be stated here that as a device of persuading boys of the higher castes to marry girls of the lower castes, the system of dowry was encouraged. Under this system, the women were reduced to the humiliating position of pawns in the game of status building. The girl from a lower group was always conscious of her lower status. The absolute neglect of the girl's happiness in such marriages is evidenced from the fact that certain families gave their daughters in marriage to persons of higher castes of a different region, where sometimes even the language was different making communication between the husband and wife very difficult.

Another implication of this system was that the highest caste group was left with a surplus of girls. When the members of such a group accepted wives from the lower groups, the chances of marriage for the girls in that group went down correspondingly. As the system implied the marriage of persons of different caste groups, the highest caste group was left with the choice of either forcing their women to remain unmarried or of committing female infanticide.

Among the Kulin Brahmins of Bengal, who had a highly complicated system of social (or caste) hierarchy, the highest class (Kulins) experienced the utmost difficulty in finding suitable husbands for their daughters. This state of affairs led to polygamy among certain high castes. This has been dealt with in detail in a previous section.

Hypergamy was also prevalent among the Anavil Brahmins and Leva-Patidars of Gujarat, Rajputs of Rajasthan, Marathas of Maharashtra and Nairs, Kshatriyas and Ambalavasis of Kerala. Hypergamy was known in ancient Hindu society as *Anuloma* and *Pratiloma*. *Anuloma* signified a marriage in which the man was of a caste higher than that of the woman. *Pratiloma* signified a marriage in which the man belonged to a caste lower than that of the woman. Such a marriage was not only disapproved of by society, it called for punishment under the ancient Hindu law and contemporary social traditions.

LAW OF CONSANGUINITY

The bilateral law of consanguinity governing marriage is stated to have been prevalent in Hindu society, especially in northern India. In ancient Hindu literature, we find certain references to consanguineous sexual relations between near of kin among the divine beings, for example, Yama and Yami, who were brother and sister, are stated to have had sexual relations between themselves. Similar was the case of the Aswins and Surya. The divine creator, Brahma, is said to have been enamoured of his own daughter. These consanguineous sexual relations were, however, believed to be restricted to the divine beings and we do not find any parallel in human society, which was actually bound by a well-defined code of specific rules.

A well-known example of the epic period is that of King Dashrath of Koshala with his cousin Kaushalya. In India, cousins are called brothers and sisters in common parlance. Buddhist-Pali literature also contains certain stories of marriage between cross-cousins, for example, Nandia married his mother's brother's daughter, Revati (*Harvard Oriental Series*, vol. 30).

Even the custom of sororate (marriage with one's wife's sister) was also not quite unknown, as evidenced by the episode of Nabhi who married twin sisters, one of whom (Marudevi) gave birth to the Jain Tirthankar Rishabha.

According to common Hindu tradition, marriage within certain degrees of relationship, both on the father's as well as the mother's side, was prohibited. This rendered the choice of a spouse a complicated matter. This state of affairs was worsened further by the concept of *sapindas* (persons whose common ancestor is not removed farther than seven degrees on the male side and five degrees on the female side).

Among some of the higher castes, especially in Bengal, there prevailed a rule enjoining the wife to be taken from a particular section and generation. For instance, a Dakshin Rahi Kulin Kayastha must marry his eldest son to a girl of one of the Kulin sections belonging to the same generation as himself (A. K. Sur. *Sex and Marriage in India*. New Delhi: Allied Publishers, 1973).

The law of consanguinity has, however, certain relaxations in south India where, simultaneously with the general rule of clan, there existed the principle of preference for certain types of consanguineous cousins. Thus, the south Indian marriage differs from the northern one, which is based upon the *sapinda* rule or the avoidance of marriage among kin as stated earlier.

The consanguineous marriage prevalent in south India involved a preference for

1. uncle-niece, and
2. cross cousins.

Thus, a man was often obliged, or at least had a right to marry the daughter of his father's sister or of his mother's brother. In southern Maharashtra, quite a number of castes allow a man to marry the daughter of the maternal uncle, but no other first cousin. In Madhya Pradesh, the Gonds, Baigas and Agaria tribals have a custom of marrying a brother's son to his sister's daughter, which they term *Doodh Lautana* (giving back the milk), representing the idea that the loss of a woman to a family on marriage is compensated by the return of her daughter in marriage to the paternal family. Among the Hos and Santhals there prevailed a peculiar precondition for marriage of cross-cousins, namely, a man could not marry his mother's brother's daughter as long as the mother's brother was alive, nor could he marry the father's sister's daughter as long as the father's sister was alive.

It may be stated in this connection that ortho-cousins, or parallel cousins, never mate in Hindu society. Before concluding this chapter, it must be stated that the rules relating to caste, gotra, pravara and sapinda played no role in the dynastic marriages of the royal houses, which were normally contracted without any consideration of these concepts.

The advantage of marrying into a known family was that the girl was not placed suddenly in an entirely new environment making an adjustment with the new family a difficult process. This was, however, not without its disadvantage. Some psychologists aver that sexual adjustment between the husband and wife who know each other since childhood often involves some inhibitions.

LEVIRATE AND NIYOGA

There was a form of marriage, known as levirate, prevalent among certain castes in which a woman was taken as wife by the late husband's younger brother. The system could be justified in case it was based on the idea of the widow's remarriage to her late husband's younger brother. But actually it assumed the form of a restricted polyandry, as even during the life time of the elder brother, the younger brother exercised tacit sexual rights over the wife of the elder brother. Till quite recently, this practice prevailed among certain communities of Haryana and some castes in Uttar Pradesh and Orissa.

Tracing the origin of this custom in ancient Hindu society, we find that in the *Rig Veda* (X. 18. 7-8), a bereaved wife is described as sleeping near the funeral pyre of her dead husband and, in the next verse, she is urged to get up and join the world of the living by marrying the younger brother of her dead husband. Again, in the *Rig Veda* (X. 402), the widow is stated to be leading the *Devri* (husband's younger brother) to bed. This, however, did not involve the remarriage of the widow. When the elder brother died, the younger lived with the widow of his elder brother in sexual intimacy. A linguistic analysis of the period has provided interesting revelations in this regard. There existed different terms to signify 'father', for example, *pita* and *janita pita* meaning sociological and biological father, respectively. The term 'sociological father' has no connection with 'godfather'. The concept of sociological father as distinct from biological father indicates that society tolerated the sexual relations of the woman with a person other than the husband. There was another term used for the father, *pitritama,* meaning the foremost among the fathers. Evidently, this refers to the father who had married the woman and not to the other fathers having sexual rights with the woman by virtue of the customs of levirate and *Niyoga.*

The prevalence of the levirate form of marriage is further substantiated by certain references in the *Ramayana* as well, for example, Sugreev married Tara, the widow of his elder brother Bali, Vibheeshan married Mandodri, the widow of his elder brother Ravana.

As in the Vedic period, the younger brother had sexual rights over the elder brother's wife, the elder brother's dying without a son did not necessitate the adopting of a son. But later on, this general right of the younger brother gave way to the *niyoga* practice, that is, raising of a son on the widow in compliance with the religious duty of begetting a son. In this connection, the *Mahabharata* states that the right of raising an offspring "in the field of Vichitravirya" was first offered to the elder brother Bhishma, and on his refusal, to the elder stepbrother Krishna Dvaipayana. It seems that the *niyoga* practice developed on the basis of this senior-levirate system.

The concept that a departed soul could attain peace in heaven only if the son performed the *Shradha* or sacrificial ceremony here in this world, developed into a tradition enjoining on everybody the religious duty of begetting a son. So much so that during the *Mahabharata* period, the main aim behind marriage seems to have become begetting progeny rather than the gratification of sexual impulse. Consequently, there was a persistent demand among men and women for begetting more and more sons. There are many references in the scriptures in this regard. Agastya, who married Lopamudra, the daughter of the king of Vidarba, asks her: "How do you want me to raise sons on you? Do you want one, a hundred or a thousand sons?"

According to custom, there was a strict discipline enjoined on a widow going in for *niyoga.* She was required to lead a life of austerity for six months and then she was required to come to the man appointed for begetting a son from her. A son raised under the *niyoga* custom was called *kshetraja,* signifying a fruit grown on another's field. By the time of the Hindu lawgiver Manu, the practice of *niyoga* came to lose its earlier social approval. In the earlier context, Manu tolerated *niyoga* (ix.59) and said that the practice could be resorted to only where there was no offspring, meaning thereby that it could be invoked even during the life time of the husband. The man commissioned for the *niyoga* was, however, only a close kinsman of the husband. The Vedic and epic traditions do not confine *niyoga* to any *varna.* However, most of the examples of this practice contained in literature refer to the Kshatriya princesses and occasionally to the Brahmins (S. C. Sarkar. *Some Aspects of the Earliest Social History of India*. Oxford, 1928). In the later period it came to be restricted to the Shudras from the early centuries of the Christian era. According to Manu, *niyoga* could not take place in the marriages performed according to the mantras. Thus, *niyoga* was not permitted for the twice-born (*dvija*), learned in the Shastras, thereby meaning that *niyoga* was later restricted to Shudras only. Further, Vishvarupa also confirms this view, stating that *niyoga* was prescribed for the Kshatriyas by foolish and ignorant people out of greed (Kane. *History of Dharmasastra*).

This institution of *niyoga* has sometimes been treated to harsh criticism and even equated to prostitution with religious approval. In this connection, it would perhaps be worthwhile to distinguish between these two institutions. Marriage is admittedly an institution that evolved through the ages and has religious, legal and social approval, not only in regard to the regulation of sexual relations but of all the activities of the two persons united by marriage. The begetting of children through the matrimonial union has, thus, social approval throughout the world. Despite all the problems caused to parents in bringing up children, children are looked up as divine blessings and the parents are universally obliged to ensure their well being. Among Hindus of ancient times, this very concept of divine blessing in the form of children became an indispensable duty on all to leave a son in order to ensure the salvation of one's soul after death. In *niyoga,* the extramarital relations were not for sexual gratification but for procreation and, after begetting two sons, the two parties to *niyoga* were no more united sexually. Therefore, the institution of *niyoga* did not grant any sexual freedom.

Prostitution stands for promiscuous sexual intercourse for hire, devoid of all spiritual attachment or love between the two parties. In prostitution, there is also no element of abstinence, which sets it apart from the institutions of marriage and *niyoga.*

—oo(O)oo—

5

SATI AND WIDOW REMARRIAGE

LITERARY evidence confirms beyond doubt that the lot of the widow in India has been very hard, in the family as well as in society.

Tradition granted the widow the usufruct of the property left behind by her husband. It further provided that nothing of the husband's property shall be taken away from her. However, this noble provision applied only in cases where there were no sons. Thus, a widow with sons had no direct right of inheritance to her dead husband's property. The provisions relating to the rights of women to inheritance are contained in a separate chapter.

It is a fact that human beings, especially women, do not live on bread alone; they need love and freedom as well. Widows in ancient India who were not childless had something more for which to live and on which they could count on. The *Ramayana* and the *Mahabharata* vouchsafe this. The marriage of a woman for the second time is referred to in many passages of the *Mahabharata* as well as in Hindu law books. Such a woman was called *punarbha* (one assuming life again). In the *Vishnu Purana,* there is an episode of Ulupi, which relates that the husband of the daughter of Airavata, having been killed by Gauda, the widow was given in marriage to Arjuna. Another famous episode is that of Nala and Damayanti, in which, on getting no news about Nala (the husband), Damayanti is stated to be contemplating a second marriage by way of *swayamvara.*

Most of the law books of the Hindus held the view that women could remarry if the husband was missing or dead, or became an ascetic or was impotent or had lost his caste. They further stated that if a spotless maid had been unwittingly wedded to a man with a lasting or obnoxious disease, she could leave such a husband and choose another. Later on, this liberal attitude towards women's remarriage lost its prevalence and there developed a new concept of the chastity of women.

The term 'chaste' was made synonymous with '*pativrata*' meaning 'the one devoted to the husband'. This meant that the ideal of a wife was one of dancing to the will and command of the husband. From the epic period, there are many examples of a wife entertaining a stranger at the bidding of her husband, as a token of hospitality. Under the *niyoga* practice, she had to share her bed with her brother-in-law or some other close kinsman appointed for the purpose of begetting a son either during the lifetime or after the death of the husband.

Later on, this practice lost its usage and came to be categorised as adultery. Thus, sexual relations came to be strictly disciplined and restricted to persons united by matrimonial ties. Hindu law books as well as *Puranic* literature prescribed severe punishment for offences against this moral law. This concept of chastity came to be implemented so strictly that even the thought of sex with another individual came to be considered adultery which comprised eight forms: *Smarana* (thinking of it); *Keli* (dallying); *Prekshana* (viewing), *Guhyabhashanam* (secret discussion); *Sankalpa* (will to copulate); *Adhyavasaya* (resolve to perform) and *Kriyanishpatti* (actual accomplishment). Among all types of adultery, that with a teacher's wife was considered to be most heinous, calling for the severest punishment.

Among the higher castes, namely, the Kshatriyas and the Brahmins, an absolutely chaste life on the part of a widow was subject to a higher rule of conduct. There are, of course, stray references indicating the prevalence of the custom of remarriage of a widow among the Kshatriyas. This justifies Damayanti taking another husband when Nala, her husband, had disappeared. In higher society, the custom was that the wives of the conquered kings (who were usually slain) were not taken by the conqueror; he was supposed to protect them and to grant them all facilities for leading a chaste life.

According to the Hindu concept of matrimony, relations of husband and wife are sacramental rather than contractual. Hence, these relations could not be repudiated even upon the death of either party. The association between chastity and power is shown in a woman to such an extent that it became proverbial, that is, "is there anything greater than a woman who is a citadel of chastity?"

It may be particularly stated that the chastity referred to means primarily devotion to the husband. As indicated earlier, *Puranic* literature contains innumerable episodes on this subject. An ironic example is:

> A king's magic elephant was injured. The king went on fast and prayed for cure but with no success. Eventually he resolved to sacrifice himself before the deity by cutting off his own head to fall at the feet of the deity, thereby hoping to attain divine favour. However, he was prevented from do so by a voice from heaven, which announced that the touch of a chaste woman's hand would effect the cure. The king made his wives and all the women of the city touch the ailing magic elephant, but the elephant was not healed (*Katha Sarit-Sagar*).

A love affair with a widow called for punishment and the widow bearing a child from her lover was to be banished from the land. In regard to celibacy, there is a difference of opinion. Crooke, in his book *The North-Western Provinces* writes that

> ...in this part of India, 24 per cent of the population prohibits widow marriage, while 76 per cent both permits and even encourages the practice...As a matter of fact, among all but the very richest castes, every young widow finds another mate, and the levirate (the custom by which the younger brother-in-law takes over the widow of the deceased elder brother) widely prevails.

In the course of time, the fate of the widow worsened progressively and ultimately the widow came to be considered ill-omened. Besides enjoining on her a highly chaste life, she was deprived of the right of participating in religious and social festivities. So much so, that the very sight of her was considered a bad omen and she was virtually reduced to the position of a slave, dedicating her life to the service of the family of the deceased husband, leading a highly chaste life as enjoined by society or religion and hoping for liberation by death.

Despite the miserable lot of the widow, the institution of *sati* or widow-burning was not prevalent in the epic age, and the references found therein to this effect seem to be later interpolations. The *Ramayana* gives only one instance of a Brahmin woman giving herself to be burnt along with her dead husband. However, the seventh book does not belong to the original poem and hence this episode is evidently of a later date.

GENESIS OF THE INSTITUTION OF *SATI*

The assertion that it is the duty and nature of a good wife to follow her husband in death is found more in the other epic, namely, the *Mahabharata,* but it also is not firm proof of widow-burning as a common custom.

Death by self-immolation by the woman has been observed among the Kshatriya (warrior) class, the forefathers of the Rajputs, who seem to be endowed with the strongest feeling for private property in regard to their wives. In the course of time, there developed a tradition of self-immolation by widows among the Kshatriyas, which ultimately led to the development of a custom called *sati,* of burning the widow alive on the funeral pyre of her dead husband. Later on, this custom got so much religious and social sanction that the glory of the *sati,* the merit of the widow's immolation and the ritual ceremony of the burning of the widow on the funeral pyre of her dead husband was the subject of elaborate discussion in the *Puranic* period (*Guruda Puran Sarod*, x, 35-55).

This development of the tradition of *sati* has, however, not remained unopposed. The wife's faithfulness being misconstrued to the extent of *sati* was emphatically stated in the *Mahanirvan Tantra* (x. 79-80), which states that every woman is a reflection of the great goddess, and if a woman in her blindness refuses to climb on to the dead husband's pyre, then she goes straight to hell. It may be mentioned that the root of the belief in the glory of *sati* lies not merely in the idea that the departed one must not go into the other world as a wifeless wretch, but also in the superstitious fear of his vengeance if this property of his is withheld from him or even taken over by a successor in the marriage.

There are ample references, however, in the *Mahabharata* and the *Dharma Shastras* indicating the marriage of a woman for a second time. A woman marrying for the second time was called *punarbha.*

In regard to the husband's remarriage, the majority opinion has always been favourable. However, in regard to the marriage of the woman, there has been, and still continues to be, a difference of opinion among the different castes. In any case, the mass sentiment towards the remarriage of women was that of disapproval and it was considered verging on the scandalous. As against this, chastity, dedication to the memory of the deceased husband and devotion to the children or the family of the husband were considered to be the proper and virtuous activities for a widow.

A radical change in the way of life of a widow is characteristic of Indian society. Widowhood is associated with the gravest misfortune not only for the widow but also for the family and society at large. The association of inauspiciousness with widowhood still continues and widows themselves avoid participating in various ceremonies to avoid humiliation. The austerities and privations enjoined on the Hindu widow were, by far, harsher than committing *sati* which attracted glory and religious and social approval.

The absolute identification of the wife's personality with that of the husband sought and achieved as a willing equation would be an example of an extremely devotional love, but its imposition by society on unwilling persons turns the ideal into a crime. This happened with the tradition of *sati* which was believed to symbolise the unity of the husband and wife through death into the next birth.

Obviously, this signified a complete annihilation of the woman's individuality. She was even degraded to the position of an animal, living and dying at the will of her master. There are ample references to this in the *Ramayana* and the *Mahabharata* which, even if they are later interpolations, testify to the miserable lot of the women. This compares to the Nietschean injunction: "Goest thou to women, forget not thy whip."

In regard to the custom of *sati,* caste distinctions played a very important role. In the *Dharma Shastras,* the custom of *sati* is discussed at length as to how and by whom the custom was to be followed. The Brahmin women were specifically precluded from performing *sati* in most of the texts. Strictly speaking, the practice of *sati* was mostly confined to the Kshatriya caste comprising rulers and fighters, among whom a sense of possession and love for a good family name was the strongest. According to Brihaddevata, the practice of *sati* was valid for Kshatriyas only.

Further, the *Padma Purana* (work of the early medieval period) states that *sati* could not be allowed for the Brahmins. Almost all the instances of widow-burning relate only to the Kshatriyas. After the middle of the first millennium, the custom increased in frequency, but then too, it was restricted to those claiming Kshatriya status. There was hardly any example of a Vaisya or Shudra woman committing *sati.* Thus, the practice of *sati* was typically an aristocratic tradition confined to the noble class called the Kshatriyas.

On having acquired political control in India, the British were especially shocked by the custom of *sati,* which Indian society held with great veneration. So much so, that many widows mounted the funeral pyre willingly. However, as in the case of all human behaviour, this willingness was largely based on various formal and informal (social as well as religious) sanctions against the woman who refused to be burnt alive with her dead husband, especially among the noble class. The tragic lot of a widow, as indicated earlier, outweighed the horror of being burnt alive, especially because the latter alternative promised her a seat in heaven along with the husband.

According to Altekar, not more than two to 10 per cent of the widows ever committed suicide. Actually, not more than one widow in a thousand became a *sati* in the general population (A. S. Altekar. *The Position of Women in Hindu Civilisation*. 1938). It may be stated in this connection that the custom has not completely died out despite all social and legislative measures against it. Stray instances sometimes occur even today in a State like Rajasthan.

As a result of the incessant efforts of our social reformers right from the earlier part of the 19th century, the groundwork was laid for legislative measures penalising the practice of *sati* (vide Bengal Sati Regulation, 1829, which was later adopted by the Madras and Bombay Governments in 1830). In the beginning, all attempts to abolish *sati* met with relatively little success, especially because widow remarriage was not permitted, and the life of the widow in her former husband's family was extremely intolerable.

Thus, the anti-*sati* Act of 1829 had little effect till positive legislative measures were taken for permitting widow remarriage in 1856. However, despite the legal protection, a widow's remarriage normally gave rise to public incidents of casting out of widows, repression, direct and indirect social sanctions and even violence.

The tragic lot of the widow can well be imagined from the fact that sometimes girls married in their infancy were widowed even before they attained puberty. In 1881, 19 out of every 1000 girls in the 10-15 year age group were widowed, whereas in the year 1901, eighteen were widowed (*Census of India 1901*, vol. I, part I). In the later period, that is, during the first half of the last century, their number decreased progressively.

It would be worthwhile to mention here that the efforts to give the Hindu widow the right to remarry were viewed as releasing her from an extremely humiliating and depressing situation, rather than the granting of an ordinary human right to live a happy married life (W. J. Goode,. *World Revolutions and Family Patterns*). Besides the legal measures for the abolition of *sati* and for prompting widow remarriage, the strong efforts made by certain religious and social reformers, for example, Raja Ram Mohun Roy, Ishwar Chandra Vidyasagar, Swami Dayananda and others resulted in growing approval for widow remarriage. In 1901, the Census Survey indicated that among the upper classes, particularly in the big cities, public opinion approved of the remarriage of virgin widows (*Census of India 1901*, vol. I, part I). Later, with the progressively growing education among women, widow remarriage started gaining increasing social approval. Thus, it may be safely said that widow remarriage has become relatively common despite disapproval in certain small sections of society.

It is well known that despite the progressively increasing approval to widow remarriage, reverence is still shown in certain parts of the country (Rajasthan, for example) for women who committed *sati* in the past. As a symbol of reverence to the self-immolating widows, newly married couples are taken to some *sati* memorial to obtain the *sati's* blessings.

According to the 1951 Census, there were 22 million widows comprising 12.3 per cent of the female population. According to the 1961 Census, 10.8 per cent of the female population were widows, whereas 3.7 per cent of the male population were widowers. The 1971 Census showed 23 million widows as against eight million widowers.

The present condition of the widows needs to be considered from the social and economic points of view, which are often indistinguishable from one another on account of a sharp contrast in the social attitude towards widows among people of different socio-economic strata. It is regrettable that although the Widow Remarriage Act was passed as early as in 1856, the attitude of some tradition-bound sections of Indian society towards this unfortunate group has not changed considerably.

—oo(O)oo—

6

DIVORCE

AS stated earlier, among the Hindus, matrimonial relations were irrevocable and hence there was no provision for divorce. While the women could not remarry even after the death of the husband, the men could remarry even during the lifetime of the wife. Adultery on the part of a woman deprived her of various privileges, but divorce was not allowed to her even in such circumstances. The only exception to this rule was that the tradition of *Sambandham* form of marriage prevalent in the Nair community of Kerala allowed certain relaxation to allow *Sambandham* relations with other men. This type of *Sambandham* marriage has been explained earlier in the previous chapter. However, as this custom entitled women to take more than one husband, the relationship in such cases assumed the form of polyandry which cannot be inferred as a right to divorce. In the history of human society, divorce has always been evidently considered a misfortune or a tragedy and the high divorce rate in the West is a clear indication of the increasing tension in husband-wife relations. A majority of the world's societies have evolved the institution of divorce as an escape from the tension in which the two parties to a marriage find themselves.

Divorce is different from the other solutions adopted in this regard; for example, annulment or polygyny, in which women are free to find another husband. However, till a little over 50 years ago almost everyone who divorced was viewed as having lost respectability to some extent. After the First World War, divorce began to attain increasing social approval. Further, legislative measures taken by many countries in this connection have made it easier to obtain divorce. The expansion of education and the economic self-sufficiency of women coupled with the possibilities of remarriage both for the husband and the wife have also increased the divorce rate. So much so that for persons above 40 years of age, the chances of eventual marriage are believed to be higher for divorcees than for those not married earlier, because the divorce does not mean a rejection of marriage but a lack of proper adaptability between the two partners. The divorcee realises better than the single person that married life, at large, is satisfying, and this consciousness makes them plan to return to it by re-marriage. In the case of wrongly combined marriages, divorce is evidently better than desertion, informal separation, swapping of partners and other similar evasive devices.

During the past few decades, divorce has aroused much moralistic fervour. Whereas during the late 1940s and early 1950s, the majority of Italian people were still against divorce, the general social sentiment in this regard underwent a radical change. According to a sample survey undertaken in 1949, about 34 per cent of the people were in favour of a law instituting divorce. This was the view of 38 per cent people residing in cities with a population of over a hundred thousand, whereas in Milan more than 62 per cent were in favour. Even in Rome, where social life is significantly influenced by religion, 39 per cent were in favour (L. F. Pierpaola. IInd volto, *Sconoscuito dell' Italia*).

Another survey undertaken in May 1955 showed that 40 per cent were generally favourable by that time and about 60 per cent approved of divorce in certain extreme situations (such as attempted homicide of the spouse, abandonment of family for a long period, etc.).

The justification given in support of divorce is its rapid increase in whichever society in which it has been permitted, which testifies to the desire of individuals going in for it to get rid of the person with whom they have been united without sufficient sentimental conciliation. The increasing number of divorces has further been accompanied by an almost corresponding increase in the chances of remarriage and a progressive decrease in the stigma attached to it earlier. In these circumstances, it seems to be proper to examine the scope of the significance of divorce. It is sometimes asserted that the new freedom for women is primarily responsible for the increasing number of divorces. In a sense, it may be partially acceptable, but it is an admitted fact that the husband demands the majority of divorces. The recognition of women as legal entities coupled with their social freedom and the decline of religious authority and community control on the state of matrimony was bound to lead to greater sexual laxity that struck at the heart of family stability.

Divorce signified a personal tragedy, an outcome of the disintegration of the family and a legal dissolution of the marriage bond, which ultimately went to create a social problem. Divorce is merely a process of giving legal recognition to a relationship already shattered by irreconcilable disparity in the character of the two partners or by unkept pledges, broken faith, tension and painful disillusionment. It is a fact that despite all the liberalism of the modern generation, any failure to abide by traditional notions of sexual morality entails grave risks for all women, married or unmarried alike. No man or woman would be willing to accept promiscuity on the part of the partner.

Evidently, emotions form a very important part of marriage and of its dissolution. Hence, in analysing the various aspects of divorce, it is very difficult to dissociate emotion from reason or custom from eternal truths. To make an objective appraisal of marriage, it would be necessary to take into consideration established practices which have ensured the institution's religious sanctity. Marriage and family imply social notions of respectability, imperious urge of sex, economic dependence of women, children's need for love, protection and upbringing. The history of matrimonial institutions reveals that the development of marriage laws has been progressively restricting the licentiousness on the part of men with a corresponding increase in the responsibilities imposed upon husbands and fathers.

In dealing with the causes of tension and discord between the partners in a marriage leading to divorce, that is, marital failure, the socio-psychological description of the interplay of the personality of each party is fundamentally based on wishes, attitudes and sentiments. Thus, for ensuring harmony in marital relations, an adjustment and adaptation to the wishes, attitudes and sentiments of both the partners is necessary. Evidently, the fact of living together calls for an adjustment to the needs and demands of both the parties consciously or unconsciously and ultimately leads to the natural process of interpenetration and assimilation of the two personalities united by the matrimonial tie.

As stated in an earlier chapter, in course of time, husband and wife tend to become identical with the progressively growing process of assimilation. The degree of realisation of this ideal of assimilation is, however, different from person to person, depending on one's own temperament as also the cultural surroundings in which one lives. Matrimonial harmony depends on the degree of this assimilation, which in turn depends on the receptivity of the two individuals coupled with their own habits, traits and attitudes, etc. Most psychologists and sociologists would agree that in the most successful marriages, the degree of assimilation and identity must be necessarily high. Only those persons who fail to make the necessary adjustment with their marital partners to arrive at an intimate relationship are heard complaining about the validity of the institution of marriage. Such persons, mostly, are those who want to ensure for themselves the security which a successful marriage otherwise offers without making any adjustment in regard to their personal freedom and the relative lack of responsibility, which they have enjoyed as single persons.

Caste considerations played an important role in the matter of dissolution of marriage. Caste endogamy being a vital prerequisite for marriage, the loss of caste by the husband vested a right in his wife to abandon him and to take another husband (Narada, XII, 97., cf. XII. 37). Such dissolution of marriage was, however, not divorce, which, according to the *Dharma Shastras* could be effected unilaterally on the grounds of adultery, barrenness, disobedience, etc.

Although marriage was considered an irrevocable bond among orthodox, high caste Hindus, divorce was allowed among certain depressed classes. According to Kautilya, divorce was permissible in the case of the four approved kinds of marriage that meant that only the lower castes, which were permitted to go in for the unapproved forms of marriage, could resort to divorce. Further, Kautilya has offered a number of options to the wife, whose husband has been absent for a long time, for example, remarriage and levirate, etc. Divorce could, however, not be forced upon an unwilling husband. Because of the contact with the West, marriage in India started being secularised in the sense that legal provisions were for divorce and the right of inheritance to women. The Special Marriage Act of 1954 provided for

1. Marriage by registration (that is, without undergoing the ritual formalities), whereby persons belonging to different faiths could marry,
2. Neither party to the marriage should have a living spouse at the time of marriage, and
3. The parties to the marriage must not be within the prohibited degree of relationship.

However, this Act did not become popular because of a strange element incorporated in it that the parties to a marriage under the Act were presumed to have separated from the joint family and their share in the family property was regulated by the India Succession Act of 1925. The compact traditional structure of the Indian family did not allow even the educated strata of society to go in for marriage under this Act. The different practices prevailing among different sections of Indian society were later unified by the passage of the Hindu Marriage Act, 1955, thereby allowing divorce to the entire Indian population.

Evidently, a monogamous marriage without the right of divorce constitutes a great hardship to both the partners of a marriage. The concept of the sacramental nature of marriage signifying an indissoluble union for life has been progressively losing importance in India. The law pertaining to marriage and divorce has been justifiably engaging the attention of our legislators. The different forms of marriage recognised by law today are

1. The sacramental marriage,
2. Marriages registered with the Registrar of Marriages, and
3. Any other form of marriage recognised by customary law.

The growing sentiment in favour of divorce was observed in a minority motivated by the Women's Rights Movement. Under the laws in force in the 1940s, the grounds for divorce were evidently harsh, for example, under the Bombay Hindu Married Women's Right to Separate Residence and Maintenance Act of 1946, the woman could claim maintenance and residence away from her husband on grounds such as

1. Loathsome disease contracted by the husband, but not from her,
2. Such cruelty as would make life with the husband unsafe,
3. Desertion without her consent, or
4. The husband has contracted a second marriage.

Some other States passed laws with similar restrictive provisions also.

Under the Hindu Marriage Act of 1955, all endeavours have been made to raise the status of the wife to bring her at par with that of the husband. According to this Act, divorce is permissible in case the spouse has been insane for three years or has disappeared for seven years or has suffered from leprosy/venereal disease for three years, or has converted to another religion or committed adultery or renounced the world to pursue the life of an ascetic. This Act granted to the women, for the first time, the right to seek judicial separation, annulment of marriage and divorce.

The grounds for divorce enumerated above are perhaps cumbersome and hard to prove. Due to this, as also Hindu society's fundamental characteristic of clinging to traditionalism, the number of divorces was low. In fact, mass sentiment about divorce is intertwined with the proscription against remarriage, which was considered something quite scandalous. Divorce seems to be viewed at par with widow remarriage, or an escape from a difficult situation rather than the chance to establish a new life because a marriage has failed.

In the tradition-bound Indian society, despite certain revolutionary legal provisions, a number of inequities and inadequacies are still continuing in this field. For example, the law provides a waiting period of two years for instituting a divorce petition even after obtaining a separation. Further, under Section 14 of the Hindu Marriage Act, except in certain circumstances, a party cannot apply for divorce within three years of marriage. Even after a decree of divorce has been obtained, there is a mandatory provision, whereby a divorcee is prohibited from remarrying until another year.

Divorce, which is admittedly a relief from the painful life of a bad marriage, is hardly enough to re-establish the individual socially and psychologically. It is evidently a public admission of the failure of marriage and even after the divorce, the aggrieved or relieved party does not find himself or herself in the same situation as before marriage. The wounds inflicted in an unsuccessful marriage have to be borne for a lifetime. Despite this fact, the cumbersome legal proceedings one has to undergo for seeking relief in case of failure of the matrimonial tie, the customary rights and ceremonies make the grant of relief to the aggrieved party well nigh impossible. For example, bigamy is prohibited by Section 17 of the Hindu Marriage Act, 1955, and is punishable under Sections 494 and 495 of the Indian Penal Code. However, the interpretation of a legally valid marriage based on the traditional ritual ceremony provides loopholes to the guilty party. In a case decided by the Supreme Court some time ago, the parties were married in 1941. During the subsistence of marriage, the husband married again. The first wife filed a complaint against the husband under Section 494 of the Indian Penal Code, but the plaint, even after being pursued up to the Supreme Court, could not bring relief as the second marriage was not performed with all essential ceremonies of a Hindu marriage (*havan* and *satpadi*) and, therefore, the husband could not be held to have married again.

The legal provisions about divorce applicable to other communities in India are also similar. For instance, Christians have to allege and prove adultery in order to establish a matrimonial offence, a cognisable ground for obtaining divorce under the Indian Divorce Act. Among the Parsis, divorce proceedings are held and decided upon by a jury of 10 assessors chosen from the community. It is extremely strange that none of the laws (except the Special Marriages Act of 1954) mentions the possibility of divorce by mutual consent. Thus, the consenting parties are left with no alternative but to resort to change of religion which is accepted as a ground for divorce. When mutuality is universally accepted as a basis of marriage, in all fairness it should be accepted as a basis for divorce.

—oo(O)oo—

7

THE FUTURE OF MARRIAGE

IN the wake of revolutionary changes in sexual behaviour in the West coupled with the economic independence of women brought about by industrial development, the institution of marriage is facing a grave challenge today. This calls for a realistic appraisal of the whole institution of marriage. The question that arises is: Does the institution of marriage have a future?

With the radical change in the structure of the family, family living is no longer compulsory. A tendency is developing that a man's domestic needs can be met cheaper and with less fuss without a wife. At the same time, women can provide for themselves and live more comfortably through their own efforts without depending on the income of the husband. This state of affairs makes marriage seem a luxury that also carries the potential of problems such as parenthood, divorce, etc. However, despite this, people continue to marry and re-marry in large numbers.

Evidently, marriage in its evolved form, will remain an indispensable part of the individual and social life. Humanity, in its search for happiness, will naturally continue to crave intimacy and experience the mystic union propounded by *Tantra Yoga* offers. It is true that marriage as it exists today is inadequate to meet modern emotional requirements and has to adapt itself to present circumstances. The continuing desire among most young people to marry means that marriage is still held to be a source of warmth and stability.

The earlier concept of marriage was a symbol of settling down in life but since the last century the concept has changed to mean a successful and meaningful partnership. The new concept of marriage which demands a truly vital relationship means not settling down but a starting place, a search to enable the attainment of happiness.

A marriage involves the pairing of two individuals who present their better selves by interacting with each other ensuring the growth of both of them. In such a marriage, individual egos would be replaced by assimilated identity which does not, however, submerge either personality. In other words, marriage today is a medium of personal growth in which both men and women grow as individuals in a spirit of co-operation as against competition.

One could argue that such a marriage is far from the accepted ideal marriage which promises perpetual bliss. Actually, a growing and healthy relationship generates its own excitement based on the personality of the partners. Such a dynamic element could also result in creation of new interests which sometimes conflict, but it will help in enriching the personalities of both the partners.

Thus, romantic marriage or the so-called love marriage has to give way to the 'vital' marriage, as a purely romantic marriage ignores the vital relationship of the couple. In the absence of a vital relationship, the element of romance diminishes, transforming the union into a burden on both the parties. As against this, a reasonable amount of personal independence together with some common ground of interests and outlook, as also physical compatibility and warmth would lead to a rewarding and enriching marriage. For enhancing the quality of marriage there is also need of a sense of commitment and profound involvement with each other.

These qualities presuppose well-based personal maturity and serenity. Consequently, the vital relationship envisaged can be expected to develop among persons with age and experience. The rising age of marriage among men and women offers hope in this regard. One can expect that in the future, marital relationships will be characterised by increasing mutual understanding and frankness. The overwhelming role given to the role of sex in analysing the bases of marital harmony will give way to a realistic attitude towards sex. With the passage of time, sexual attraction may strengthen in some cases and decrease in others. This problem, of course, is still without a solution. However, such cases can be minimised if the couple, with profound faith, strive for mutual fulfilment through broadened interests.

It is very difficult to predict the future of marriage and the family, because the functioning of these institutions is dependent on the cultural background of different societies. The present challenges these institutions are facing would result in certain modification, but their total elimination is not likely.

UNIVERSALITY OF MARRIAGE

In the Vedic age, the participation of the wife was considered indispensable for the successful conclusion of all ceremonies and sacrifices on the assumption that as man alone is spiritually incomplete, he is not competent to offer oblations to the gods. This was similar to the Avestian concept of bachelors being spiritually impure. Thus, in the Vedic age, marriage was a religious and social duty for attaining happiness in this world and beyond.

Therefore, until quite recently, Hindu society had a tradition of universal marriage, enjoining on every individual a religious duty of entering into matrimony, based on the belief that a male descendant was necessary who could offer *pindas* (sacrificial offerings) for peace to the departed soul of the deceased father.

From the discussion on the position of women, it is clear that marriage and motherhood came to be considered an indispensable aim of life for a Hindu woman. In a sense, marriage was not a personal matter but a cultural need. This fact is dramatically evidenced by the prevalence of so many special *vratas* (fasts) which the Hindu woman observes for getting a suitable life partner, continued married state, long life and welfare of the husband, and for motherhood and securing special protection for the sons. For example, there is an annual *vrata* in commemoration of the steadfastness of Savitri, who followed the god of Death and brought back her husband through the virtue of her penance. Similarly, there is an annual worship of Parvati, who performed difficult penance to win the heart of Shiva.

From the reference made earlier explaining the custom of *niyoga* it is clear that the tradition of enjoining a duty on the parents or guardians to get their children married was almost universally accepted. The epic *Mahabharata* also contains references in this connection, namely, Bhishma tells Yudhisthar: "One who does not marry his daughter to a suitable groom, commits the sin of killing a Brahmin." However, despite all the religious and social provisions in favour of marriage, it was not made compulsory until about 300 B. C. and then too only for girls.

This belief in turn resulted in the introduction of another evil tradition of child marriage, which continued for a long time and, despite the various preventive legislative measures taken by the Government, persisted till quite recently, to a small degree, among certain backward sections of society. However, with the various legislative checks and the incessant efforts of social reformers, these traditions have disappeared almost completely.

It may be worthwhile to state that a similar belief was prevalent among the followers of the laws of Moses and Confucius to beget children for ensuring salvation and true immortality. It was believed that with a son, a man obtains victory over all people and with a son's son, one enjoys immortality. One of the reasons why Jewish women considered sterility dishonourable was that each of them secretly hoped that she might become the mother of the promised Messiah. But when the Jews ceased to hope for the deliverer that was to come, then the incentive for child birth was gone. Thus, to a Jew, Chinese or Brahmin, the absence of a son was not merely a misfortune, but a life of failure.

—oo(O)oo—

SECTION II

Man-Woman Relationships

8

LOVE MARRIAGE AND FREE LOVE

AS against the traditional system of combining endogamous marriage in India, marriage in Europe is based on the independent decision of the two partners to the marriage, who are guided mainly by romantic love, sex attraction, companionship, rapport, sympathetic understanding, idealisation, etc. In view of the increasing degree of marital discord in present-day society despite the prevalence of an absolute independence of free choice in regard to marriage, even the term 'romantic love' needs to be redefined in the wake of the changing mores and standards of values in its physical as well as social-psychological aspects.

It is a psychological fact that to ensure happiness, it is indispensable to prepare oneself for marriage, especially in the adjustment techniques. Evidently, the personality of an individual starts taking a definite shape right from childhood, with the child's attitude towards different members of the family. These impressions and attitudes in the child's mind may prove to be either highly congenial to adjustments later with one's marital partner or even insuperable impediments.

From the point of view of ensuring success and happiness in life, preparation for marriage actually involves a preparation for life itself, that is, a capacity to deal with various situations. For this purpose, it is necessary to ensure intellectual and emotional development simultaneously, so that both parties to marriage may assume adult responsibilities not only ungrudgingly but also with an attitude of spiritual devotion. Marriage is undoubtedly a situation to be taken up with the courage of a realist and not to be evaded like an escapist. Evidently, escapism offers no solution to a problem, especially when it concerns marital relations.

Some people believe that marriage is an abrupt and jolting change from courtship and engagement, which is no longer true in modern conditions, where the transition is admittedly a gradual one. During the period of courtship and engagement, couples have the opportunity of experiencing varied situations, testing adaptability of both the parties and the extent of reciprocal assimilation of the two personalities. They are fully conscious of each other's personality traits. The prospective husband is aware of the type of make-up used by his prospective wife and how she looks in a bathing suit or in a housecoat. They see each other under both favourable and unfavourable physical and psychological conditions.

There is also a widely prevalent notion that the success of a woman is judged mainly in terms of her marital status, whereas that of a man is judged with reference to his occupational achievements. This indicates a distinct psychological situation in which the two sexes find themselves, whereas the prevalent social system induces a woman mainly to enhance her appearance and social relations, thereby making herself more attractive to the opposite sex.

Marriage implies a satisfactory orientation towards the culturally defined concept of 'love', which is often seen as somewhat mysterious, irrational and a highly individualistic affair because of the progressively increasing stress on rationality. The concept of the so-called romantic love as the only basis of marriage often creates problems, both social and psychological. The traditional ideal requiring a woman to be physically attractive and not too bright, at least pretend to be such, entirely subservient to the man, has faded in the wake of the progress of education.

The change from Victorian sexual mores, prevalent during the 19th century towards the modern attitude to sexual relations, is also often associated with the woman's status. The concept of sin in sexual mores, both in and outside of marriage, is losing significance. In certain countries (including India), abortion has been legalised and children born out of wedlock are given full legal and social approval. It has been observed that there has been a progressively increasing parity concerning behaviour patterns in the field of sex mores, marriages and family living.

Despite all this freedom, adolescent girls are usually encouraged to turn their attention towards marriage and family matters. About their relation with boys, girls are advised to be relatively passive and to set limits to sexual intimacy. Thus, the burden of responsibility falls on the woman, who is denied the initiative, a rather curious combination of rights and obligations. However, this state of affairs is undergoing a rapid change. The custom that the young man always pays when the couple goes out no longer holds true indicating that both partners now share initiative and decision making equally.

The question arises as to whether this relaxation in the sexual pattern confers on the woman an advantage in comparison to her traditional position. There are divergent opinions in this regard. The supporters of tolerant sexual mores plead that apart from providing natural sexual satisfaction, this would ensure a harmonious development of the personality, guarding against double standards in behaviour, thereby avoiding complexes and psychological distortions. Against this, the opponents of more tolerant sexual mores apprehend a disadvantageous position for the young girl leading to premature sex-indulgence.

As stated earlier, the institution of love marriage is known in India. The *Gandharva* type of marriage was nothing else than a love marriage in the strict sense of the term. In the *Gandharva* marriage, the main deciding factor for marriage was love.

During the post-Vedic period, the prevalence of *Samana* festivals, in which girls freely participated and looked for a suitable husband testifies to the prevalence of love marriage in India right from the earliest times. This was especially more prevalent among the lower classes, among whom women have always enjoyed more freedom in regard to marriage, partially on account of their active participation in earning income. Among certain Indian tribes, for example, the Murias of Madhya Pradesh, there exists a tradition of practising a form of free love that combines the logic and impulse of sexual attraction. They have an institution called the *ghotul* which provides for unmarried young men and women to live in sexual intimacy till they find the person of their choice for marriage. This institution of absolute freedom is prevalent among them even today, more or less in its original form. But among rural and urban societies, the institution of free love went through radical change, towards degeneration, with the development of the tendency of exploitation which took different dimensions, for example, in the name of religion, caste, sex, etc. The Rishabdev Mela (fair) of Rajasthan is reminiscent of the old *Samana* fair.

In urban society, on festival gatherings and similar occasions, there are often opportunities for young men and women to make friends. Even so, parents kept a watchful eye on their progeny and if such friendship became serious and the young couple wished to get married, the boy's parents usually approved if formal permission was sought by the parents of the girl.

In the *Swayamvara* marriage, prevalent among the noble class, the girl was given absolute independence to choose her husband from among the gathered suitors. However, later, the institution of marriage based on love came to be restricted to a very small minority.

The freedom enjoyed by young people in the West to form friendships necessarily means that a higher proportion of marriages are based on love and free choice within the social limitations. However, in Europe too this freedom was attained by the urban middle classes or aristocracy after the First World War. Before this, arranged marriages appeared to have been more common (Joel M. Halpern. *A Serbian Village*); for example, in Serbia all negotiations were carried on between the heads of the two families concerned.

Further, this freedom was not absolute. Parents continue to play an important role in their children's decisions in varying degrees, depending upon regional and cultural conditions. Certain field studies made by some sociologists in this connection are quite revealing.

In a study of a French village, Wylie states that "all the people of Peyrane, whom I questioned on this point, agreed that the most important condition for marriage was not only love" (Laurence Wylie. *Village in the Vauchuse*). The increasing participation of women in almost all spheres of social, administrative, political and industrial activity, coupled with the decreasing authority of the parents over their children, has made the institution of love marriage universal in the West.

During the last five decades in India, there has been a significant expansion in educational facilities, industrialisation and urbanisation which has led to a debate on women's emancipation in India. The prevalence of arranged marriages in India has been exposed to much criticism and there has been an incessant struggle by urban educated women for free choice. It would be worthwhile to consider this matter from the historical point of view.

In India, there prevails a system of joint family in which, normally, three generations live together in a patriarchal system which administers the various affairs of the family. Thus, the elders are held in great esteem and have almost irrefutable authority. Young family members who fail to adhere to their advice and decisions are subject not only to the displeasure of the elders but to social opprobrium as well.

In this state of affairs, even the younger generation which is otherwise supposed to be highly modern in their outlook on life, is compelled to turn to the parents in matters of matrimony. It is considered a sacred duty of a daughter in a traditional Indian family to submit to her parents' selection of a husband. There may be some girls who are aggressive and resourceful enough to choose their own life partner, but even in such cases, the approval of the parents is usually obtained. Apart from such exceptional cases, it is the privilege as well as the responsibility of the parents to find a suitable match for their daughters. To do so in a society bound by traditions of caste endogamy, *gotra,* and village exogamy and by the evil of dowry, is a gruelling task and some parents naturally seem to be secretly wishing that their daughters solve this problem for themselves. If the girl in such a family is fortunate and courageous enough to do so, the parents readily acquiesce despite some tacit social disapproval.

In these circumstances, the marriage, which is a strictly personal affair, is transformed into a vulgar display of one's social status and the marriage ceremony, instead of being a gathering of close friends and relations, often becomes an unmanageable crowd involving much wasteful expenditure by the bride's parents. The marriage party from the groom's side, which could be huge, adds no ritual or social significance to the marriage. By the time the bridal couple gets ready to exchange their marital vows, the crowd has normally left. The girl's parents who normally observe a fast for divine favour till the conclusion of the marriage, can heave a sigh of relief only at the conclusion of the sacrificial fire ceremony sanctifying the marriage.

Increasing education and contact with the West has naturally had its own effect on the state of affairs, and today the educated Indian seems to be picking up courage, of course with certain reservations, to hold that marriage being a matter of profound social importance, should be left to the free choice of the young. The standard of values and behaviour seems to be undergoing a radical change, so much so that virginity as a pre-requisite to marriage is perhaps not as significant today as it used to be, and the young talk freely about sex and conceding that a woman's physical need is as great as a man's, implying that both have an equal right to enjoy sex before and outside marriage. However, this revolutionary attitude is not in accord with actual behaviour. An insignificant minority of urban educated women share these ideas partially on account of the irrational restrictive behaviour of their parents and also their own economic independence. In a sample survey of Delhi and Agra university students, one respondent said: "I am free to do whatever I feel like doing, and intentionally do things that my parents hold to be sinful and immoral." A survey made in Poona University in April-May 1975 and another in Delhi University in 2001 substantiated the prevalence of a similar tendency.

The most evident change in this regard is the open discussion on sex. The young generation feels that parents should discuss sex freely with their children. Although it is still difficult to comment on the actual change in sexual behaviour, in matters of dress at least, the younger generation feels less embarrassed to expose their body. The concept of love making, too, has undergone a significant transformation. An enquiry made in this connection suggests that today it means 'rational love', resulting from the knowledge and assessment of the material and emotional assets of the prospective husband. Now compatibility is the watchword instead of the old-fashioned romance. Further, consideration of personal and social factors is also shaping the educated Hindu woman's idea of love from the 'romantic' to the 'calculated'. Evidently, love marriages among educated working women is becoming more common and the concept of the traditional institution of marriage as a permanent and sacred contract is now being substituted by the concept of a practical contract suited to both parties. A large number of young people marry for material reasons. Another development is the 'neo-arranged marriage' in which the parents select a suitable boy and then the boy and girl are allowed to meet a few times and take a final decision themselves.

This situation does not signify a total revolution in the Indian woman's ideas on love, sex and marriage. Instead, it indicates an evolution in a certain direction which needs to be given a proper lead.

In the present transitional stage, the urban educated Indian woman seems to be developing an increasingly superficial and materialistic attitude which has an impact on their attitude towards matrimonial relations and parent-child relationship. The degree of affection for children is often low and leads to development of distorted personalities. The confusion about the standard of values is manifesting itself in various ways, for example, increase in juvenile delinquency, student unrest, disobedience, etc.

As stated earlier, the Indian woman's struggle for rights is limited to her role as a wife. Since Indian society at large is still clinging to traditionalism, modern educated Indian working women find themselves in a state of ambivalence and high tension, or with a sense of guilt as well which needs to be removed by the conscious co-operation and understanding of men who, normally, tend to traditional values which are tilted in their favour.

—oo(O)oo—

9

ARRANGED MARRIAGES

IN India, there is a notion that the honour of the family rests with the women who can violate it by conduct that is against the principles of the concept of ritual purity. Thus, marriage is not an independent affair of the boy and girl, but an affair of significance to the entire families of both spouses who seek to strengthen their relations, already existing or new, through matrimonial alliance. This led to an elaborate restrictive control on sexual and marital norms.

In these circumstances, a natural question is whether, in India, a man or woman exercises some control over the selection of his or her spouse. As would be clear from an earlier chapter, the nature of marriage as an institution in India is significantly different from that in Western societies. Whereas marriage based on romantic love has been prevalent in India in ancient times, its prevalence in the West does not seem to have originated earlier than the 20th century. This conceptual difference would be evident even from a linguistic study of certain kinship terminology. For instance, the relatives by marriage are 'relatives in law'; signifying a mere legal relationship as against natural or fundamental relationship indicated by the term 'relatives by blood'. The quality of affinity-based relations in Indian societies is similarly different from that prevailing in the West. In the West a spouse is free to behave with members of the family of her husband according to her will or in conformity with the latter's mode of behaviour. In India, however, a spouse is obliged to love and honour her husband's relatives in much the same way as she is expected to love and respect her own parents. In fact, she may do neither, but that is a different matter.

Until quite recently, marriage in Hindu society depended not on the free mutual choice of the young people, but on the will and choice of the parents or other elderly relatives. In the old days, endogamous marriages were arranged by the parents and elderly members of the family in consultation with the family astrologer. In such matrimonial alliances, the social status of the two families was the most important factor and the personalities of the bride and bridegroom hardly played any role. Thus, the marriage was arranged by an intermediary who was called *sambhal* in Vedic times. Later, the *sambhal* came to be called *ghatakas* or match makers, who kept the genealogical records of every family for consultation before concluding matrimonial relations between the two parties. This procedure avoided intermarriage between persons belonging to the same *sapinda* or consanguineous group.

After consulting the genealogical records, the parents or elderly relatives of the bridegroom were approached and, if they agreed to the proposal, the next step was to consult the horoscope of the bride and the bridegroom to see that both the parties conformed to each other in their fundamental temperament. It is well known that Hindu astrology embodies various rules pertaining to marriage. These rules are quite elaborate and complicated and for the perusal of a horoscope to arrange a successful marriage, the services of expert astrologers were used. These experts prescribed the date, exact time and place for solemnising the marriage with a ritual ceremony. With the change of values over time and in the wake of industrialisation and urbanisation, it became harder to arrange for endogamous marriage, that is, within the members of the same caste in a circle of acquaintances. This called for the extension of the area within which a marriage was sought. Earlier, marriages were arranged between persons residing within a radius of 50 km, later it was extended to a radius of 500 km. As an aid to finding prospective brides and bridegrooms of the same caste, matrimonial advertisements in newspapers came to be used. Such advertisements crept into periodicals published by various caste organisations as well. The element of freedom of the young partners in a matrimonial alliance has been dealt with in detail in the chapter on Free Love.

Despite the spread of education, the Hindu family structure still continues to be traditional, especially in regard to marriage which is still arranged by the parents of the young ones with the main consideration being caste endogamy and *gotra* exogamy and dowry. Village communities, especially, adhere to this procedure. However, in cities the position is slightly different. The young boys and girls studying in universities or other institutions of higher learning come to know each other. Often, friendship develops, but if the question of marriage comes up the boys may be disinclined to do so and the girls usually submit to the will of the parents who are invariably guided by considerations of caste endogamy. Although the ideal of a shy, chaste and submissive woman is gradually losing significance with the spread of education, the psychological impact of ambivalent values is still an obstacle to the young in conforming to their convictions. Society, largely, is liable to misinterpret the character of any person, especially a woman, who is truly frank, bold and claims independent views on sexual mores. In these circumstances, even the woman who is profoundly convinced of the mismatch inherent in an arranged marriage normally consents to it. Economic independence and social status of the educated working woman in urban society is still overshadowed by the feudal concepts of the upper middle and higher classes in regard to marriage as a means to economic and social security. This ambivalent attitude towards the educated working woman has led to increasing mental conflict and tension.

After intensive interviews with more than 500 educated working women between 20 and 40 years of age, Dr. Promilla Kapur writes in her book *Marriage and the Working Woman in India,* that the percentage of women preferring arranged marriages has gone up in the last two decades of the previous century from 37 to 52 per cent. However, this preference has been accompanied by an emphasis on knowing their selected partner well before the marriage. This is clearly a progressive step and a deviation from blind tradition, and indicates a line of thought which is distinctively individualistic and motivated by a wider experience. In other words, the modern girl is playing it safe by placing the responsibility for mate-selection on the parents while, at the same time, demanding the right to know the partner before marriage. Radhakrishnan's view that "we do not marry the woman we love, but we love the woman we marry," is bound to be reversed in the course of time. A tendency is evident among the youth in favour of the concept that marriage is a social institution evolved primarily for the personal satisfaction and benefit of the two individuals. This signifies that marriage is now becoming a social tie rather than a religious one, which in turn, involves doing away with the cumbersome rituals of the Vedic ceremony. The Hindu Marriage Act of 1955 has made a decisive change in the concept of marriage in India from the sacramental to the contractual.

Today, the method of selecting the marriage partner has changed, especially in urban areas. We find that the tradition of parental selection without consulting the young ones is being replaced by the custom of self-choice with subsequent consent by the parents or the parents' choice is subject to the approval of the parties to be married. The demand for self-choice, however, is emerging very slowly, partly due to the traditional respect for parents and partly for avoiding uncertainties in this important aspect of life. Another type of marriage called 'neo-arranged marriage' has also come into vogue. In this type of marriage, the two families come to an understanding, introduce the girl and the boy and grant them restricted freedom to meet and find out about each other. Even in such cases, the young ones invariably submit to the choice of the parents.

Apart from these traditional types of marriage, there exists in India, the so-called 'civil marriage' based on mutual love and concluded by registration in a court of law. As against this, the traditional type of marriage is arranged according to caste, sub-caste and horoscopes of the boy and girl. Such a marriage virtually brings forth an alliance between the two families.

The traditional type of marriage requires that the bridegroom, accompanied by his parents and relatives and friends, goes to the bride's house where a religious ceremony is held under the supervision of a Brahmin priest. The ceremony includes chanting of rituals before the holy fire fed with sandalwood, *ghee* (clarified butter) and incense. On the conclusion of this ceremony, the bride moves into her husband's family. The wife shares the husband's prestige in the family. Thus, a young Indian does not set up a house on his own on getting married, but brings his bride to the joint family home. This too is changing with rapid urbanisation.

—oo(O)oo—

10

MARITAL RELATIONS

FAMILY structure in India is very compact and united and, in rural areas where the impact of industrialisation and urbanisation is lesser in degree, the normal way of life in a joint family is such that the women members of the family form a compact group with its own activities and hardly any interaction with the menfolk during the day. Relations between husband and wife are generally restricted to the nights.

The bride, finding herself in a lonely and often intimidating situation surrounded by strange elderly women, finds relief in the physical proximity of the husband who, in course of time, assumes the same authoritative position in her heart as her father had in childhood. Thus, relations between husband and wife developed characteristics of a master and servant, the former taking over all the responsibility of providing the necessities of life and the latter being expected to be utterly respectful and unquestioningly obedient. This state of affairs hardly left any chance of emotional integration between the two. Further, the impersonal pattern of the joint family also contributed to the development of a somewhat mechanical sexual relationship, devoid of emotional significance. This is evidenced by Apastambha's comment that the bride was given to a family and not to an individual. One might object to this observation with the argument that this situation did not apply to the whole of Hindu society or to every woman and thus did not constitute a serious problem. Psychologists' contention that too much cruelty makes an individual callous is well observed in the behaviour of many women who, because of their innate force of character, were not ready to meekly submit to unjust infliction. This moral discontentment manifested itself in taunts, slighting remarks and innuendo among the women.

However, refusal to acquiesce to the traditionally prevalent injustice is not an innate characteristic of most individuals and, thus, the Indian woman's emotional devotion to the husband was almost on par with that of the mystic towards the object of his adoration. Lack of education among Indian women also contributed to their submission to the tradition in relation to the husband, family and society at large.

The worldwide sexual revolution in modern times is bound to have a far-reaching impact on sexual relations and standards of behaviour between the sexes in Indian society. Among educated women of different age groups, a conviction is growing that the prevailing sexual relations and concept of sexual morality in Indian society need serious and ritualistic reappraisal. The progressively declining appeal of religion and adherence to tradition, increasing contact with the West by virtue of education and tourism, the availability of unobtrusive contraceptives, urbanisation and industrialisation leading to the development of a nuclear family are bound to transform the sexual patterns in Indian society. The new generation is already becoming acquainted with the liberalised sexual mores prevalent in the West, and it may be assumed that with the development of education and freedom to associate, the ideal of a relatively de-sexualised husband-wife relationship in a joint family is bound to give way to the development of a dynamic state of reciprocity. The transition in this direction is discernible from the fact that during the post-independence period, emotional religiosity has been giving way to emotional reciprocity strictly in consonance with Indian cultural values, especially among the middle classes where women are increasingly striving for education and economic independence.

PREMARITAL SEX

Premarital and extra-sexual relations have a special significance in the social structure of a society. The traditional Indian attitude to sex reflects a striking absence of guilt, quite distinct from the Judaeo-Christian tradition. Until the impact of Christian missionaries in India, Hindus considered sex sinful only where it was socially illegitimate.

Far from being considered a sin, the sexual act was symbolic of creative energy. This resulted in a dual attitude towards women, namely, as mother on the one hand and as an erotic being on the other.

Evidently, the equation of freedom (enjoyed by women earlier) with licentiousness gave rise to an assumption that moral standards for men and women should be different. Further, the concept of matrimonial fidelity enjoined upon women the duty of avoiding all acts that might be regarded by a jealous husband as a threat to his sexual monopoly on her. Thus, a woman came to be expected to avoid all situations in which any man might find an opportunity to court her. The concept of virginity enjoined upon girls an absolute prohibition of sexual relations before marriage and a girl deviating from this rule exposed herself to social contempt; she was not considered a suitable marriage partner and often ended in the undesirable situation of having to live as a spinster in some relative's house. However, these restrictions on premarital sex did not apply to men in the past. In view of the strict restrictions imposed on girls and women in relation to premarital and extra-marital sex, men's sexual contacts were restricted to prostitutes.

To discuss this aspect of Indian society in the earliest times, one has to take recourse to literary sources. These references indicate that premarital sexual relations were tolerated during the Rigvedic period. The prevalence of the *Samana* festival (a sort of modern fair in which girls participated in search of a husband) confirms this. During the age of the *Mahabharata* also this type of relationship was permitted, for example, the Vedic Rishi Parashar, enamoured of Satyavati (the virgin daughter of the fisherman Uparichara Vasu) says to her: "Darling, satisfy my desire." Satyavati replies: "How can I do it here in the boat as the people on the shore may see us in the act." Thereupon, Parashar created fog all around which engulfed the area in total darkness. Under the cover of this fog, the Rishi satisfied his lust and the girl gave birth to a son. The Rishi granted her a boon that despite this sexual union, she would ever remain a virgin.

Kunti, the mother of the five Pandava brothers, had premarital sex with Surya and had given birth to a son, Karna, the brave rival of her later son, Arjuna. Even after sexual intercourse and the birth of a son, she continued to remain a virgin with the blessing of the sage

Durvasa. The Madhavi-Galav episode also refers to the retention of virginity even after giving birth to sons from different men. The existence of the concept of different kinds of sons, namely, the one born before marriage and the other born after marriage, confirm that pre-matrimonial sexual relations were socially tolerated in contemporary society. In the *Mahabharata,* Krishna tells Karna: "Two kinds of sons may be born to a virgin, namely, *Kanian* (a son born before marriage) and *Sohodha* (a son conceived before but delivered after marriage).

All this indicates that during those days, premarital sex relations not only existed but were also generally tolerated.

During the medieval period, the average age at marriage fell very low and left virtually no chance for premarital sex. Marriages were arranged at a very early age.

During the last century there has been a sexual revolution in the West with consequent progressively increasing sexual freedom. With industrialisation and urbanisation, the upper classes in India have also come under this influence. This involves various questions; for example, whether there has been an actual increase in this sphere. Have the people of different classes different attitudes towards premarital sex? Do the increasing opportunities for economic self-sufficiency encourage greater premarital sex among women?

It is hard to assess the extent of change of attitude in this regard. While the changes are evident in the public behaviour of the upper classes, other sections of society appear to be more prudent in public. However, private attitudes contrast with public attitudes concerning sexual freedom.

Despite disapproval, premarital and extra-marital sex relations exist in the West as well as in India. The difference in this connection is that the West has accepted it by now as a normal aspect of life. The idea of virginity as a precondition for marriage is progressively losing importance and the attitude of tolerance towards children born before marriage also substantiates the belief.

Throughout human society, premarital and extra-marital sex relations exist which makes them natural human behaviour. The distinguishing feature in India is that they are indulged in more as an act of defence than of belief. The consciousness of guilt remains implicit.

The increasing tension in social and family behaviour is developing an outlook that excessive or unrestrained sex is perfectly normal and that chastity is an outdated concept.

Interviews with young boys and girls of lower, middle and upper classes of society reveal that promiscuous premarital and extra-marital sex, largely, is rooted in emotional disturbances created at home. Among the rich, the parents normally feel that they have fulfilled their obligations by providing material comforts to their children. Further, in the wake of progress, modern social and economic pressures compel the mother to earn an income because of which she has to stay away from the house for the greater part of the day. This lack of direct contact between the parents and children often results in the development of distorted personalities. There is sufficient evidence that children of a family where the mother does not work, or works part time, have generally a more stable personality than those where both parents are full-time earners. The domestic tension so created often finds release in premarital sex as far as girls are concerned.

In cities, working girls, living away from home and enjoying economic self-sufficiency have more freedom in this respect.

GIRL FRIEND AS A STATUS SYMBOL

Contact with the West and the expansion of education have given young boys and girls more opportunities to meet each other. This developing friendship between boys and girls often leads to sex relations as well. Among the more sophisticated students, having a girl friend has become a status symbol. Boys boast of the number of girl friends they have in a strange reversion to the medieval age when the number of wives and concubines signified power and status.

This race for sexual experience has resulted in a lack of emotional unity between the two partners. Even very young school children are tempted to explore sexual relationships. Drugs and pornographic literature have given impetus to the growing promiscuity.

In the Scandinavian countries where society is most tolerant in regard to sex, young boys and girls experience sex before and after marriage and bored husbands and wives in a bid to introduce novelty in their sexual relations explore multiple marriages and practices such as swapping partners. People are starved of genuine human relations and become easy victims of husbands and lovers.

The United Nations Charter says: "Since wars arise in the minds of men, it is in the minds of men that the battles must be fought." Thus, the need in the case of sexual relations is not free indulgence and annihilation of inhibitions but for proper understanding of the working of sex and development of a sense of proportion in this regard. The Indian concept of the humanity of an entity made up of two inseparable components, namely, *Purusha* and *Prakriti* (or Self and Non-Self) representing the male and female sexes signifies that the attraction between the two towards each other is a natural phenomenon that makes a complete whole entitled to attain happiness. Disproportionate indulgence in sex leads away from happiness in the same way as over-eating causes damage to health instead of maintaining or improving it.

EXTRA-MARITAL SEX

The institution of marriage gives the husband exclusive sexual rights with his wife. However, the history of human society shows that this right has been abrogated temporarily at the will of the husband, who is the sole owner of this right and can even transfer it to another. Such abrogation was generally a token of hospitality that existed in certain societies in ancient times.

Sexual hospitality was based mainly on the awe, fear or magic by which the danger signified by a stranger (or a guest) was warded off. In course of time, it came to be believed that extending hospitality to the extent of including sex could avert the potential danger of a guest. This custom prevailed at different times in different societies, for example, among the Marquess Islanders, the ancient societies of Arabia, Ireland and perhaps even in early medieval Europe and in ancient India.

It is worthwhile to notice that the term 'chastity' had a somewhat different connotation then. By the period of the Epics, and particularly in the age of the *Ramayana,* this concept assumed a different form, for example, a chaste woman came to signify the one devoted to her husband, obeying him in all matters including the rights to her person. This absolute surrender to the will of the husband expected of a chaste woman resulted in cases of a wife giving herself to a stranger at the bidding of the husband. The *Mahabharata* offers certain direct and indirect references in this connection. The story of Sudarshana clearly refers to the prevalence of such a custom.

The *Mahabharata* presents another well-known incident of the mother of Svetaketu, son of the great sage, Uddalaka. Duryodhana, the hero of the *Mahabharata* on the Kaurava side, was willing to give away his wives and children to anyone who could tell him where his rival Arjuna could be found. These are stray references to sexual hospitality. However, the custom of such extra-marital relations lost its social approval in later times when the term 'feminine chastity' acquired an altogether different connotation and the system of 'lending' the wife was discontinued altogether. Extra-marital relations in later times were those resorted to in compliance of religious duty enjoined by the *Dharma Shastras* to beget a son on the widow of a man who died without begetting a son. This custom was known as *Niyoga* and has been discussed in detail elsewhere.

These practices were approved by society under the influence of different concepts, either because of religion or contemporary social exigencies.

Another type of extra-marital sexual relations was that permitted by the *Tantras,* believed to be a form of yoga for spiritual development through gratification of physical instincts as against the path of austerity and self-negation propagated by *Rajyoga.* According to the *Tantras,* for example, *Niruttara Tantra* and *Gupta-Samhita,* etc. the union of male and female energy assumes an esoteric aspect and the worship of the mother goddess is incomplete without sexual intercourse with women who represent female energy (called *Shakti*).

Another type of extra-marital sex relations was that of a woman dedicating herself to the service of a deity enshrined in a particular temple. Such women were known as *Devadasis* (female servants of the god or goddess) and served the deity even to the extent of offering their bodies to the temple organisation. Some of the most important Hindu temples in the south and the eastern part of India had vast colonies where these so-called servants of the deity lived. In ancient times, the temples were the main centres of all social and artistic activity and this institution of *Devadasis* went a long way in developing the dance form that is performed as an offering to the deity. The dance became a traditional art form of the *Devadasis*. However, because of various social and legal measures, the institution of *Devadasis* has disappeared.

The extra-marital relations referred to above had social or religious sanction and, therefore, did not constitute adultery or illicit relations. Hindu law books have vehemently denounced adultery, prescribing various punishments for different forms of adultery. The most heinous type of adultery was intercourse with one's teacher's wife or with a woman ascetic. The sexual offence for which the Hindu law books prescribed heavy punishment was sexual intercourse with a woman of a higher caste. In such cases, the punishment was equally severe for the man as well as the woman.

Despite all the social and legal sanctions against extra-marital sex, social behaviour is controlled by human instincts and not merely by social rules. Instinctively man tends to be polygamous and woman polyandrous. The institution of marriage is evidently an attempt by society to discipline the sexual behaviour of the individual and to ensure the smooth functioning of the smallest social unit, namely the family. Thus, it was evolved as a means to ensure maximum happiness to both the parties to a marriage and for the harmonious development of the children born of the union. As each social institution is exposed to good as well as bad influences, marriage, too, came to be used as a means of exploitation. It is a historical fact that right from ancient times, the husband was normally in command of all affairs. In the earlier agricultural and feudal economies, men took all pains to subject the woman to a secondary position, depriving her of her rights to education and inheritance, thereby making her economically dependent on the husband. In a further step, even religion was used for this purpose and the wife was put under a religious and sacred duty to be unquestioningly obedient and faithful to the husband.

Marriage has always been believed to be a lifelong companionship based on mutual love, mutual sharing of pleasure and grief, satisfaction and disappointment; a working together to build the kind of life considered desirable for the husband and wife while giving the children the opportunity to prepare themselves to face the vicissitudes of life to the best of their ability.

It may be mentioned in this connection that there has been a grievous mis-interpretation of the term 'marriage' accompanied by confusion about love and lust. Education and urbanisation have emancipated the woman from economic slavery to the husband and thus a tendency has been gaining ground, in the name of women's liberation, that the current rules relating to marriage should be radically changed, basing them mainly on free sex. It is asserted that women, who are socially, financially and intellectually equal to men should, in all fairness, be as free as men in their search for happiness from whatever source they prefer.

This state of affairs presents a grave challenge to the institution of marriage. Young men and women are developing a tendency to avoid marriage as far as possible. The tendency towards self-assertion and the lack of capacity to adapt oneself with the partner results in a good number of marriages turning out to be unhappy, often resulting in sexual aberration, homosexuality, lesbianism, etc.

Women have begun to feel that they have been victims of double standards over extra-marital relations. Never a cause of humiliation in the case of men, even the slightest slip in the case of a woman may completely ruin her whole life. For a woman, to love a man and give herself to him joyously is the highest compliment to a man. To a sensitive woman, the thought of giving herself to anybody without love is highly repugnant. Present-day society appears to be providing her with a choice that may not be wise but is being forced on her.

If a marriage is satisfactory, there should be little or no desire to seek satisfaction elsewhere. A successful marriage is often considered a matter of fate or chance, but it is something the individual has to work for constantly. It is not an unchanging or unchangeable relationship. Matrimonial happiness requires time and effort coupled with a sense of proportion and understanding and mutual adaptability.

—oo(O)oo—

11

Promiscuity in Indian Society

In 1961, a German scholar, Bachofen, brought out his epoch-making work *Mutterecht* suggesting that a state of promiscuity existed in human society before the establishment of the institution of marriage. He quoted many passages from the classical literature of many countries. His conclusions were further supported by other scholars, namely, Maclennan, Morgan, Lubbock, Spencer, etc. However, other anthropologists like Darwin and Westermark refuted this theory and reiterated the view that the institution of marriage existed right from the commencement of the human race.

In ancient Indian Vedic literature, there is virtually no direct reference to the existence of promiscuity. However, this social phenomenon is indirectly presented by certain well-known myths; for example, Prajapati was enamoured of his daughter; Pusan wooed his mother. But a study of the ancient literature brings forward that the code sanctioned for the gods is invariably different from that applicable to men. Thus, even the Vedic gods named above are shown to have had incestuous relationships with daughter, sister, mother, etc. (S. C. Sarkar. *Some Aspects of the Earliest Social History of India*. Oxford, 1928). These references clearly indicate the existence of a society with minimal sex taboos.

Later, the Epics and *Puranas* also refer to the practice of parental incest, the most famous example being of Manu, the father of mankind, who was begotten by Brahma on his daughter Satarupa (S. C. Sarkar.

Some Aspects of the Earliest Social History of India. Oxford, 1928). There is another reference in the *Aitareya Brahmana* indicating that for begetting sons, men united with their mothers and sisters.

In the *Mahabharata,* there are indications that promiscuity prevailed in the earlier period. The *Karna Parva* (Kumbkonam edn., 37.23) refers to the prevalence of many such traditions among the people of Madra Pradesh where the women were very licentious and self-willed and considered a blemish on mankind. As it was not possible to determine birth in their caste, the sisters and not sons were the heirs. The reference in the *Rajatarangini* about the Brahmanas of Gandhara living in incest (Kalhan. *Rajatarangini*, i. 308) indicates the prevalence of such a tradition in north-west India also.

The absence of restrictions on social intercourse as enjoined by the institution of monogamous marriage among the Madra and Bablika regions is confirmed by other references to the prevalence of certain traditions, namely, *Strirajya, Strivabya* or *Narivaisaya* in north-west India (Vatsyayana's *Kamasutra,* Niranaya Sagar edn,; *Santi Parva* IV, 7; *Brihatsamihita,* XIX, 22).

Certain statements made by Pandu about an age in which women were uncontrolled, licentious, self-willed and independent are further evidence of the prevalence of promiscuity. Their pre-matrimonial relations with men did not involve any sin on their part. Pandu states further that such practices prevailed in Uttarkuru even in his own time.

The most glaring example of the existence of promiscuous sexual relations is contained in the story of Uddalaka and his son Svetaketu which says that once Svetaketu was standing by the side of his mother, when a Brahmana caught her hand and snatched her away. The angered Svetaketu was calmed down by the father, who said that there was no point in getting furious on this account because all the women in the world were uncovered and self-willed and that this had been the practice since time immemorial (that is, Sanatan Dharma) (*Adi Parva, Mahabharata*, 128, 4-5).

However, the son did not accept this explanation and made a rule that the woman who neglects her husband and the man who violates an unmarried girl shall be guilty of destroying the embryo. Some scholars have attempted to dismiss this legend of Svetaketu as mere fiction, but it is so much in keeping with various other traditions of that period that it can hardly be ignored.

Certain practices reminiscent of the prevalence of promiscuity in the earlier ages lingered on until the time of the *Smritis,* when the institution of marriage was well established. This resulted in the introduction of a legal provision for sons born as a result of intercourse with a man other than the husband. Such sons were called *Gudhotpanna.* Provision was also made for children born of unmarried and widowed women. In all, four categories of such children are enumerated in the law books.

All these references confirm the prevalence of promiscuity in India in ancient times. However, it is not possible to determine the extent to which it was prevalent or whether this practice was confined to the Aryans, the non-Aryans or both. The references to Madra and Gandhara indicate that in the Punjab and north-west India, women enjoyed more liberty than those in other parts of the country.

As things stand now, one would not fail to observe an increasing tendency for unabated discussion on sex among the urban educated classes and the various sociological surveys conducted reveal that quite a number of women view sexual desire as a biologically, socially and psychologically normal phenomenon. Despite this liberation of the modern generation, there is no gainsaying that any failure to abide by traditional notions of sexual morality entails grave risks for all women, married and unmarried alike. No man would be willing to accept promiscuity on the part of his wife.

PLEASURES OF VENAL LOVE

The master work of Vatsyayana, *Kamasutra* (third century A.D.), a treatise on the science of love in an exquisitely healthy manner is known world-wide. This is not the only work on the subject, but due to the lack of an earlier surviving text, it has become a landmark in the history of the erotic. Further, the erotic element in Indian art, namely, sculpture, painting, literature, etc. indicates that despite the glorification of a life of abstinence and chastity (*Brahmacharya*), the sexual aspect of life has been given detailed treatment.

The *Kamasutra* is often confused with sexual mysticism represented in the temples of Khajuraho (Madhya Pradesh) and Orissa or in *Tantrik* literature pertaining to the Buddhist *Mahayana* and Hindu *Shaiva* and *Vaishnava* cults. Actually, the *Kamasutra* is not based on the concept of the identity of sexual passion with divine passion. It is the product of a courtly culture in decline. Its appeal was evidently restricted to court circles and the nobility who craved for sensuality.

The *Kamasutra* may be called a standard manual on the techniques of sex for erotic specialists. The author has mentioned in the book a list of various types of lovers, each with a different point of view and has offered advice to each in conformity with the Indian principle of ethics suited to the individual's nature. He has dealt with the subject with systematic thoroughness and moral consistency, thereby instructing men and women in the legitimate pleasures of the senses to ensure matrimonial harmony. He says, "of all the lovers of a girl, only he can be her true husband who possesses the qualities most liked by her, and only such a husband enjoys real superiority over her, because he is the husband of love."

This detailed treatment of eroticism in the face of the expectation of absolute fidelity on the part of woman goes to show that Indian society has always been tolerant towards women who sell their favours. Although the penitent lived in the forests, meditating on the deepest mysteries, cut off from the world and strove earnestly for stainless chastity, in towns and cities the harlot, often highly educated, went about the street in her splendour, taking in the fiery hearts of the men along with their purses. India is a land of sharp contrasts. A major part of classical Sanskrit literature is filled with praise for the public woman as the very embodiment of perfect womanhood. In the Epics too, as early as in the Vedas, the woman as entertainment for the individual or in public was a matter of course.

Right from the very early periods, the public woman, open to the visits of all (*nari parkasha sarvagamy*) was not marked out as something criminal or vulgar. Although her class was low in the social order, it was for the reason of distinguishing her for the greater ease and comfort of the world of men.

Strumpets were shown in the Epics, as elsewhere in Indian literature, to be an important part of urban society. In the *Mahabharata* when the armies march out to the battlefield of Kurukshetra, the forces under Duryodhana are accompanied by professional singers and *ganikas* (women of pleasure).

In the *Ramayana* (ii, 36), Dashrath gives orders for a splendid army to be fitted out for his son, Rama, and adds (shloka 3), "women that live by their beauty, those skilled in words, shall adorn the well drawn up troops of the prince."

It is thus clear that *veshyas* or strumpets were an indispensable part of any expedition (whether for battle or for hunting or for diversion in the countryside or pleasure gardens). Often we find references that 'city beauties' danced on joyful occasions (*Markandeya Purana*, cxxvii, 9). It was believed that the mere sight of them brought good luck, a belief that can be observed in the more traditional sections of Indian society even today. The strumpet was thus not only an adornment of the royal courts or camps, but a highly appreciated ornament of civic life. They have been considered protectors of dance and music throughout the ages.

The Tantra Yoga (a branch of Yoga) exalted the position of prostitutes still further. In the Tantra Yoga, Shakti (the female embodiment of divine active power) plays an important part in formal worship. In some Tantrik literature, this role of Shakti has been shown to be assumed by certain categories of harlots, namely, *raja veshya* (the harlot of the kings), *gupta veshya* (the secret harlot or woman belonging to a respectable family secretly following this profession), *nagari* (the city harlot), *deva veshya* (the harlot of the gods or temple dances, also known as devadasis in south India) and *Brahma veshya* (the harlot of the centres of pilgrimage). From this classification, it is clear that the term 'prostitute' has had a somewhat different connotation in the earlier periods. Hindu society has evinced good sense in giving due recognition to prostitutes in the social structure, enjoining on them the duty of highly disciplined and honourable behaviour. Yajnavalkya, a Hindu lawgiver, lays down (ii, 292) that if a prostitute has already accepted her price and then refuses she should be fined double the amount given to her.

Of the different ancient works on venal love, two more have come down to us, namely, *Kuttanimatam* (the lessons of a bawd) written by

Damodargupta (eighth century, A.D.) and *Samayamatrika* (breviary of a harlot) written by Kshemendra (11th century A.D.).

In *Kuttanimatam*, the author has described the personality of a bawd (an old woman) very gay and well mannered, held in high esteem among the harlots as a source of advice, training and protection in the art and profession of venal love, highly calculating in understanding and exploiting human sentiment, dry as dust in refusing to grant gratis favour of her physical charms. While the customers detested and ridiculed her because of her avaricious eyes ever fixed on their purses, the young harlots held her in awe and respect.

The lessons imparted by the bawd to the young harlots on the art of pleasing men indicate the author's intimate knowledge of Vatsyayana's *Kamasutra*. However, from the literary point of view, *Kuttanimatam* is not a compact work and some passages are even incoherent.

Samayamatrika, apart from being a compendium of warnings to men against the bewitching and enticing ways of the harlots, is a literary masterpiece, compact and unified, bristling with cruel wit and cynicism. In the epilogue, the author says: "Now you have learnt that the cultural benefits mean nothing to a bawd and also how she cheats her daughter's lovers." Despite all the warnings, he seems to be convinced of the human tendency of succumbing to the enticement of venal love in the same way as the gazelles in the forest run headlong into the snare despite knowing they are heading towards destruction. Unheeding the discussion among learned circles and the preaching of moralists and saints warning against the evil of associating with harlots; the various punitive measures in this life and threats of punishment in the next, most men succumb to the snares of the harlots.

—oo(O)oo—

12

PROSTITUTION IN INDIA

PROSTITUTION is, strictly speaking, a category of extra-marital relations and is legally defined as promiscuous sexual intercourse for hire.

The prevalence of prostitution in ancient India is referred to in Vedic as well as Epic literature. The prostitutes, normally referred to as 'city beauties' or 'city wives' (*Nagar Vadhu*) were specially invited to dance on various festive occasions.

In Indian society, although prostitution was looked down upon, prostitutes always enjoyed an honoured place right from ancient times. The *Matsya Purana* sanctifies prostitutes, declaring them to be *gopis* or milkmaids of the legend attributed to Lord Krishna (*Matsya Purana,* LXX, 24-68). They were granted special privileges by kings as well as religious authorities. Prostitutes' houses were looked upon with pride and the prostitutes themselves were seen as ornaments of the city (P. Thomas. *Hindu Religion, Customs and Manners*). They were also considered as exponents and protectors of the dance and music forms. In all religious and festive gatherings, processions, etc., participation of harlots was indispensable. In classical Sanskrit literature, they have been glorified as the heroines of various plays and romances. Buddhist *Jataka* literature is replete with references to harlots. In a *Jataka* tale, a harlot has been shown as receiving a thousand gold pieces for a night, and in another she demands five hundred elephants for a single hour.

The glorification of prostitutes is further evidenced by a description of Vijainagar, one of the most important medieval Hindu States. There, every Hindu temple had a number of *devadasis* (handmaids of the gods) and the prostitutes living quarters were one of the sights of the capital. These *devadasis* were perfect dancers and singers and many of them amassed enormous fortunes.

Sighting a prostitute while setting out on a journey was considered a good omen. Kings used to keep them in their inner apartments. They even constituted an essential part of the retinue on the battlefield. A visiting prince was entertained and invited into the prostitutes' quarters; these women escorted the august guests from outside the city gates.

Before considering this issue further, it seems to be necessary to understand an important distinction between the position of women belonging to the upper and lower (working) classes, which manifested itself in the area of sexual mores. Upper class behaviour was characterised by double standards in that everything was permitted to men while being forbidden to women. To enforce conformity by the women to matrimonial fidelity and virginity, the upper classes adopted various measures making it well nigh impossible for a woman to even talk to a man not directly related to her. It was believed that man and woman were only sex symbols to each other and their desire to talk or meet together could be only with the intention of sexual intercourse. In these circumstances, girls were given no opportunity to fall in love. Further, due to lack of education, girls had neither the maturity of judgement nor courage to object to the spouse chosen for them by their parents (Raphael Patai. *Women in the Modern World*).

The two contradictory moralities, one granting men wide latitude in sex and the other imposing all possible restrictions on women, resulted in the need to provide sex objects which, in turn, led to the belief that prostitution was an indispensable institution. Thus, prostitution was allowed to develop basically on a false notion. Further, prostitution was given an impetus by the role of Hindu women in the medieval period who were reduced to domestic drudgery and the bearing and rearing of children which left no time for education or develop traits that would be attractive to men. As against this, the prostitutes concentrated all their attention and effort to enhance their attractive aspects by adornment of the person and proficiency in the fine arts, namely, dance, music, literature, etc. The men of the upper strata of society, with a different code of morality than their wives, bored by their wives and craving gratification, were attracted to prostitutes who provided them with a sense of conquest. In the sphere of love, the prostitutes with their highly developed and attractive behaviour provided easy access for the satisfaction of male egos. With this background, there developed in Hindu society two classes of women, one reduced to domestic drudgery in holy wedlock and the other free to move around and develop themselves and provide men with venal pleasure.

Apart from enjoining a strictly disciplined behaviour on prostitutes, the following characteristics were expected to be well developed, namely, she should have a beautiful body, amiable behaviour and a developed sense of appreciation of the qualities of her customers. She was not supposed to entertain those who were in ill health or sickly, or harsh and avaricious in their temperament, and those men whose infidelity would wreck their marriages.

The earliest book written on the subject of prostitution is that written by Dattaka, pertaining to the prostitutes of Pataliputra (modern Patna). However, Dattaka's book did not come down except in an abridged form in Vatsyayana's famous erotic work, the *Kamasutra.* A perusal of Part VI of the *Kamasutra* will clearly indicate how elaborately the personality of a prostitute has been analysed.

According to certain Hindu law makers, sexual intercourse was permitted in the case of certain classes of women, and they could be freely visited without causing social, religious or legal offence. Such women included public harlots, called *veshyas* (A. K. Sur, *Sex and Marriage in India*).

Prostitutes were divided into different categories according to their physical charm and artistic as well as literary accomplishments. Of all the categories enumerated, the *Ganikas* were those with the highest accomplishments, proficient in the fine arts, well-mannered, exceedingly beautiful, highly intelligent, adept conversationalists, liberal towards the poor, patrons of men of learning and highly respectful to their superiors. Because of these virtues they were known as the jewels of the city in which they lived. The position of honour enjoyed by these

Ganikas can be evidenced from the fact that the kings or maharajas sought to attract the famous *Ganikas* from neighbouring kingdoms by offering special favours in order to enhance the reputation of their own kingdoms.

Before going further into the subject, it would be worthwhile to study the institution of the so-called temple prostitutes in certain parts of India.

THE INSTITUTION OF *DEVADASIS*

In certain religions one observes the idea of women identifying themselves with the brides of god for their rapid spiritual progress. The *Bhagwat Purana* shows that milkmaids left their husbands to be united with Krishna, one of the reincarnations of Vishnu. One well-known example is the case of the Rajput princess, Mira Bai, who claimed that her true lord was Krishna and not her wedded husband, the Rana. Another similar example is the Tamil saint-poetess, Andal, who regarded herself as married to god.

In course of time, this concept of symbolic marriage to god gave rise to the institution of the *devadasi,* signifying god's maidservants whereby girls were given in marriage to the deity by their parents in the hope of accomplishing their desires in return for making such an offering. Thus, the *devadasis* were dedicated to the performance of certain rituals (including dance and music) in the service of the temple deity. Further, they were expected to lead a highly austere life observing frequent fasts and devotedly pursuing the fine arts.

In the beginning the girls were offered by their parents, evidently motivated by religious fervour as an offering of one's dearest object. Later, however, the rich started offering girls bought from others with a view to seek favours of the deity. It was believed that by making such an offering, one could ensure a place in heaven for oneself. The *devadasis* were not allowed to marry, as they were considered irrevocably married to the temple deity. However, during the reign of the Chola, Pullava, Pandyan, etc. dynasties (*circa* 600-1300 A.D.) a great number of affluent temples were established and this resulted in an increase in the number of *devadasis.* In course of time, these *devadasis,* who were not allowed to marry, came to be exposed to sexual exploitation and this provided a further spur to the expansion of the institution of *devadasis.*

MARRIAGE OF THE *DEVADASIS*

In the beginning, the devadasis were symbolically married to the temple deity along with a sword, which signified that in case of her going astray from the path of devoted service to the deity, she would be killed with that very sword. Girls who dedicated themselves to the service of the temple deity were also called Daughters of God, and were treated as sisters-in-religion by the people.

When a girl, with the requisite qualifications of chastity and trained in dance and music, offered herself as a *devadasi,* she was adorned as a bride and taken to the temple where she was symbolically married to the deity. The custom of putting a yellow mark on the forehead of the bridegroom according to the Hindu marriage ritual was performed by putting a yellow mark on a coconut. Such a marriage with the deity left no chance of widowhood because the deity was immortal.

It is gathered from certain ancient Hindu scriptures that there existed seven categories of *devadasis,* namely:

1. *Data* or those offering themselves in service of the deity of their own volition;

2. *Vikrita,* or those who sold themselves for the service of the deity;

3. *Bhritya,* or those who served as *devadasis* to earn a livelihood for their families;

4. *Bhakta,* or those who entered temple service with a sense of devotion;

5. *Hrita,* or those who were stolen from their families and offered to the temple;

6. *Alamkrita,* or those whom the raja or feudal chiefs considered appropriate to be dedicated to the temple and did so by adorning them with ornaments; and

7. *Rudra-Ganika*, or *Gopika*, who performed dances in the temple for regular payment.

It may be mentioned that sexual exploitation under the camouflage of religion is not unique to India. Similar exploitation is evidenced by certain ancient traditions of other countries such as Greece, Babylon, Egypt, Thailand, etc. In the Sumerian culture of Mesopotamia, some women were attached to temples to attend to menial services or as concubines of the priests. It would be more appropriate to say that the institution of devadasis in India traces its origin to the contact with Greek culture after the invasion of Alexander the Great.

There is a theory that temple prostitution was introduced by the Dravidians as a practice borrowed from Egypt and Mesopotamia and the bronze figure of a dancing girl excavated at Mohenjodaro represents, in all probability, a sacred prostitute. Under the influence of Dravidian culture, the Vedic god Indra was made the divine patron of arts whose court was crowded with celestial singers (*gandharvas* and *kinnaras*) and dancing nymphs (*apsaras*).

The institution of devadasis is said to have developed first in the Karnataka region of south India. Later, its prevalence extended rapidly to almost all the flourishing temples of south India. Apart from performing various ritual services of the temple deity, they were required to present music and dance performances on special occasions. Thus, the *devadasis*, apart from being devoted servants of the temple deity, became the principal exponents of the art of music and dance.

In recognition of these services, they were granted gifts of land and cash from the temple estates. The introduction of this system of granting gifts resulted in a rapid increase in the number of *devadasis*. People started looking for pretexts to offer a girl to the temple, even by purchasing her from others. Such an offering became a status symbol and a matter of pride.

It is a fact that not all people engaged in the service of religion are motivated by religious fervour alone. This was the case of the *devadasis*. The young *devadasis*, fed up with the restrictions of celibacy, looked for secret sexual relations. This state of affairs was fully exploited by those associated with the temples and gave rise to the development of prostitution in the living areas of the *devadasis*. This moral degradation was, however, restricted to a small number. Despite this, the tragic fact is that the *devadasis* came to be exploited to satisfy the sensual craving of the priestly and ruling classes in the feudal ages. The institution of *devadasis* was given religious sanction by making it an indispensable part of the temple complex and no pains were spared to promote and protect the institution.

In order to overcome public resentment against this state of affairs and the prohibition of *devadasis* from marrying, rules were amended allowing them to marry on condition that the first daughter born of a *devadasi* would be dedicated to the temple as a *devadasi*. This was about the 15th century A.D. and this relaxation continued for about a century, preventing the number of devadasis from decreasing. It may be mentioned here that until about 60 years ago almost all important Hindu temples of south India maintained a large number of *devadasis* (called dedicated prostitutes) and when legislation was introduced to abolish this institution, an internationally renowned interpreter of Indian art and culture as well as an ardent supporter of the tradition, Ananda K. Coomaraswamy, defended it and denounced the reform. Even today, traces of the institution exist in certain villages of south India where a number of devadasis can still be found, most of them devoted to the flesh trade than to the deity. Some sociological studies of red light areas in big cities have shown that a majority of the prostitutes were ex- *devadasis*.

With the expansion of education among women, the system of *devadasis* attracted public resentment and legislative measures were taken to uproot the institution, for example, the Devadasi Protection Act of 1934. However, in tradition-bound Indian society, traces can still be observed in some parts of Karnataka and Maharashtra. This Act prohibited the marriage of girls to idols. However, it is a law that is not always followed. Idol-marriage is still performed clandestinely by some priests with the active co-operation of ignorant villagers and relatives of the girl. So far, there have hardly been any convictions under the Act. The other legislative measures to curb this evil are:

1. The Madras Devadasi Prevention Act of 1947.
2. The Bombay Devadasi Protection Act of 1854.

PROSTITUTION IN NORTH INDIA

Prostitution as it was in vogue during the early Hindu period, continued during Muslim rule as well, when the role of prostitutes assumed still greater importance and respect in contemporary society by virtue of their having received special patronage of the royal court. Prostitution, in common parlance, is considered to be a category of extra-marital sex and is legally defined as promiscuous sexual intercourse for hire. However, in India, especially during the Muslim period, the role of the prostitute, instead of being an object of promiscuous sex enjoyment was transformed into that of a community dedicated to the maintenance and development of dance and music. Prostitutes came to be considered to be highly cultured and young nobles visited them to learn art and social manners. This is evidenced by the Kathak school of dance, which was developed in the royal court during the Mughal period. Thus, the contribution of the Mughals in presenting this community as protectors of the fine arts is commendable.

With the changing position of prostitutes in Indian society, the *ganikas* have disappeared from public life, and the responsibility for developing and preserving the fine arts is no longer a responsibility of the section of society that carries this ill-famed designation.

During the British period, the term 'prostitute' again assumed a reprehensible connotation. British policy aimed at restricting prostitution. Still, effective legislation was not enacted to discontinue the brothels except by a few States, namely:.

1. Bombay Prevention of Prostitution Act of 1923.
2. Madras Suppression of Immoral Traffic Act of 1930.
3. Bengal Suppression of Immoral Traffic Act of 1933.
4. Punjab Suppression of Immoral Traffic Act of 1935.
5. Mysore Suppression of Immoral Traffic Act of 1936.

Abbe Dubois has commented that India was free from the dissoluteness of European towns like London or Paris, which reckon a huge number of prostitutes. The increasing number of prostitutes in the principal tourist centres of the East, Bangkok, Hong Kong, etc. clearly indicates that prostitution, in its vilest form, is growing rather than decreasing.

Humiliating conditions and lack of opportunity to earn a decent living often compel some people to submit to this social evil which, coupled with a traditional sense of guilt, retards the development of the character of the individual. Some people often comment that prostitution is a social evil, and demand strengthening of legal curbs to re-establish our spiritual heritage. However, so far, a punitive legal approach and spiritual preaching have proved of little success.

There is another group that holds a contrary view. They aver that prostitution is neither a social evil nor an immoral act. They plead, further, that prostitution has been in existence in some form or the other concurrently with society's attempts to regulate and control sexual relationships through the institution of marriage and family and that, if there had been no prostitutes, sexual offences and illegitimacy would have increased enormously. Today, societal norms, at least in urban areas, do not absolutely condemn dating and friendship between the sexes. The evil of prostitution cannot be rooted out merely by an appeal to the people or through religion or preventive measures. A cynical poet once said in this connection: "Thou mayst shut up thy doors with bars and bolts. It will be impossible to make them so fast that a cat and a whore master cannot find a way through them." There is, evidently, a strong case for regulating the institution of prostitution. However, legalising the institution constitutes a grave violation of human rights and dignity of a group of persons. The institution of marriage was evolved by society to provide, *inter alia*, a natural outlet for sexual needs, the concept being that those who look for sexual gratification without undertaking the consequent responsibilities do not deserve the consideration or sympathy of society.

The institution of prostitution needs a new, positive, radical and realistic approach that would probably require the reorientation of the whole social and legal structure in this connection. At the international level, the League of Nations appointed a special body in 1927 to analyse the problem. The general conclusion of the study was that "the existence of licensed houses provides incentive to traffic both national and international." Another body appointed by the League of Nations for studying the situation in the Far East also gave a similar opinion. The eradication of prostitution can hardly be achieved merely through legislation or administrative action. It is a disease that spills over into society and becomes more intense so rapidly that mere statutory reforms serve no purpose. Prostitution can be ended only through a total transformation of the system of values overthrowing outdated and diseased concepts of the social order. In a society where there is no prostitution, women may claim to possess that fundamental freedom which is a *sine qua non* for real liberation.

Before arriving at definite conclusions, however, it is necessary to take into consideration different values as practised in real life. For a realistic solution one has to do away with the temptation of allowing society entertainment that is centred on women and the exposure of their physical charms. Fashion parades and beauty contests indicate distorted notions of femininity. And all these aspects constitute gross injustice to women.

Human history testifies to the unfortunate fact that sexual exploitation has always existed in one form or the other. In all fairness, society is neither justified nor capable of imposing standards of sexual behaviour on its members without introducing a radical transformation of the standard of values. Similarly, the State has no reason to interfere in the sexual activity of consenting individuals.

Strictly speaking, prostitution needs to be viewed not merely from the traditional or historical angle but also taking into consideration its social and emotional causes. According to the principal elements of prostitution, for example, payment, promiscuity and emotional disturbances, prostitutes can broadly be divided into two main categories, namely professional and non-professional (clandestine). The first category comprises those in brothels, street walkers and call girls. The second category is hard to define exhaustively. The Committee on Moral and Social Hygiene under the Central Social Welfare Board (India) in its 1958 report divided prostitutes into four categories:

1. Hereditary (as observed among certain extremely backward communities or tribes);
2. Religious or traditional (*devadasis*);

3. Victims of social conditions (kidnapping, seduction, losing parents or guardians); and

4. Those having developed an abnormal attitude towards sex (due either to a high sexual drive or unbalanced mental disposition).

It is clear that the attempts made so far to eradicate prostitution through the religious or spiritual approach, by appeals to the good sense of the people or through legislative measures have not brought about the desired results. Therefore, a campaign based less on preventive and punitive measures and more on the importance of education of the people about the implications and hazards this institution poses, coupled with creation of more employment opportunities would go a long way to eliminate this social evil.

—oo(O)oo—

13

SEXUAL MORALITY

ANCIENT Hindu philosophers have prescribed not only the spiritual path but also moral discipline including social duty. Right from the time of the *Vedas* and the *Upanishads,* they have been concerned with such matters as moral conduct, marriage, longevity, obligations of the individual towards society and so forth. For example, the great epics, the *Ramayana* and the *Mahabharata* have emphasised the ideal of chastity in women, brotherhood and piety.

In Indian social life, the guiding principle has been *Dharma* (truth). From birth till death, all activities (individual as well as social) are inspired by this principle which, at the domestic level, has been the basis of family ties and, at the social level, has welded society into a compact unity saving it from disintegration under the force of external elements.

Dharma is perhaps the most comprehensive concept in Hindu thought. It is often translated as 'religion,' which is a grave mistake. Insofar as religion denotes 'faith' in a particular theology, *Dharma* signifies certain sacraments encompassing different aspects of life. Thus, *Dharma* is based on the truth of life rather than on religion.

Right from earliest times, Indians approached life as an integrated whole. They recognised the oneness of the inner and outer world, based on the fundamental principle of truth. This attitude towards life is different from that of speculative formations and institutionalised organisations.

To understand the complexity of Indian history and culture, it is imperative to examine the concept of *Dharma* that has been defined variously by different scholars at different times. With a slight variation in outward significance, *Dharma* has all along been guiding Indians in a particular direction. We find that during the Vedic period, *Dharma* signified a transcendental law, whereas in the Upanishadic period it concerned individual growth and development. Thus, *Dharma* has two broad implications:

1. An individual ethic referring to the individual development of personality; and

2. Collective or social obligations referring to the castes and occupations (*Varnas* and *Ashrams).*

The combination of individual ethical and social duty is a characteristic feature of Indian society. Individual moral performance is equal to doing one's own social duties. This combination is also represented in the concept of *Karma,* which is applied to all human relations on the one hand and to political and economic problems on the other.

In India, when an individual's behaviour is criticised for any reason, he is inclined to justify himself based on his own social duty as determined by caste duty.

It would, thus, be clear that the fundamental psychological and sociological principle of *Varna-Ashram* ensured an organic unity in Hindu society which, despite the ravages of time and the cruelty of its rulers, protected Indian society from disintegration.

THE INDIAN CONCEPT OF SIN OR GUILT

In India, the concept of sin is equivalent to evil (that is,. *paap*). However, the criterion of sin does not depend on god but on *Dharma.* Human action sanctions the superior obligatory character of *Dharma.* Thus, in India sin is considered as an evil to be purified by one's own self. Indian thinkers were not concerned with the question as to whether human nature is essentially good or evil. Therefore, Indian thinkers did not discuss the conflict between the forces of good and evil. Instead, they were concerned with discussion on ignorance (*Avidya*) rather than on evil. By removing ignorance, evil would automatically be removed. Thus, it would not be proper to say that we do good or avoid evil action. Man is himself full of paradoxes and is blinded by his own ignorance. When man recognises the paradoxical structure of human existence, ignorance is controlled. As against this, the Western concept of determinism is associated with a belief in god who is said to control or determine human choice, thus freeing humanity from the responsibility of behaviour and values.

OCCIDENTAL CONCEPT OF GUILT

In Western moral life there is an absolute standard based upon the law of god, which is applied universally as against the Oriental standard based on human relations. In the Orient, there is no such concept that the law of god can be violated by human beings.

Westerners have their inherited pattern of conscience based on the concept of the relationship of man with god. Thus, the reaction to the apprehension of punishment by god is a feeling of guilt that sanctions good behaviour. This explains the existence of the system of confession among Catholics to relieve themselves of guilt. In the West, there has also been a persistent tendency among thinkers to challenge this tendency in the interest of moral freedom. Among them, Jean Paul Sartre may be mentioned. He believed that if moral freedom is to be retained, the existence of god has to be denied...Freedom is the birthright of each individual who has to create or invent values. However, he further states that with this freedom to create or invent social values, morality would become relative to each individual, ultimately leading to moral anarchy. Sartre's suggestion for the solution of this problem is that the man choosing or creating a value should hold himself responsible not only for himself, but for the whole of humanity (Jean Paul Sartre. *Existentialism*).

In most modern civilised countries, religious and personal feelings have been replaced by patterns of organised institutions set up by various organisations like community, society, foundations, firms, etc. In this setup, the individual has been reduced to a non-entity, more a slave to society. In such circumstances, personal responsibility of the individual seems to be losing significance. In this sense, today, there is hardly any individual freedom.

In the wake of rapid industrialisation and urbanisation after the First World War, various social institutions and standards of values have undergone radical transformation. Instead of large families, the nuclear conjugal family has come into existence. Sexual behaviour has also changed. There is more freedom of sex compared to the situation prevailing 50 to 75 years ago. However, social disapprobation of unrestrained sexual behaviour still forms a criterion of morality, and the ideal of chastity is still jealously guarded. Sex (pre- or extra-marital) may be indulged in, more as an escape from the bitter realities of life than as a conviction. The consciousness of guilt is implicit.

Concerning the Indian concept of the ideal woman guarding her chastity, an Air India advertisement issued some time ago is relevant. It began: "Would you like to date an Indian girl?" This caption infuriated the moral susceptibilities of Indians and caused a discussion in the Indian Parliament. It was said that the advertisement "violated the dignity of Indian womanhood."

—oo(O)oo—

14

PUNISHMENT FOR ADULTERY

PROTECTION of women and private property as the main obligations of civil authority is referred to in the *Mahabharata* which says that when people resolved to set up a civil society, an important point of agreement was that they should abandon the person who encroaches on another's property and violates the chastity of another's wife.

The views in ancient Hindu law books and the *Puranas* on extra-marital sexual relations is quite strict. So much so that in the case of adultery, the man's penis and testicles were to be cut off and in case of evil doings with a maiden, the man's property was to be confiscated. The *Mahanirvan Tantra* (xi, 53) enjoins that if a man comes upon his wife in another man's arms, and kills both, then the king must not punish him. The prevalence of this tradition is vouchsafed by an incident from Rajput history related by James Tod (James Tod, *Annals and Antiquities of Rajasthan*). Prince Gopinath of Bundi went in the night to a Brahmin's wife. The husband saw him and bound him, went to the sinner's royal father and announced that he had taken a thief who had stolen his honour. He asked the father what the man deserved. "Death" was the spontaneous reply, whereupon the injured man hurried home, beat in the prince's head with a hammer and threw him into the street. The king, on coming to know his son's fate, remained silent.

The *Brahmaivarta Purana,* a work of the early medieval period, states that virtuous men never interfere with the wives or property of others, the source of all trouble (*Krishnarjuna Kanda*) . A latter work of the 11th century, namely, *Agni Purana,* reiterates the same view. The *Garuda Purana* enjoins that on no account should one use another's property or take another's wife (*Garuda Purana*).

Thus, we find universal condemnation of the man who covets the wife and property of others. The *Garuda Purana* also states that to lie in another's bed with another's wife are inequities which may force even Indra to go abegging (*Garuda Purana*). Another reference in the *Agni Purana* states that paying court to another's wife should be regarded as a characteristic of those who are released from hell.

It is thus clear that social condemnation was further backed by religious sanction as well as expiation through punishment of the guilty people. The offence of wrongful possession of another woman could be atoned by performing *Candrayana Vrata* (*Agni Purana*). So much so, that even thoughts of another's wife was a sin which could be expiated by prayer (*Agni Purana*). Coveting another's wife could be expiated by reading or hearing the *Puranas* (Markandeya). There is also a reference of a person violating the chastity of another's wife being condemned to *Vaitrani* (hell) (*Garuda Purana, Uttar Kanda*).

Infidelity on the part of men as well as women has always been subject to control by social and legal sanctions.

—oo(O)oo—

15

SHOULD THE INSTITUTION OF MARRIAGE BE ABOLISHED?

THE institution of marriage appears to have been evolved with a view to discipline sexual relations and ensure proper care of children and their intellectual and psychological development in a congenial family atmosphere. However, in course of time, this institution developed certain problems and in the wake of modern civilisation that brought a radical change in human values and standards of behaviour, dissatisfaction and pressures influence marital life. The development of science and technology has radically changed human relations and given them a new direction.

From a historical appraisal of the institution of marriage, it is clear that the responsibility for the care and development of children was entrusted to parents by religious as well as social sanction. Further, legal measures were adopted to strengthen this responsibility. In course of time, women were forced into a secondary position, which they accepted because of their economic dependence on men and dedicated themselves to the care of their husbands and children.

On considering the socio-cultural setting of marriage in the Orient as well as in the Occident, it is evident that the lack of marital status was seen to be undesirable. This gave rise to the exaltation of the role of wife and mother as against that of the unmarried woman who was exposed to ridicule and pity. In this development of the institution of marriage, the fundamental distinction between a happy and unhappy marriage has been ignored. Many unhappily married couples are those who were either unprepared for marriage and unequipped to deal with the various situations that arose in married life, or took to marriage as a matter of doing what was required of them to avoid the social disapproval that followed a spinster or a bachelor.

With the advent of the industrial revolution and the development of education throwing open avenues of economic independence to women, human values, especially those pertaining to husband-wife relations, underwent a radical transformation. There has been a progressive increase of pressure in the relationship. Women's literacy and consequent increased economic independence resulted in a loss of harmony in the family which was based on the tradition of exploitation. Thus, there developed a more permissive attitude in the matter of sex, encouraged by the availability of improved contraception methods, declining religious inhibitions, increased awareness of the psychology of relationships and, above all, the movement for the emancipation of women.

Modern woman is in revolt against her exploitation in the name of religion and social exigency. In this state of affairs, mental disequilibrium and sexual distortions increased. The outcome of the rapidly changing social mores has been a peculiarly ambivalent situation. The old codes of sexual behaviour are losing their value while new values suited to the changed social conditions are yet to be fully evolved. Hence, there exists a kind of double standard in morality, that is, that which was mandated and actual practice. In the latter, there is less of hypocrisy than before. In urban societies, young girls think nothing of spending time with their male friends. However, the exponents of the mandated attitude, namely, judges, ministers of religion, so called leaders of society and others, seem to ignore the rapidly changed perception of sexual morality and condemn those deviating from the traditional path of virtue subjecting them to punitive provisions.

The rising number of divorces or separations is a clear indication of grievous shortcomings in the institution of marriage which need to be removed to meet present-day needs, if the institution of marriage is to be saved from total disaster. The solutions suggested so far are the introduction of contract marriage, combined marriage, unmarried couples living together, and so on. It is clear that in modern society, the institution of marriage is facing a grave challenge. It is often argued that male-female relations which develop because of friendship and fellow feeling, free from any social control or pressure, would be useful and constructive. The search for a new dimension to counter the monotony of marital relations is also subject to the same conditions.

Marital relations should be fundamentally based on constructive and reciprocal interests, coupled with love. Marriage is admittedly an institution for establishing sentimental relations leading to reciprocal identification, but now it has been reduced to a mere social tradition devoid of its original sentimental element, and the two parties united by matrimony often remain irreconcilable entities. This indicates that we should meet the requirement of a sound and firmly based companionship for young people and devise a more effective system of mate selection.

One of the manifestations of this state of affairs is the development of so-called illicit relations. The spiritual gulf between the husband and wife, if not spanned, leads to constant bickering, misunderstanding and even extra-marital relations. However, considering the necessity of disciplining human instincts, the challenge posed to the institution of marriage is irrational. Actually, the matrimonial tie unites the two parties on a sound basis, provided both of them are of equal economic, social and intellectual standards. The oft-quoted plea for adjustment hardly arises in such cases where, by virtue of equality of status, both the parties are free in their pursuits and because of their mutual sentiment, there is little urge to indulge in extra-marital relations.

Some people plead for the abolition of the institution of marriage. They argue that marriage is an abrupt change from a courtship concluded with certain elements of romanticism and idealisation. According to them, the increasing marital conflicts and disintegration of the family in modern society are also attributable to this. However, considering the many opportunities available to the two partners to understand each other's personality traits, this argument appears to over-emphasise the end of the romantic phase as a cause of marital conflicts.

Further, their belief ignores certain more important but less apparent factors, for example, emotional immaturity, dominant personality trends, escapist attitude to life, lack of adjustment skills, early inhibiting sexual influences, etc. (Becker and Hill. *Family, Marriage and*

Parenthood) Such persons plead for unrestrained sexual relations. This is perhaps based on the concept of equality of man and woman and the fact that infidelity on the part of the man has, in all societies, been condemned less than in the case of the woman. It may, however, be stated that the disparity in the degree of condemnation does not challenge the justification for the institution to which the offence relates.

It is admitted that quite a good number of conflicts in attitudes towards sex have their roots in certain childhood happenings, and early definition of sex as something unclean or unnatural, coupled with lack of sex education, which leads to seeing sex as something lewd, licentious and beastly. Thus, the consciousness of guilt behind sexual experience manifests itself in psycho-sexual immaturity and escape mechanisms to avoid sex, for example, psychosomatic illnesses, workalholism and similar other factors. Pre-marital sexual irregularities and sexual inhibitions create a tendency to look at sex as undesirable, and a pre-marital sexual experience sometimes creates hostility and ambivalence because of guilt consciousness and lack of respect.

In certain cases, conflict in marriage arises out of difference in the standards and the cultural setting of the two partners which includes behaviour, mores of their respective social groups, age, dress habits, mannerisms, recreational and aesthetic interests, conventions, religion, education, language and so on. Normally, these cultural differences are obstacles or hindrances to unification of the two partners. Of course, these cultural differences may not result inevitably in conflict if the two partners in marriage are otherwise held together by bonds of common interests, sympathies and association.

A plea for the abolition of the institution of marriage seems on par with a demand for the abolition of the concept of morality, because the number of offences against moral codes has been increasing. Innumerable psychological problems and distortions in children because of dissatisfaction and disharmony among parents, and consequent lack of adequate parental care, has manifested itself in increasing disobedience and juvenile delinquency. A tendency has also been observed among today's youth to avoid marriage because they apprehend conflict at a later stage, and this has resulted in pre-marital relations and illegitimate births. Of course, the negative aspects of liberalisation—

coarseness, molestation, vulgar manners—are not likely to be permanent even if they continue for some decades.

Sex is admittedly an indispensable part of human life and there is no escape from it even if humanity decides not to bother about procreation. In this connection, the prevalence of test tube babies is significant. The union of a man and woman would be reduced to mere sexual satisfaction devoid of sentiment and love.

Just as a child needs the love of its mother for healthy development, men and women need each other's love for harmony in their physical and mental health. Maladjustment between the husband and wife can lead to various complications. No couple can remain united unless there is a spiritual rapport between them. The sexes are inter-dependent in a manner that is biologically fundamental, their functions are basically reciprocal and they are so delicately related to each other that any lack of adjustment may lead to serious personal and social consequences (Ashley Montaigne. *The Natural Superiority of Women,* London: George Allen and Unwin Ltd, 1954). Thus, there is a dire need to evolve a new type of relationship between the sexes for which men and women will have to work together in a spirit of co-operation rather than competition. By collaborating in absolute harmony, men and women will be able to benefit each other. The psychic and spiritual significance of marriage may not be very evident during youth, but by middle age the difference in life with and without a marital partner becomes obvious.

No one, of course, is totally satisfied with his marital state. Conjugal happiness is dependent on the physical, mental and spiritual state of the two partners, coupled with their ability to adapt to the needs and attitudes of each other. There may be some ambitious women who refuse to accept subjugation of marriage and choose to be independent. For them, earlier, there was a place in religion where no man's caprice could master them. However, spiritual pursuit is not the lot of everybody. Further, in most unfortunate marriages neither party is at fault. The problem is that when two normal persons are yoked in matrimony without a proper appraisal of whether they are suited to each other, the painful discovery of their disparity brings out the worst behaviour in each of them. With the passage of time, it becomes impossible to maintain even a facade of a happy marriage. The only remedy for breaking the bonds of matrimony is still regarded as somewhat degrading by society.

Today, considerations influencing marriage may be said to be mutual sexual love in the West and endogamy and exogamy of castes in the East. No consideration is given to the psychological profile of the two individuals and this usually leads to problems in married life.

When Charlie Chaplin faced divorce proceedings initiated by his wife, these were the reasons she gave for the suit:

> "He is a man of strange moods, who wanders down to the sea shore and stays there alone for hours; he is a silent man, indulging overmuch in thought, he is a solitary and frequently walks away from society into the Californian hills."

Evidently, Mrs. Chaplin was too young in body and soul to understand that if Charlie's genius was to survive, he had to do these things. He had to practise solitary self-communion (Paul Brunton. *Hermit in the Himalayas*). His withdrawn mood and silences were the price he had to pay to nourish the genius bestowed on him.

Conditions prevailing in most modern societies indicate that in respect to women, the criterion of success is their marital status, whereas for men it is judged based on occupational achievements. This indicates the fundamental differences between the social and psychological behaviour of the two sexes. The woman's goal of marriage makes her enhance her attractiveness to the opposite sex and occupational proficiency has little role to play. Women are further expected to orient themselves to the concept of love which, in its romantic state, is often seen as mysterious and irrational and is hardly compatible in the present context of rationality based on scientific and technological progress.

This leads to psychological conflict among girls who experience grave difficulty in reconciling the feminine ideal with the intellectual ideal, for example, the feminine ideal calls for assumption of the behaviour of a non-intellectual. This is not a totally new phenomenon. In the past, too, there have been irreconcilable conflicts or disparities among the partners to a marriage and, despite the various restrictions of religion and tradition, certain devices were evolved to make a divorce or separation possible. But in most cases, the solution lies not in divorce but in unravelling and clarifying each strand of the conflict with understanding, patience and sympathy. In tense marital relations, the services of a psychologist may be required. The courts can adjudicate on the claims of contesting partners according to legal provisions which can never be so extensive as to cover the problems of all individuals brought up in different circumstances, of different cultures and adhering to different values. Recourse to legal action is the last resort after psychological and social measures prove futile. The Hindu Marriage Act and the Special Marriages Act have made it obligatory for courts to try and bring about a reconciliation between contesting parties in consonance with the nature and circumstances of each case. This injunction is adhered to only perfunctorily because of lack of time and machinery at the courts' disposal.

In these circumstances, a viable solution to the problems facing marital harmony can emanate only through spiritualism which would ensure the inculcation of a sense of proportion and development of the standard of values. An attitude of co-operation based on proper understanding between partners to a marriage is bound to ensure marital bliss as the husband and wife would tend to identify with each other.

—oo(O)oo—

SECTION III

Egalitarianism

16

EQUALITY OF THE SEXES

THE term 'egalitarianism' refers to the position of women in society as well as in the family. It is easier to assess her position in society from the availability of opportunities of participation in social and productive activities as also of gainful employment. However, her position in the family is difficult to evaluate. In this connection, the Yugoslavian sociologist, Ilija Stanojcie has said:

> "...the creation of the socialist family type is founded on individual and reciprocal sexual love and on the true equality of the spouses. It is necessary to confess, however, that in Yugoslavia, this type of family is found rather rarely at the present time, especially with respect to the latter characteristic." (*Transactions of the Third World Congress of Sociology*, vol. 8, Amsterdam International Sociological Association, 1957).

This clinging to traditional behaviour and standard of values is further evidenced by West Germany's Constitution which asserted that there was to be full equality of the sexes in all fields without any qualification and that legislation had to be made to conform with this new provision. However, in the process of legislating, a grave difficulty came up in respect of the reconciliation of this constitutional provision with the practices and values of the German family. Indeed, they did not succeed in rewriting the legislation and eventually had to leave specific decisions to the German judges in specific cases (Sophie Grinberg-

Vinauer. 'The Status of Women Throughout the World'. *Marriage and Family Living*, August 15, 1955).

It is evidently a grave mistake to speak of women as a homogeneous class. It is undesirable that, like men, all women be treated as having the same social and intellectual status. Further, the disabilities to which women have been exposed in the past have not affected all women in the same way and to the same extent; nor did all inequalities apply to all women. For example, the lack of employment opportunities for women applied only to the middle class, as peasant women were occupied in agricultural activity along with their menfolk, and the women of the higher classes had hardly any wish or necessity to take up employment.

Tradition restricted women to the home and this adequately describes the woman's role in pre-industrial society. Even after the advent of the industrial revolution, maldistribution of the newly created wealth ensured that the beneficiaries were only those belonging to the prosperous middle class, leaving the women of the lower classes to face the same age-old miseries. The growing urban middle class, which was thriving on the expansion of trade and industry, developed a tendency towards idleness, especially the women, and made it a status symbol in the name of culture and tradition akin to that of the ruling and landed nobility of medieval times. This state of affairs has been described by Viola Klein as unde--

> "Daughters were brought up to be decorous, modest and chaste and they were closely guarded and chaperoned so as not to stray from the path of virtue. Knowledge and initiative, intelligence and experience were discouraged. The education of women was aimed at producing accomplishments—a smattering of music, art and needlework as well as social manners... (R. Patai. *Women in the Modern World*).

This situation applied, in varying degrees, to almost all societies in the world. However, the outbreak of the World War, coupled with the tremendous progress of science and technology transformed the whole social structure from the economic as well as the psychological points of view.

By and large, it can be said that in the West, women have fought for and achieved the fullest measure of equality with men in all fields of life, namely, in the family, law, society, economic opportunities, cultural achievements, etc. It is of significance, however, that women in the West are realising that the primary satisfaction which life holds for them is found in the house from where they started on their feminist crusade just two or three generations ago (R. Patai. *Women in the Modern World*).

Today, the more advanced debate is no longer restricted to the status of women. It has been extended to the whole complex pattern of men's and women's social roles. Actually, women in the West have achieved a high degree of legal and professional equality with men, but the traditional concept of male and female roles still holds a strong influence on the actual behaviour in various sections of society.

In the West, women generally occupy a fairly strong position as equal partners of men in most spheres of life. Both may marry after the attainment of puberty without parental consent. There is no gainsaying that woman has obtained considerably greater freedom than she possessed half a century ago. In Western countries, the old patriarchal family is now uncommon but in regard to family behaviour, the husband is admittedly dominant in every family system in the West (William J. Goode. *World Revolution and Family Patterns*).

It is sometimes argued that the position of women depends on their economic contribution in the family. However, the conditions prevailing in different societies (patriarchal as well as matriarchal) do not substantiate this assumption. For example, among the hunting and food-gathering tribes who constitute the best example of a surviving primitive form of economy, the division of labour between men and women is such that the women are engaged in food-gathering and the men do the hunting. Although from the economic point of view, food gathering is by far more important than hunting, most of the tribes have a patriarchal system. Further, in the matrilineal societies, the woman's economic contribution is in no way higher than her contribution in the patrilineal societies. Thus, an approach to this problem, purely in utilitarian terms, is bound to be misleading, as an improvement in the earning potential of the individual without a fundamental transformation of his or her whole personality is bound to bring about more problems of ambition and caprice.

With the increasing earning capacity of women, the weakening of the old (patriarchal) system of the family, the woman's position in the family is becoming progressively stronger. Further, the ever-increasing number of women taking up employment has brought about ambivalent attitudes in family behaviour, for example, in Poland a press report indicated that "young husbands of the working wives, who left the house cleaning and even cooking to them, grumbled that 'progress' had come too fast" (Arthur Olsen. 'Polish Chefs Pay Women a Tribute', *New York Times*, March 9, 1962).

Evaluation of the various conflicting comments and the data published in different sociological records seem to lead to the conclusion that the claims of fundamental egalitarianism in the West are not correct and that an unequivocally egalitarian family is rarely to be found (William J. Goode. World *Revolution and Family Patterns*). Normally, all family relations are determined by the male. Even when the husband performs the household duties, he gains power through his participation in those activities that were so far the monopoly of the women, and thus gets more opportunities for exercise of prerogatives in making decisions. There are, of course, women in almost every society, rather in many families, who manage to dominate men.

The women's liberation movement aimed at achieving rights for women in regard to marriage, property and franchise. With the incessant effort of various social reformers, women got the right of separation and divorce, to inherit patrimony and to vote. The various legislative measures coupled with the expansion of education among women have radically changed the traditional concept in regard to the role of men and women as being fundamentally different. In the wake of industrialisation creating potential of employment in industrial, educational and administrative spheres for women equally with men, their role is now considered inter-changeable in the economic sphere.

In Indian thought, there is a fundamental affirmation of the female principle. *Brahman,* the transcendent and imminent Absolute is neuter, beyond the differentiation qualifications of sex, beyond all limiting of individual characteristics. However, one of the principal manifestations of the godhead is *Ardhanarishwara,* signifying that the Lord, who is half man and half woman, signifies the unity of man and woman. Another similar manifestation is the dynamic symbol of the divine couple.

In all forms of Indian art, namely, sculpture, painting, dance, etc., the gods and goddesses are the self-revelation of the Absolute, the male specifying the passive aspect (known as Eternity) and the female personifying the activating energy (or Shakti or the dynamism of time). Thus, both male and female are essentially one.

Ancient Indian thought recognises no fundamental distinction between the two sexes and both are considered inseparable parts of the human soul which have a natural attraction towards each other which manifests itself in sexual attraction as well. This concept resulted in the development of a unique standard of behaviour and values in which people cared more for giving than taking. Both the partners of the matrimonial tie tried to add to the happiness of each other. This ensured absolute harmony in their relations and an ever-increasing contribution of both men and women to the welfare of society at large.

Historically, Indian women enjoyed high respect in the Vedic and up to the post-Vedic period. However, from the post-Vedic period there came a decrease in the respect granted to women, mostly in the economic sphere. Thus, there have been attempts to deprive her of her religious and ritual equality as well, for example, Mahavira and Buddha, the two greatest religious reformers of the sixth century B.C. (and founders of two of the most important religions, Jainism and Buddhism) did not grant them equal rights of admission to monastic life. It was with the persistent efforts of Ananda, the favourite disciple of Buddha, that women got permission to enter the religious order of *Sangha*. In these circumstances, there have, of course, been reactionary movements in favour of women that often assumed incredibly high levels. So much so, that woman was raised to the position of divinity. Thus, the woman was not merely a symbol of sex, but an object of adoration for the attainment of ultimate happiness.

It is unfortunate that the Indian woman has been subjected to cruel and unjust behaviour in regard to her role as wife. As and when she chose to reject that role, whether in ancient or medieval times, and assume that of a philosopher, religious devotee, fighter or artist, she was treated as an equal. The contribution of women seers to Vedic and Upanishadic literature and the protection and continuity of artistic traditions during the medieval period, as also the role of women in modern Indian social and political sectors speak for the honourable position enjoyed by Indian women.

Even in villages and small towns far from modern urban influence, where women still observe *purdah* on certain occasions and are considered subservient, male prejudice is almost non-existent. Unfavourable conditions in difficult regions and insecure borderlands naturally spur men and women to more equitable adjustments in status and rights. In the urban areas, the working woman, whether in offices or in the educational, social, political and industrial sectors, is being accepted as a professional equal.

The fundamental differences between the women's liberation in the West and the one in India is that in the West it involved a struggle for acceptance as equals in all spheres of life, but in India it pertains only to the woman's role as wife. In India, woman has never degenerated into a sex symbol. She has, rather, been treated with divine reverence. As stated earlier, her cause has been upheld by men themselves, and hence the Indian woman carries no bitterness against man as a class.

The rapid change in the standard of values and behaviour attempted by Mahatma Gandhi and some of his enthusiastic followers could not bring the desired results because society was not prepared to accept the Gandhian ethic in sexual matters, which called for a highly developed standard of sincerity. This state of affairs resulted in the development of hypocrisy in the sense that whatever was propagated and accepted publicly was rejected in private. Men tried to evade the call of the times by adopting double standards and women, newly freed from their domestic subjugation, did not see a clear way out of this situation.

This resulted in moral confusion that took different directions and distorted sexual behaviour and the standard of values. In the matter of equality of rights, one cannot fail to observe a sharp distinction between the roles and spheres of the two sexes. True parity, granted by the Constitution of India, could be achieved only when the conceptions and attitudes of the people are brought on par with it.

With the expansion of education and urbanisation since the attainment of independence, Indian women are getting more opportunities to enter almost all spheres of social, administrative, legal and political activity. During the past few years, much thought has been given to the principle of egalitarianism between the sexes on the individual level. It appears that human society is conceived to consist of two sexes hostile to each other. This tendency is fundamentally very unfortunate from the point of view of the larger interest of humanity. However, every social trend is based on certain historical facts.

In the West, talk of egalitarianism is based on economic self-sufficiency of the woman. The progress of science and technology and industrialisation have laid open to women all kinds of jobs, technical as well as administrative. Almost everywhere women are achieving positions which were once considered beyond their capacity. The most exclusive scientific societies have opened their doors and admitted women to the highest honours (Montaigne Ashby. *The Natural Superiority of Women*. London: George Allen and Unwin Ltd. 1954), for example, Madame Curie, Semla Lagerlof, Grazia Seledda, Sigrid Undset, Pearl Buck, Gabriela Mistrel, and many many more.

It is sometimes said that among women, there have been very few great musicians, poets, painters, scientists, inventors, technologists and philosophers. This contention might have been valid until the dawn of the 19th century, that is, before which women were deprived of all opportunities to prove and develop their faculties and genius. Now they can vote and occupy various high positions in all spheres including the legal, political and diplomatic. The increasing demand for skills to fill jobs created by industrialisation has been the most important factor leading to this state of affairs. The demand of industry has crossed all racial, ethnic, national and sex barriers. Most of the highly industrialised countries of the West had to allow even foreigners to work in their industries. In certain countries, the number of foreigners working in industry had gone beyond the number of the natives so engaged.

Further, the economic philosophy of John Locke introduced in Western ethics and philosophy the concept of equal opportunity to develop oneself. Thus, the industrial needs as also the ethical assertions worked simultaneously in favour of the struggle for egalitarianism.

To develop skilled workers needed by industry, the educational set up was expanded laying all branches of study open to men and women equally. Thus women got an opportunity to prepare themselves for all types of jobs at par with men, thereby attaining economic independence. This state of affairs benefited the women of the lower strata, who learnt skills for getting employment while women in the middle and upper strata could attain economic parity with men due to their traditional apathy towards participation in occupations.

In course of time, this led to two independent trends among the lower and upper classes; for example, the menfolk of the lower classes conceded fewer rights than their women obtained while men in the upper strata conceded more rights ideologically than their women did, in fact, achieve (William J. Goode. *World Revolutions and Family Patterns*).

These ideological tensions are non-existent in Indian society. As stated earlier, the Indian woman's struggle is limited to attaining parity in respect of her role as wife. With increasing education, academic as well as professional, they will soon attain this parity in all respects and regain the position of respect they held during the Vedic period.

The relationship between husband and wife is one of partnership in which each looks after the interests of the other. As the elevation of the soul consists of self-negation, the ideal of husband and wife looking after each other is evidently conducive to worldly happiness and spiritual elevation. The proper ideal of Indian womanhood is self-fulfilment by means of self-effacement.

Ancient and medieval literature of the West confirms the prevalence of a similar concept of the ideal woman, that is, the personification of devotion, sacrifice and submissiveness to her husband. From the modern point of view, we find an element of consent and mutual co-operation as the basis of married life among the members of the lower castes, whereas among the upper castes there is a strong sense of possession over property and wife alike.

Besides this, women of the upper castes, not themselves engaged in productive or economic activities, were fully dependent upon their husbands whereas women of the lower castes enjoyed much more freedom and economic independence due to their equal participation in productive activities.

Although it is very difficult to define the term 'equality' in any universal form, a beginning has been made to transform relations, frame policies and set up goals. There is no gainsaying that the two sexes need to be brought closer through mutual love and understanding. It is time to realise the significance of an effective social equality of the sexes.

—oo(O)oo—

17

WOMEN'S LIBERATION

DOES women's liberation constitute a supra-social concept, quite distinct from the fundamental problem of liberating toiling people from slavery of every kind, gross and subtle, direct and indirect, imposed upon them by a small minority leading a life of ease and luxury at the cost of the former? The term 'women's liberation' has often been misinterpreted as it is a comprehensive concept. Phenomena do not exist in isolation and the question of women's liberation needs to be examined in the context of an integrated view of social life, in the absence of which women would never enjoy true liberation in a society which is based on an exploitative and repressive system of organisation. This is evident from the fact that despite all claims made in Europe and America on behalf of women, their liberation is far from reality. At the same time, it is admitted that they enjoy a certain amount of quantitative freedom, which seems to be a new bondage resulting from frustration in a society that has become commercialised to the marrow. A social worker engaged in the task of ameliorating the lot of women commented:

> "I am not a women's lib exponent in the popular sense. I sincerely feel that co-operation rather than confrontation with men is the real answer to the problem of equality for women, and the best way for women to achieve a better status in society is to work hard and secure better positions in their chosen fields. In regard to the availability of opportunities for the development

of personality, women are in no way in a disadvantageous position. The fields of education, employment, social, cultural and political activity are equally open to women as to men."

Leaving apart the extravagant claims of the movement, it is undeniable that it has brought to the surface the topic of the role of women in society in general, in contradiction of the traditional roles assigned to the sexes on the basis of biology and cultures of different societies. It aims at bringing about some concrete benefits to under-privileged women in developing countries as well as those in more advanced countries who resent being treated as mere sex symbols. There are people who believe that women, whether in India or elsewhere, need to identify themselves and struggle for a better place in society and that the task of the women's movement is not yet over.

In the West, Fredrika Bremer established the first women's liberation organisation in Sweden in 1845. In 1884, the Norwegian National Association for the rights of women was formed. The Western Women's Liberation movement got its inspiration from the declaration of Women's Rights in the French Revolution and the development of certain new theories in the field of biology, genetics, etc. The exponents of women's liberation complain about the generally inferior status of women, that is, she is relegated to the backwash of social, administrative and political life, in spite of her qualifications being comparable with or even better than those of men, and that this male chauvinism constitutes the biggest hurdle in women's advancement.

Strictly speaking, the women's liberation movement offers nothing fundamentally new, as right from earliest times people have been commenting on the energy and faculties of women. In the history of the evolution of the family, 'woman' power was considered to be best utilised in the household and in bringing up children. In the primarily agricultural society before the Industrial Revolution, social and political structures were extremely simple and feudal in nature, where all the power of decision-making was vested in the feudal heads (who might be men or women) or the heads of the village communities of religious organisations. In these circumstances, the people were not very ambitious to establish their identity or assert themselves. Both men and women devoted themselves equally to the pursuit of religious, spiritual, philosophical, artistic and literary activities without the least tinge of self-assertion. Most of the ancient literary or artistic works do not contain the name of the author. This is evidently due to a peculiarly Indian approach to life in which all activity, conscious as well as subconscious, was considered a medium of devotion to the divinity. Giving one's name to literary or artistic creations was deprecated. The whole of Vedic and Brahmanic literature evidences this.

In these circumstances, women as well as men have been participating equally in all fields of social activity, and all went well in the name of religion and tradition. With the advent of industrial development even in the tradition bound sections of society, the women's liberation movement was ushered in. It created an awareness all over the world that the position of women must be reconsidered both in the family as well as in society. The number of books and articles written, the various commissions and committees appointed to study the status of women and the observance of the year 1975 as International Women's Year clearly reflected this interest.

A definition of the terms 'liberation', 'equality' and 'status' is necessary. *Prima facie,* status is discernible from the statistics pertaining to law, education and participation in social, administrative and political activity, but this is far from reality. The term 'liberation' has already been discussed briefly at the beginning of this chapter. In regard to 'equality', it is perhaps not justified to divide the whole of human society into two hostile groups which, in the garb of struggling for equality, are liable to strive for superiority over each other, even as a slave, instead of struggling against the institution of slavery, dreams of replacing his master one day when he would be able to command the respect of other slaves.

Thus, the term 'liberation' without associating it with some well-defined objectives aimed at by women as a group is quite vague. The main problem seems to be that pertaining to the standard of values and the respect given to different types of work, for example, manual, intellectual, administrative, political, etc. Accordingly, effort should be directed towards removing obstacles such as immobility, optionless occupation in menial tasks, denial of the right to participate in decision-making, etc. The present structure of society in regard to assignment of respect and remuneration for different types of work needs to be transformed if modern labour problems, which challenge modern society, are to be averted.

Similarly, it is a question of value given to domestic work, both in terms of human intelligence and use of energy and labour, which needs to be taken up in right earnest by the women's liberation movement. In this connection, it would be appropriate to draw attention to increasing juvenile delinquency in developed countries, evidently due to lack of direct contact of working mothers with children. The lack of motherly affection creates emotional conflict in the character of the child, leading to an unbalanced personality.

Thus, the value of domestic work will have to be raised to bring it at par with other professional work, or the energy and time spent on housekeeping will have to be reduced drastically by introducing labour-saving devices so that women could take to professions along with their domestic responsibilities. In this case, the participation of men in household chores has a special significance.

Each individual, man or woman, has a distinct personality and any attempt to ensure equality of groups without any consideration of the aptitude of the groups is not going to assist either group achieve happiness. Imitation of men in work and behaviour in the name of equality and liberation is not justified as it is bound to lead to a merger of the woman's identity without any corresponding advantage. Retaining one's image is a definite advantage; for example, the Negroes in America in the initial stage of their struggle for equality with the Whites sought to merge their identity with the latter by imitating them. However, this defeated the whole purpose of their struggle. They now assert their colour to gain equality, which has brought them more respect than the earlier approach of imitation.

Thus, the main problem pertains to the standard of values and behaviour, and it is more realistic to bring about a comprehensive transformation of the human personality through a well-phased programme of education suited to modern requirements conforming to the traditional structure of each society. The assertion of the distinct features of womanhood and their advantages is bound to improve the status of women.

The other point for consideration is whether women would like to set distinct goals for themselves irrespective of what men have, or aspire to, and whether women identify themselves as a category with a definite set of dispositions and interests, distinct from that of men. The age-old traditional assumption that women are, by nature, more suited to domestic duties and rearing of children has already met with challenge in the West, based on the conviction that there is no fundamental difference in the drives and dispositions of men and women and hence men should share or take over domestic responsibilities just as women are struggling not to be an economic burden on men.

Similarly, 'status' is a term based on the pattern of relationship between men and women, which in turn depends on the image that the two parties have of each other. Status has hardly any fundamental relation to material possessions or rights to such possessions. Instead, it depends on the state of development of the personality which the beholder or companion is bound to appreciate and respect. In regard to the image of a developed personality, there may be some difference of opinion between societies and generations with distinct cultures, and any attempt to bring about a uniform approach by different societies is bound to serve no fruitful purpose.

There has admittedly been a great difference between the position of women belonging to the upper and middle classes, and those belonging to the lower or working classes. With the advent of the industrial revolution, this gap widened further due to the newly-created wealth through increasing trade and industrial activity. But after the Second World War, the labour movement gained ground and the gap between the once wealthy middle class and the lower or working class started narrowing and, ultimately, both classes joined at a median point, where most of their differences on standard of values and behaviour gave way to a joint approach to various social problems.

In regard to the attitude towards women, the middle class standard of values and behaviour have yielded to those prevalent among the lower or working classes, for example, the middle class women, whose field of activity was earlier restricted to the home, started entering into all types of gainful employment, whereas only 50 years earlier, a middle class woman seeking employment outside her home was the object of suspicion and even ridicule. Now, like the per capita income, literacy, and life expectancy, the extent of women's participation in the labour force of a country is considered an index of its advancement.

Another feature emanating from this fusion of the earlier middle and lower working classes is increased sexual freedom, which was earlier restricted to the lower classes. The traditional concept of family honour requiring zealous guarding of girls and women does not hold good any more even among the middle classes except in a few countries.

Simultaneously, with these changes and the development of new standards of behaviour, there arose an increasing demand for women's rights, denied to them so far. The liberation movement has sensitised the role of women in society at different levels, from the most banal to the most esoteric, thereby illuminating human and social relationships.

Women's liberation, as a product of the urban middle class in the Western industrial society with an overwhelmingly large segment of women trained in different professions suited to modern industry, administration and politics, does not have immediate relevance to Indian social conditions. The movement for the amelioration of the status of women throughout the world may be broadly summarised as comprising a struggle for achieving greater equality with men, both within and outside the family, namely, in the sexual, social, legal, economic, occupational, political and cultural fields. The earlier concept of the woman's role being confined to domestic service, as servants or, at the most, as helpers to their menfolk has yielded to the new and dynamic concept of assigning to women different roles on the basis of equality; within the home as wives, mothers and home-makers and outside as collaborators of men in all types of enterprises.

History shows that the traditional relationship between men and women in the patriarchal set up in most societies had the following characteristics:

1. The family was headed by a male member.
2. Women were considered property and whatever they owned was their father's or husband's.
3. Men enjoyed more free sex, namely, men were allowed to have more wives or concubines whereas women were subjected to strict pre-marital chastity and marital fidelity.

4. Women were confined to domestic work or to helping their menfolk in agriculture.

5. A woman's merit depended on her ability to bear children.

The institution of *sati* (burning of widows on the funeral pyre of their dead husbands) and *purdah* (complete segregation of women) indicate that women were considered nothing more than private property to be dealt with according to the whims of the master or possessor.

Despite all the sociological developments, starting with the dawn of the 19th century, women continued to be subjected to a secondary position and to severe restrictions in regard to their activities and interests. Even the advanced countries of Europe were reluctant to grant women the right of voting until 1913 in Norway, 1915 in Denmark, 1918 in England, 1920 in America and 1921 in Sweden.

The position of women in different sections of society before the onset of the women's liberation movement was that in the middle and upper classes they lived in idleness and were expected to be refined and charming ornaments of the world of men. Thus, they were life-long dependants on the male—on the father during childhood, on the husband during youth and on the son during old age. This absolute economic dependence of women exposed them to extreme vulnerability in case the source of economic dependence was eliminated. Besides facing social opprobrium to earning a living, she was totally unprepared to take up gainful employment.

Prior to the industrial revolution, this aspect applied only to a minority of women because the majority comprised the lower or working classes engaged in agriculture, petty trading, crafts or allied services. The legal rights of these classes were at par with their counterparts in the upper and middle classes.

—oo(O)oo—

18

EMANCIPATION OF WOMEN

THE struggle for women's emancipation went through three stages:

1. The fight for women's rights;
2. The moral emancipation of women; and
3. Liberation in which the very fundamentals of the equation in male-female relationships are questioned.

How far have Indian women consciously asserted their rights and rebelled against their traditional principal role of wife and mother? This aspect needs to be discussed and also whether Indian women have freed themselves from their moral and economic subjugation to men.

In India, there have been infinite variations in the status of women, in accordance with the cultural milieu, structure of the family, caste, class, etc. Strangely enough, the struggle for restoration of the status and dignity of women which they enjoyed in ancient India was undertaken by the men themselves. Major issues like the abolition of *sati,* etc. were taken up by early social reformers like Dwarka Nath and Raja Ram Mohun Roy. Again, it was a man, Ishwarchandra Vidyasagar, who created a social consciousness which ultimately made it possible for legislative measures to legalise widow remarriage. The practice of child marriage was abolished in 1929. Indian women were given voting rights in 1935, that is 10 years before French women and 11 years before Italian women.

Another important step in this regard was of a legislative nature when, in 1956, the Hindu Divorce Act came into being, providing for divorce without the interference of any religious or social institution. This was the first legislation of its type in the world. From 1971, even abortion was legalised under certain special conditions.

As stated earlier, under the leadership of Mahatma Gandhi, Indian women proved their merit in the political field by their active participation in the struggle for independence. It was, therefore, natural for them to acquire some of the highest positions in government and outside. The Indian Constitution provided for social, economic and political justice to every citizen and equality of opportunity in public employment.

Thus, women were given equal rights to adequate means of livelihood and 'equal pay for equal work' with men. All careers were opened to women. They started outnumbering men in educational services, and a spate of women joined the lower income groups as well as highly paid groups. Women became engineers, pilots, lawyers, politicians, vice-chancellors of universities, etc.

Some of the honours bestowed on women in the post-independence period were: in 1947, a woman became the governor of a State, another became a minister in the Central cabinet and still another the first woman ambassador in the world. In 1966, not only the masses but the hard core intelligentsia opted for a woman as Prime Minister of the country.

However, despite this and the various legislative provisions to look after the interests of women, statistics show that a lot has still to be done, particularly in rural areas, where the literacy rate among women is very low. The findings of the 2001 Census in this regard is encouraging. The overall literacy rate in 2001 was 65.38 per cent (75.85 per cent for males and 54.16 per cent for females).

In rural areas, the female literacy rate varied in different States, for example, in Rajasthan it was as low as 4 per cent, 6 per cent in Bihar and Madhya Pradesh and 7 per cent in Uttar Pradesh. The highest literacy rate was in Kerala (90.92 per cent), Mizoram (88.49

per cent) and Lakshadweep (87.52 per cent) while the lowest was in Bihar with 47.53 per cent.

In the post-independence period, the school enrolment rate for boys increased from 60 per cent in 1950-51 to the high seventies in 1973-74, while in the case of girls it rose from 25 to 66 per cent during the period. In the 11-14 age group, the enrolment increased from 21 to 48 per cent for boys and 5 to 22 per cent for girls. In the 14-17 age group, the number increased from 9 per cent to 31 per cent for boys and from 2 to 12 per cent for girls. Enrolment ratio at the primary stage has gone up 42.60 per cent in 1950-1951 to 92.14 per cent, the number of primary and upper primary schools has gone up from 2.23 lakh in 1950-1951 to 8.17 lakh in 1998-1999 and the number of teachers in primary and upper primary schools is 31.80 lakh in 1998-1999. Secondary education serves as a bridge between elementary and higher education to prepare young persons of the age group of 14-18 for entry into higher education. In 1999, there were 1.10 lakh higher secondary and senior secondary institutions, 272 lakh enrolment, 101 lakh enrolment of girls and 15.42 lakh teachers.

Although there has been a progressive increase in the enrolment of girls, the target for universal enrolment, originally set for 1980, has yet to be achieved. There has also been an increase in the number of girls entering professional courses, namely, law, medicine, engineering, etc. The Constitution of India guarantees equality to all citizens and prohibits discrimination on the grounds of sex. The Fundamental Rights and Directive Principles of the Constitution provide for the emancipation of women. Indian society, however, is tradition bound and conservative and in some cases, even sections of women oppose the demand for their own rights.

The Constitutional guarantee for equal rights to women having proved inadequate, and with a view to accelerate women's interests in society, the Government constituted the National Committee on the Status of Women in September 1971. The terms of reference of this Committee were to examine various constitutional, legal and administrative provisions bearing on the status of women and their impact on the position of women in India during the previous two decades. With progressively increasing education, women are coming out of their traditional role of housewives and mothers and entering different fields of social, political and industrial activity, proving their ability to play a full and powerful role in building the nation.

It is evident that the Indian woman's struggle is centred on liberation from the prejudices governing her position as a wife. This involves asserting women's rights without any challenge to the standard of values. There is evidently no conscious attempt to change the pattern of sexual equations and to question its fundamentals. Women's liberation in India is, thus, fundamentally, different from that in the West.

In the West, certain emancipationists have stressed the need of preparing women psychologically and academically for alternating between the family role and employment, with provision of facilities for adjustment to both fields. With increasing industrialisation and women's entry in administrative, legal and industrial fields, certain radicals have gone to the extent of saying that the idea of 'two roles for the woman' needs to be substituted by a system in which women could take up all occupations and careers along with men. Such a programme involves a radical, revolutionary change in housekeeping, childcare, etc. The psychological problems of children who lack close personal care of their parents has been dealt with in detail elsewhere.

There was a belief during the International Women's Year that Indian women were joining hands with their counterparts in the West to fight against male dominance and exploitation, which had the support of religion and tradition. In this connection, it should be said that the struggle for the restoration of the status and dignity of women, as enjoyed by them in ancient times, was undertaken by men. In the last century, Mahatma Gandhi was mainly responsible for involving Indian women in the national struggle for independence, thereby proving their equal importance in society. However, the name of Mahatma Gandhi is hardly referred to in the cause of women's liberation, perhaps due to the fact that the Gandhian attitude towards women's liberation is not properly understood.

Mahatma Gandhi loved the Hindu traditional framework of society in which the man and woman are complementary. He considered the home to be the best place for women, whereby he stood for the maintenance of the *status quo* in the man-woman relationship where the man is the wage-earner and the woman, although economically dependent on him, maintains and looks after the affairs of the home, including bringing up the children. Thus, *prima facie,* Mahatma Gandhi was a chauvinist who wanted to restrict women to the four walls of their houses. However, his ideas in this regard are clarified in his speech at a meeting of mill workers in Ahmedabad in February, 1920. He remarked:

> "Work is not for women. It is not for women to work in the factories. They have plenty of work in their homes. They should attend to their children. If women go to work, our social life will be ruined and moral standards will decline."

This was in conformity with the particular social structure prevailing in India as he was not unaware of the changing role of women in the industrial world. He took up the cause in a highly realistic manner, saying:

> "It is libel on all women to call them the weaker sex and that is man's injustice towards women. If by strength is meant moral power, then woman is immeasurably man's superior. Has she not greater intuition, is she not more self-sacrificing, has she not powers of endurance, has she not greater courage? Without her, man could not be. If non-violence is the law of our being, the future is with women."

Conscious of the potential of women, Mahatma Gandhi made a commendable contribution in liberating Indian women from exploitation by extending their field of activity and involving them in the freedom struggle. His passive resistance especially suited the general ethos in which Indian women lived, and thus the Indian woman joined the mainstream of nationalism and began playing a significant role in the Indian struggle for independence.

The independence movement gave a definite impetus towards bringing a change in the attitude towards women. In order to extend the movement among the masses, a number of depressed groups, namely, untouchables, peasants, workers and, above all, women, were included in it. The participation of women in the movement was intended partly to mobilise entire families and partly it drew inspiration from the Jaina and Bhakti ethic which stressed the equality of women. It may have also been inspired by the tremendous success attained by women politicians in ex-colonial countries. Mahatma Gandhi realised that by awakening national consciousness among women and involving them in the struggle for independence, they would come out of their traditional restricted domestic role. He provided Indian women with an opportunity to break from tradition. Consequently, a great number of women, rural and urban, literate and illiterate, from all sections of society, joined the freedom struggle. This gave women a consciousness of equality with men and brought them to the forefront of thought and action. An overwhelming number of women politicians distinguished themselves in the national struggle for independence.

Dr. Annie Besant's entry into politics encouraged Indian women to join the freedom struggle. In 1917, she was the first woman to be elected President of the Congress Party, a post which has since been occupied by two other women, Sarojini Naidu in 1925, Indira Gandhi in 1959 and now (2002) by Sonia Gandhi. While Sonia Gandhi's mettle has been seen to quite a large extent, both Sarojini Naidu and Indira Gandhi fulfilled the concepts of political leadership in India. Their courageous challenge of outmoded traditional social values was a strong source of inspiration to Indian womanhood. Another woman, Basanti Devi, wife of Deshbandhu Chittaranjan Das, was the first woman to be arrested for participation in the freedom movement. The Quit India movement in 1942 also involved participation of women, and leading women workers such as Aruna Asaf Ali, Sucheta Kripalani and Usha Mehta even had to go underground to avoid arrest.

As women's first major participation with men was in the struggle for freedom of India, their emancipation had no elements of man-woman antagonism which plagued women's movements in the West. From time immemorial, the Indian woman in tribal and rural society has been an equal partner with man. Decadence in this regard has been only in urban society, and that too among the higher classes. Women's liberation as it was preached in the affluent West is not in consonance with the Indian situation. The economic independence of women does not have the same significance in a society which is mainly agricultural and follows the joint family system.

—oo(O)oo—

19

WOMAN'S ROLE IN THE FAMILY

WOMEN have a dual role in the family: first in their parents' house and after that in their husband's home. The circumstances under which the birth of a daughter was considered unwelcome have changed, and although the treatment meted out to a daughter in Indian society is still not on par with that of a son, she is not denied care and affection by her parents.

As among the upper and middle classes during the medieval period, the ideal occupation of girls was considered to be preparation for marriage, which comprised some formal education in household chores, social and religious ceremonies as well as family and caste traditions. The importance of education, academic or otherwise, for girls was considered to be of little importance. In the parents' house, the girl was supposed to help her mother in domestic work, look after the younger brothers and sisters and obey her elders in all respects.

Among the higher classes, women were trained to be decorous, gifted in music and dance, well mannered and to serve their husbands. Among the middle classes, the most important occupation for young girls was the same as among the higher classes. This type of upbringing consisted of an intensive training in the art of pleasant conversation (based on an introductory study of history, art and modern literature) and the art of discreet flirtation. Even at the beginning of the 20th century, women of the upper and middle classes were chaperoned when they went out.

The situation, however, varied with the region, period and society and there have been occasions when women gained control. Even today, despite constitutional provisions for equality of the sexes, there is virtually no distinction between femininity and submission, sacrifice and economic dependence, etc. There are certain literary references proclaiming the woman to be the ruler of the household, but in fact, she has been put in the position of an inferior being. Her field of activity was restricted to the home, comprising her role as daughter, sister, wife and mother and it never extended beyond the house. The only alternative to home was a monastery and this too depended on the wishes of the family, for example, for gaining social prestige or to follow the tradition of widows having to lead a monastic life.

Among the lower or working classes, living conditions did not allow strict imposition of the ideal of female chastity and fidelity cherished by the middle and upper classes. Girls and women working in the fields or carrying water or other items of domestic necessity could hardly be restrained from meeting other young men or from resorting to planned meetings. This aspect of life in Indian society has been discussed in the chapter on pre-marital sexual relations.

Religion bestows its own status on the woman. Even in temples dedicated to male divinities, homage to the consort is considered indispensable. Frequent propitiation in various forms is made to ward off the wrath of the *Devi* (Kali and Mariamma). However, despite this religious attitude, woman generally has been reduced to playing a subservient role.

Processes such as modernisation, urbanisation and socio-economic changes in post-independence India have brought in their wake many fundamental and far-reaching changes. The most revolutionary change has been the emancipation of women from their tradition bound ethos into the mainstream of national life. Two of the oldest and most basic institutions of life, namely, marriage and family, have been tremendously affected by feminine emancipation.

PRESENT SCENARIO

India is among the four largest countries in the world, accounting for 15 per cent of the world's population, while its share in the land area is only 2.5 per cent. Forty-nine per cent of India's population are women. Among them 80 per cent are in the villages.

Indian womanhood has withstood valiantly the challenges and ravages of time, economic depressions, invasions, social problems, religious upheavals and political turbulence. It has adapted itself to social changes and new developments in leadership demands. The ancient religious background has given Indian women a heritage of the finest spiritual values and ideals that human imagination has created, ideals of chastity and courage. Women are the bedrock of the home and have carried forward over centuries these qualities and strengthened them.

WOMEN IN THE HOME

The Indian woman in the family plays a multiple role. Primarily, her duties centre around her life in the home and in the labour force. As a homemaker, woman is a 24-hour multi-purpose worker. Mahatma Gandhi had stated that "women by nature are intended to be soft, tender-hearted and sympathetic mothers to their children..." He had also cautioned women that domestic work output should not take the whole of their time.

In everyday life and various crises, woman displays strength and patience in carrying out her responsibilities. Through her hard work and dedication to house-keeping, child-rearing and assisting in agriculture and industry, woman contributed much to national, economic and social development. She is responsible for the food that the family consumes and for the care of her children. She takes care of food production, food processing, food preparation and serving, cleaning the household, carrying water, gathering fuel and washing dishes and clothes. Management of resources—human and material—sending children to school, meeting the needs of adolescents, improving the environment and planning for her daughters' future are also among her heavy responsibilities. She exerts great influence on the mental and social development of children. Woman is the fulcrum around which all the decisions and actions of the family revolve.

The mental resources of women are almost inexhaustible. They learn 'through' the ears and transmit orally much of the religious rites, ethical and moral codes, literature and music. They have played a significant role in the development and fostering of social, cultural and spiritual values, social relations and co-operation. Home beautification has been the prerogative of women since the beginning of civilisation.

WOMEN IN THE LABOUR FORCE

In the poorer communities, women do much strenuous physical work to eke out a living. At least 60 per cent of the rural women are involved in agricultural work—weeding, manuring, harvesting, winnowing, shelling and storing of crops. The other responsibilities include tending poultry and other domestic and farm animals. Transport of produce to the market is also their job. Such heavy work affects their health and role in the family directly and indirectly.

However, women's contribution to development has not been given due importance. The aim of women's development is to help develop 'adult women' to arrive at decisions that affect their lives and to bear the consequences of the decisions with courage. Full integration of women into total development right from the stage of decision-making of economic, social and cultural matters; and at community, regional, national and international levels is very important. Recognising the need for integrating women into development, the 20-point programme incorporates programmes of welfare for women and children and nutrition programmes for pregnant women, nursing mothers and children in tribal, hill and backward areas.

CHANGE IN THE WOMEN'S DECADE (1975-1984)

Through the effort of the International Year of the Woman in 1975, some changes have been initiated which have relevance to Indian women in the context of better family living. Through the U. N. World Conference held in Mexico in 1975 to usher in the Women's Decade, an awakening has been created which has sparked off various welfare measures, economic programmes, educational efforts and application of science and technology for alleviating the drudgery of women. The aspects which pertain to women in the family in the context of the changes which have occurred are discussed under the following headings:

1. Traditional functions of the family;
2. Patterns of family living;
3. Education of women;
4. Status of women in the family; and
5. Income support by women.

TRADITIONAL FUNCTIONS OF THE FAMILY

In Indian society, the position of women has been traditionally that of a 'dependent'—first on parents, then on husbands and later on the sons. The woman assists her mother in her early childhood; after marriage, her role is that of wife and mother. The traditional functions of the family are: transmission of culture, child care, marriage and family relations.

The family is the most important socialising agency. The task of promoting the healthy development of the child falls on the shoulders of the parents, especially the mother, who provides an atmosphere of acceptance, love and encouragement to set up and strengthen the child's self image. Rural women in 1972 were found to be more authoritarian in disciplining children. Scolding, threatening and physical punishment were found to be more common methods of disciplining them. Today, mothers feel a child thrives better on warmth, both mental and physical. They adopt mostly democratic methods of disciplining. Educated mothers are better at adopting positive disciplinary techniques.

Traditionally, among the Hindus, marriage was possible within the framework of the caste system only. The attitude of the educated middle class woman has, however, begun to change and they seem less bound by the constraints laid down by traditional patterns of marriage. There is increasing approval of inter-caste marriages among the educated middle class people.

There is evidence that modern women are more in favour of arranged marriages than they were 10 years ago. Although the ideology of romantic love marriage has gained popularity in Indian society and is regarded as a panacea by many social reformers for freeing Indian society from the stranglehold of the caste system, the vast majority of the people, both educated and uneducated, continue to conform to the traditional pattern of the arranged marriage.

Child marriage has played havoc with the physical and mental health of Indian girls. There is considerable improvement in this position in the cities and among high caste families. However, child marriages still continue to be solemnised in rural areas and in the backward sections of the city population. The education of women has tended to raise the age of marriage and lower the birth rate.

Although educational and occupational opportunities are providing women with new roles outside the home, their social position in the family remains largely unchanged because the system of arranged marriage confirms the authority of caste norms and the obligation of conformity to the traditional image of woman as wife and mother. Attitudes towards marrying a widower/widow or divorcee and attitudes towards sex, pre-marital sex and sexual freedom have been changing gradually.

The percentage of widow re-marriages increased as the educational level and socio-economic status of the widow improved. The favourable attitude towards widow re-marriage is seen more among the educated and the working women.

PATTERN OF FAMILY LIVING

Home-making is a multi-faceted task. It comprises a variety of tasks and activities such as management of human and material resources, menu planning, food selection, preparation and serving of food, selection and care of clothing, selection and use of equipment and decoration of the home.

A study of persons making decisions in two selected localities in 1975 showed that the urban man and the rural woman had a major role in taking family decisions. Wives and husbands together made decisions on food purchase, clothes, education of children, saving, health, recreation and religious activities in a majority of households, irrespective of the employment status, education and size of the families. The responsibility of managing money was entrusted to the head of the family in 49 per cent of the families while the homemakers along or with the husbands, took the responsibility of the rest. The position has changed now (2004). Women have the freedom to express personal desires in all activities. Regarding the education of children, it was found that they did not take advice from their in-laws. The husband and wife took joint decisions.

The data from a study of major activities in a household reveals that in the households of gainfully-employed women, activities such as sweeping and mopping the floor, cleaning utensils and washing clothes are carried out by paid helpers. In a majority of full-time homemakers' households also these activities are carried out by paid helpers. The major responsibility for cooking was taken up by 58 per cent of the gainfully-employed homemakers and 74 per cent of the full-time homemakers. The gainfully-employed homemakers depend more on paid helpers for most of the household activities than the full-time homemakers.

The adolescent girls of the family participate mainly in cutting vegetables, table setting, serving food, ironing, arrangement of furniture, bed-making, decorating the home, dressing up children, planning and purchase of cosmetics and clothes for themselves. Cooking was done by a majority of the girls in the absence of their mothers. In both low and high income families, wives and husbands shared the responsibility differently for purchasing different items of family goods. In high income families, children also shared the responsibility along with their parents.

FAMILY EXPENDITURE PATTERN

Longitudinal studies on Indian families carried out by Sri Avinashilingam Home Science College, Coimbatore, give details of the items of expenditure on an average for major items. The composition of family expenditure has remained more or less constant over the decade under study.

Six out of every 10 rupees earned by the household was spent on food, the remaining four rupees being shared among other items of expenditure. The rise in the percentage of expenditure on clothing and other items that include personal and miscellaneous items indicated a slight increase in the standard of living. However, the proportion of savings declined from 9 per cent to 3.5 per cent.

The food expenditure pattern shows that the expenditure on cereals ranked highest in both the years. During 1969, sixty-three per cent of the families spent 41.8 per cent of their income on cereals as against 43.9 per cent in 2001. It is notable that 45 per cent of the families in 2001 spent less (21-40 per cent) on cereals as against 16.4 per cent in 1969. This trend may be due to the fact that the increased purchasing power of the families had enabled them to include more variety in their food consumption pattern as opposed to the monotonous use of cereals alone.

Despite increases in the price level of pulses by over 30 per cent from 1979 to 2110, 34 per cent of the families in 2001 spent 21-40 per cent on pulses as opposed to only 13.3 per cent in 1979 and 31.1 per cent of the families spent 41-80 per cent on pulses in 1979 as against 'nil' in 1969. This trend in pulse consumption is a welcome change as pulses contribute not only to the calorific value of the diet but also provide protein along with calories, especially in a vegetarian diet.

In the consumption pattern of vegetables and fruits also, a similar trend is observed. But there does not seem to be any appreciable difference in the consumption pattern of fleshy foods over the decade. A very definite change was observed in the expenditure pattern for milk and milk products. While only half the population (51.5 per cent) was consuming milk and milk products in 1969, 77.5 per cent of the families spend 21-40 per cent on milk and milk products in 2001. The above figure leads to the conclusion that there is a marked trend towards the consumption of more nutritious foods. This may be attributed to high purchasing power and also the educational levels of the families.

Studies all over India indicate that in the Sixties, home-makers spent more time in cooking than in other activity. At the beginning of the new century, the time spent has been reduced considerably. In the middle class home, the time spent for food processing, preparation and cooking has been greatly reduced from about 4.5 hours per day to 3.3 hours due to the introduction of labour-saving devices, gas and pressure cooker in urban homes, In rural homes, the absorption method and use of Hay Box cooker for multiple food cooking has resulted in reduction of time taken for cooking. Introduction of the smokeless 'chulha' has resulted in reduction in the quantity of fuel used and therefore reduction in time for gathering of fuel to the extent of 20 minutes. In areas where welfare organisations had introduced education, better methods of cooking were adopted in low-income homes. The nutritious noon-meal programme has helped women to be free from the worry of feeding the pre-school child with left-over morning meals. Working women are also free of the burden of packing a cold lunch for the children.

A majority of the low-income families (76 per cent) were expending their leisure time towards creative crafts and income-earning activities as compared with 28 per cent of the middle and 20 per cent of the high-income families. The pattern of spending time in other activities has not changed much.

MANAGERIAL RESPONSIBILITIES

Among the many managerial responsibilities of a home-maker, cooking and preparing food and allied activities involve a major part of her time, energy and creative skills. Women spend 70 per cent of their time in the kitchen. In order to reduce this enormous expenditure of time and to save energy, labour-saving equipment like grinders, solar cookers, pressure cookers, hot cases, electric kettles, etc. is being increasingly used by the homemaker.

Eating habits have also changed. This is largely due to nutrition education. It has been found that the intake of cereals and fats and oils was much reduced in 1982 as compared to 2000 and the intake of protective and highly nutritious foods like green leafy vegetables, other vegetables, roots and tubers, fruits, milk and milk products, sugar and jaggery was considerably increased.

Information available on breast-feeding and weaning of infants showed an improvement. Breast-feeding has been followed commonly. However, there was a remarkable change in the range of weaning time. Breast feeding was practised even after two-and-a-half years in 1969, whereas it was observed that all children were weaned by the age of 24 months in 2000. This change in weaning practice may be attributed to the mothers' knowledge of better health and nutrition practices, their necessity to earn outside the home in order to increase the family income and also towards the provision of better amenities like balwadi in the village so that children are sent there by two-and-a-half years of age.

Cooking and dietary practices have thus substantially improved after nutrition education. This shows that Indian women are very receptive to new scientific ideas and attempt to implement them in their daily life.

STATUS OF WOMEN IN THE FAMILY

The freedom enjoyed by women of the present generation may be enumerated as

1. Economic freedom: seeking gainful jobs, having personal property, freedom to plan family budget, and the freedom to purchase;
2. Social freedom: appearing in group life, participating in group activities;
3. Educational freedom: seeking education of their own interest, academic specialisation in any aspect, locating suitable profession;
4. Political freedom;
5. Personal choice;
6. Recreation;
7. Status; and
8. Satisfaction towards life.

Though basically religious, women today appear to give less importance to going to temples, participating in rituals and indulging in superstitions. Orthodox practices have become less significant.

The status of women is associated with various positions which women occupy in society and how they carry out their responsibilities in their roles as daughters, wives, students, mothers, workers and heads of household. The actions, rewards or rights that they expect from others in these positions, and the perception of the actual rewards accompanying these positions constitute their status. The important determinants of status within the family are:

1. Extent of power in decision-making in the family;
2. Extent of freedom in spending the family income;
3. Extent of help received in discharging household responsibilities; and
4. Extent of observation of traditional customs and behaviour which are indicative of the subordinate or superior status of women.

SOCIAL PROBLEMS

The practice of dowry or bride price has infiltrated even those communities that did not practise it earlier. It has assumed the character of a sordid commercial transaction. There is greater awareness of it as a social evil now than there was more than a decade ago. As regards addiction to drugs, 11 per cent of the women of the middle socio-economic strata were found to have taken pills to induce sleep. One often comes across drug addiction in women of the high socio-economic strata of society.

Education is the foundation of human capital and yet women, who constitute nearly 50 per cent of the total population, have not received adequate attention in this sphere. Education increases women's power and self respect. The key to improvement in the position of women at home is their access to an independent income, which can be acquired with the help of education. Education is a major avenue of upward social mobility. Women's participation in economic activity is crucial to the family.

Barriers to women's participation in higher education are the family income or service and marriage as a preferable alternative to education. Furthermore, parents are usually inclined to spend less to educate their daughters than their sons due to the traditional systems of descent and inheritance through males, parental expectation of old-age support from male children, etc.

Women's participation in development effects deep and radical changes in the structure of society. They can bring about changes not only in their own status, but also in the social relations between men and women, and the basic institutions such as the family and the school. The more women are involved in developmental activities, there is no doubt that neither will they only play a significant role, but the results will be quick and demonstrable. One frequently comes across newspaper reports of how panchayats with women as sarpanches or even as members of the panchayat samiti seem to be doing better than all-male panchayats.

INCOME SUPPORT BY WOMEN

Women make a substantial contribution to the family income through home-based activities. But this is treated as supplemental as it is unrecognised, and in the organised sector women are entering new avenues; they are undergoing training programmes to improve their skills or acquire new skills. Their number as technicians in various fields is on the increase, as also in managerial and professional fields. Recognition of woman as an economic entity and as a provider for the family may help to eliminate the many ills that she is subjected to. Such recognition will promote women's access to resources and technology that can elevate her status in society.

In spite of the progress, there are still several constraints:

1. Employment is not an option but an economic compulsion as poverty pushes them to accept any available occupation;
2. The majority of working women are relegated to very low wage and low skill sectors of the economy;
3. Of the 94 per cent women in the unorganised sector, 80 per cent are in agriculture;
4. Some of the lowest paid jobs have the highest percentage of women workers;
5. Ninety per cent women are in unskilled or semi-skilled jobs; this is due to lack of access to education and training; and
6. A large number of women do not have any control over their own earnings.

Even when a woman's income sustains the household, she is considered as a supplementary earner. This is in contrast to the many research findings that highlight the crucial role women play in their family's economy and well-being. The implications of this on women's status are far-reaching. Women are willing to take up any job to support the family, Without women's wages, many families would live below the subsistence level. The majority of women contribute up to 50 per cent of the family income. Yet, familial attitudes and social norms have relegated women to the status of supplementary earners. However, certain changing trends are discernible. Social supports like creches, balwadis and hostel accommodation are being provided. Men, especially from the middle class, have slowly started sharing the responsibilities of the household.

The status of women would improve if the existing gap between the laws relating to women, their property rights, guardianship rights and personal rights and their implementation is narrowed by educating women on the legal provisions relating to them, activating legal aid committees and spreading their coverage to women, particularly in the rural areas. Already, the Committee for the Implementation of Legal Aid Schemes (CILAS) in Delhi has initiated action towards the same in its five-pronged programme as under:

1. Education and awareness of the law;
2. Taking legal aid to the doorstep of the needy and settlement of disputes through legal aid camps;
3. Mobilisation of law students through the opening of legal aid clinics in universities and colleges;
4. Instituting research in areas of law affecting the poor; and
5. Promoting public interest in legislation and creating para-legal brigades to enable dedicated lawyers to render service to the poor.

PROGRAMMES TO HELP WOMEN IN THE FAMILY

Some of the programmes and institutions that seek to bring about perceptible changes in the lives of Indian women and their families aim at:

1. Helping women to attain self-sustaining cumulative economic growth; and

2. Strengthening the synergistic relationship between good nutrition and good health.

Some of the programmes are as follows:

1. IRDP: aimed at the removal of poverty and unemployment in the rural areas through the adoption of the family as a unit of planning;

2. TRYSEM: is operated under IRDP, where one-third of the beneficiaries are women;

3. Dairying, where the implementation of 'Operation Flood' has created a noticeable impact on rural economy through an integrated approach to dairy development; and

4. The Science and Technology for Women's Scheme instituted by the DST: Under this scheme, a compendium of technologies relevant to women has been identified.

AGENCIES FOR COMMUNICATION

Mass media, of which radio and television are two important limbs, is a powerful agency for communication and can go a great deal to help promotion of nutrition and mother-and-child care, besides other aspects of women's welfare. More and more programmes should be featured on radio and television with the proper thrust of providing women the following: consumer education, population education, nutrition and health education, working knowledge of law and related matters, insight into opportunities for employment and self-employment.

In this connection, mention must be made of the yeoman service being provided to the cause of women by various women's organisations, formal and non-formal, government and voluntary, which have been set up and are now growing. These organisations like SEWA, Ahmedabad, and the Working Women's Forum, Chennai, have been trying to improve economic activity around which other activities like better health care, are also provided.

It can therefore safely be stated that the poor woman in the rural areas bears two burdens. She has to

1. Contribute to the family's income; and

2. Shoulder the responsibility of the care of the family.

When women are unable to earn an adequate income and are unaware of the prerequisites for good health such as the need for clean drinking water, sanitary living conditions, their family, particularly the children, suffer. In such a situation, mothers need to be educated in the basics of health and child care and they must be given the opportunity to earn enough to enable them to put their newly-acquired knowledge into practice.

—oo(O)oo—

20

DYNAMIC STATUS OF WOMEN

WOMEN derive the ideological and moral base for their status and their institutionalised roles from religion. The various restrictions imposed on women and our notions about their proper role in the domestic and social spheres have been influenced by religious conceptions in regard to their fundamental characteristics, the virtues and vices attributed to them, etc. which are based on various legends and myths. However, it depends on the element of dynamism in a religion which allows transformation of the values in the historical process. Further, scriptures and sacred texts are prone to diverse interpretations by different authorities at different times. For example, the different interpretations of Hinduism throughout history have brought forth new religionsor sects such as Buddhism, Jainism, Sikhism, Veerasaivism and Vaishnavism, etc.

Hinduism has a very long history during which the image of woman has undergone far-reaching changes. There is no denying that the lot of the vast majority of Indian woman has not been satisfactory. Over large parts of the country, they have been denied educational opportunities. Under the Constitution, discrimination on the ground of gender is prohibited. The principle of equal pay for equal work is enshrined in the Directive Principles but, in practice, the wages of women in rural areas engaged in agricultural operations or construction activities in cities and towns tend to be much lower than those of men.

Some people argue that women in India enjoy a very high status and in support of their contention, they point to the large number of women in public office. It is also claimed that there have been profound changes in women's position in society, family and law. Their participation in public life has been increasing. However, the presentation of exhaustive lists of eminent women in different fields of public life is often misleading.

The position of women in India has not been static; at different times they have been vested with authority and freedom or reduced to subservience. That women's lot has not always been subservient is evident from certain literary references. In the *Mahabharata,* the Madra women are described as free and even licentious (*Mahabharata, Karna Parva*). The *Satpatha Brahmana* describes the women of Uttarkurus to be as free as men (*Satpatha Brahmana*).

India is a land of extreme contrasts; in the cities automobiles ply along with bullock carts, slum colonies can be seen near deluxe residential complexes, and the lot of women has mostly been below that of men. So much so that some time ago, the Backward Classes Commission received a representation that women, as a whole, should be treated as a backward class (Devaki Jain. *Indian Women*. Ministry of Information and Broadcasting, Government of India, 1975). These contrasts signify a transitional stage through which India is passing socially, economically and politically. Even in earlier times we have two clear exceptions, Gargi, a reputed scholar in a period when learning is said to have been closed to women, and Razia Sultana who ruled in a fiercely male-dominated period.

In order to resolve these contradictions, it is necessary to consider this matter from a realistic, sociological perspective, as the position of women in society can hardly be assessed without a proper appraisal of the fundamental structure of that society. Further, even more than the socio-economic factors, the cultural background of a society governs the various responses to change. Indian society comprises people following different religions with distinct cultural variations, for example, the family law applicable to Hindus and Muslims grant different positions to women. Also, the legal position is often different from that in actual practice. To study the gender inequalities it is necessary to keep in mind a variety of social, economic and cultural differences among the different sections of Indian society which are based on caste, community, class, region, etc. In such a state of affairs, generalisation of women's status in Indian society would be unrealistic.

In Indian society, the traditionalist would present an idealised picture of women to substantiate their claims based on certain references from Vedic and classical Sanskrit literature. They often claim, with justification, that in ancient India women were encouraged to participate in all scholarly pursuits. They married men of their choice and were respected in their husbands' homes. Later, even the Buddhist social structure offered women the alternative of a spiritual mode of life in place of the marital state. Many Buddhist nuns distinguished themselves as scholars and social workers. Against this, some modernists claim that these freedoms were restricted only to principle and the actual position of women in the past has been that of suffering and privation, and that the Indian woman symbolises a curious intermeshing of low legal status, ritual contempt, sophisticated sexual partnership and deification (Devaki Jain. *Indian Women.* Ministry of Information and Broadcasting, Government of India, 1975).

In these circumstances it is important to guard against hasty conclusions based on the position of women in any particular period of Indian history or a particular section of Indian society, for example, tribal, rural, urban, upper or lower classes. The importance of kinship and of family coupled with the idea of the transfer of the girl, after marriage, from one family to another, had a great influence on the role of relationships in the family. The material differences among people living in different geographical conditions and historical development are presented most lucidly by the social structure of the Dravidians of south India as compared to the Indo-Aryans of north India. Following the same ritual orthodoxy, women of the different regions of the country enjoy different degrees of freedom in actual behaviour.

In Indian society, it is not difficult to find a sharp contrast among the customs prevalent in certain communities living in the same region and following the same religion. For example, in Kerala, the Nambudiris and the Nairs whose intimate social ties have been explained elsewhere, are quite distinct from each other. Whereas the Nambudiris are patrilineal and patrilocal, the Nairs are matrilineal and matrilocal. In the past, Nair women enjoyed a higher degree of freedom and rights than their Nambudiri counterparts.

The Indian family largely conforms to the patrilineal structure with certain differences in form and function. Before the advent of freedom and subsequent industrialisation, the image of an Indian patrilineal patrilocal family was that of a co-residential group formed by close male kin (up to three generations) with their wives and unmarried daughters. Such a family had a common residence and common hearth, with a system of pooling the income of all members and joint landed property or family business in which all the members of the family were engaged, contributing according to their individual potential.

It is sometimes said that the rights of women in a patrilocal structure of society are bound to be inferior to those of men. However, a study of the position of women in matrilineal societies reveals that this structure does not grant a dominant position to women. The matrilineal structure involved only the transfer of property through the female line, for example from the mother's brother to sister's son. In matrilineal societies, the woman is normally under her brother's control instead of the husband. Similarly, among polyandrous societies, supremacy of women was not ensured.

The most conspicuous variations in the position of women are those observed in the different strata of Indian society based on caste hierarchy, namely, the ruling, priestly and warrior classes comprise one group in regard to the treatment of women while the agricultural and lower castes have different customs sanctioned by tradition.

The position of women in the poorest sections of rural society seems to be restricted to toiling in the service of the husband and members of his family, besides bringing up the children. However, among various sections of the rural community, women enjoy a great deal of liberty and are conscious of the importance of their role in the family as well as society. This is exemplified by tribal women, Rajput women and those of the dominant communities in the village.

Early historical sources generally refer to the aristocracy and urban society including wealthy traders. The great heroines of the past depicted in Puranic literature, whether Sita in the *Ramayana* or Gandhari in the *Mahabharata,* led secluded and well-protected lives and were not, therefore, guided by common norms of behaviour. They are depicted as possessing a forceful personality, enjoying life to the full.

It is unfortunate that early Indian literature, for example, the *Brahmanas* as also later literature including the *Smritis* and *Puranas,* do not speak highly about the status of women from various points of view—civic, social, religious, cultural and economic. Concerning the position of women, the post-Vedic period (300 B.C. onwards) is very significant when Hindu law came to be compiled systematically.

Among these lawgivers, Manu (*circa* second century B.C.) was the most influential and he has been described as having placed "unshakeable shackles on Indian women for countless succeeding generations". Even today, it is his law that binds women to orthodoxy (R. Patai. *Women in the Modern World*). Manu was the first to assign to women a definite role in society as well as in the family.

Concerning the civic rights of women, the law book of Parashar (*circa* 8th century A.D.) stipulates that a person who kills an artisan, a mechanic or a woman shall perform the *Prajapatya* ceremony twice and give a gift of 11 bulls to expatiate his sin (*Shilpinam, Karukam*). The inferior position of women is further corroborated by the *Agni Purana* (*circa* 11th century A.D.) which prescribes the same penance for the murder of a woman as that of a Sudra [*Agni Purana* (Panchanana Tarkaratna edition)].

References to the lower position of women can be traced even in the works of the later Vedic period. The *Satpatha Brahmana* warns that while teaching *pravariya,* the teacher should not look at a woman, a Sudra, a dog and the blackbird because they are embodiments of untruth (*Satpatha Brahmana*). The *Prashar Griyyasutra* also has a similar rule which prescribes how, after the *Samavartana* ceremony, one should avoid seeing women, Sudras, dead bodies, blackbirds and dogs.

In the post-Mauryan and Gupta periods also, the position of women was almost similar. In the *Gita,* Krishna says: "Finding refuge in Me, they also, who may be of sinful birth, women, Vaishyas as well as Sudras, can attain to the supreme goal (*Bhagawad Gita*). This clearly indicates that though an absolute surrender to the Almighty assures women equal treatment in the next world, their social status in this world was not of significance.

It may be noted that such an attitude towards women was based not only on their low status but also on fear of being polluted by them. Women were regarded as impure on certain occasions. According to the Hindu concept of ritual purity, Manu further divided society into two groups, namely, *Dwija* (twice born) and women and Sudras. According to him, the former can attain bodily purity by drinking the water of the holy river Ganga three times, while the former need to drink it only once (*Manusmriti* V. 139). According to him, a woman's marriage was equated with religious initiation of men. He further laid down that devotion to the husband and the performance of household duties by women served the same purpose as daily worship and performance of havan (lighting of the sacred fire) by men.

In regard to the cultural position of women, the *Brahma Purana*, a text of the Gupta period, prescribes the ceremonies of bathing and saying prayers according to Vedic rituals only for the twice born, excluding women and Sudras (*Brahma Purana* 67-119). They were not given the right of performing fire sacrifice along with chanting of mantras, that is, they could perform ceremonies without saying mantras. According to Apasthambha, women could acquire a particular kind of knowledge, supplemental to the *Atharva Veda* (*Apastambha* II).

Hindu marriage rites symbolise male superiority. The concept of *kanyadaan* (giving of the daughter to the bridegroom by the parents) and the various other rites of marriage signify that marriage is the first major *sanskara* (ritual initiation) for Hindu women and that it brings them prosperity and good omens. Apart from the various other vows and exchange of promises, the bride is advised to obey and follow her husband, to serve and respect the members of the husband's family.

Two important Hindu lawgivers, namely, Manu and Yajnavalkya, held the view that woman is never independent (Manu IX.3); Yajnavalkya I. 85). While she is unmarried, the father protects her and when she is married, the husband protects her and in old age, the son protects her. So she is to be kept under the surveillance of men all her life.

The belief that women can pollute, apart from ritual reasons, at the psychological level suggests fear of someone who plays such a central role in procreation. Obviously, the socio-legal treatises, such as the *Dharma Shastras*, are not always a description of reality. More often than not, they contain social ideals and may be treated as manuals to perfect action conceived on the basis of prevailing social conditions. This state of affairs has been observed in many older societies, among whom the rights and obligations were not always distinctly demarcated. Hence, a literal interpretation of the *Dharma Shastras* to define the status of different sections of society in those days would be unjust.

On the basis of these references, attempts are made to draw the conclusion that women constituted the most condemned section of Hindu society. However, all ancient class-divided societies were fundamentally based on the predominance of man over woman, and on the domination of the priestly and warrior classes over the trading and producing masses. In this regard the ancient Indian and Roman law are quite similar.

According to Manu, the wife and son of the slave had no personal claim to property; whatever they earned was the property of those to whom they belonged (Manu, VIII, 416). The unfettered right of the head of the family over his wife, son and slave has its exact counterpart in Roman law, under which the wife, children and slaves of a Roman head of family were subject to his unrestricted power and outside the jurisdiction of the State (William A. Hunter. *Introduction to Roman Law*. London, 1934).

It would be hasty and unjust to draw inferences from these scattered references. Quite a large part of ancient Sanskrit and Prakrit classical literature has been contributed by women writers and poets. The ancient Indian tradition of hiding one's identity as a token of attributing all talents to the Almighty has made it impossible to collect historical details about women who contributed to Vedic and classical Sanskrit literature.

There is the story of the son of a great rishi being denied the hand of a princess by her mother because he was not erudite which appears to indicate that women in India prized learning over other aspects. In the *Brihadaranyaka Upanishad* there is a reference to Gargi, who rises twice in King Janak's assembly and questions Yajnavalkya indicating that she was a Brahmavadini of high status. The thirst for spiritual knowledge among women in those days is further proved by the case of Maitreyi, wife of Yajnavalkya, who preferred spiritual bequests to earthly possessions. Patanjali speaks of the person of an acharya in her own right and not merely as the wife of an acharya. In the *Vedas* and the *Upanishads*, we have many instances of women who were erudite scholars, skilful debaters, great teachers and seekers of spirituality. Later, the two major religions, Buddhism and Jainism, upheld women's status in society by instituting orders of nuns in monastic life, thereby providing an alternative position of dignity to those women who wished to dissociate themselves from the normal role of women in the family. Then, the Bhakti Movement, in different forms in different periods, developed the concept of individuals, equal relationship with a personalised deity, emphasising the right of women to Bhakti and a freer life. Thus, religious and ritual equality was further extended to the relations of men and women in general.

We now consider the position of Indian women today, as to how an average Indian woman finds herself in the social context. Is she in any way subordinate to her husband whereby her personality is merged with that of her husband's or does she retain her individuality, commanding a position of equal respect with man, or is it a mixture of the two. In recent years, the position of women has been subjected to much analysis. It should not be ignored that for assessment of the social status, Indian women could not be treated as a homogeneous group. As stated earlier, there is a wide range of contrast between the position of women among the different sections of society—tribal, rural and urban. Among the tribal population, scattered in different parts of the country, men and women participate freely and on equal terms in all ritual and religious activities as well as in song, dance and other forms of collective entertainment. In these circumstances, it is necessary to consider the image of women in various religious traditions of India, their status in the family and society at large, before and after marriage, and their status among different sections of society, from the ruling nobility to the lower sections of the community.

The role and status of women form an integral part of the prevailing socio-economic structure of any community, and the cultural norms and traditions and value system determine the woman's status in society. A characteristic feature of Indian society is the involvement of the man's prestige in the type of work in which the women of his family are engaged. The acceptance of paid work by women outside the house, until quite recently, seldom met with social approval. This explains the development of a tendency among women of the ruling classes and well- to-do communities in the medieval period and among those of the richer classes today, to lead a parasitic life. A change in organisational forms and the value system does not take place overnight, and this explains why there is a wide gap between theoretical possibilities and actual realisation. In the natal home, a girl is considered a liability and this has a far-reaching effect on the socialisation of children. In Indian families, one can easily notice a traditionally sanctioned discrimination between boys and girls over food, education and medical care. To bring about an effective change through the expansion of education and legislative measures, an attitudinal and structural orientation of society is essential.

The position of women has not lagged behind the change in the socio-economic structure of Indian society. Apart from playing her customary role in conformity with the traditional division of labour between the sexes, that is, bearing and rearing children and domestic chores, they have been making an equal contribution in the income and well-being of the family. The traditional division of labour was meant to maximise the benefit of combined social effort in accordance with the aptitudes of men and women. In the agricultural field, women and men work together and the household is the unit of labour with men and women playing complementary roles.

In terms of the authority pattern in a joint family, the daughter-in-law is under the direct control of the mother-in-law who normally exercises her authority (sometimes very strictly) as long as her husband continues to hold economic authority in the family. However, it would be unrealistic to interpret the position of the mother-in-law as indicative of the status of women in general, as the authority of the mother-in-law declines with age, widowhood and with increasing importance of the daughter-in-law. The position of the daughter-in-law starts improving with the earning capacity of her husband and when she gives birth to a son. The importance of a son in the family has already been explained.

With advancing age and experience and as mothers, old women enjoy a great amount of authority and respect in the family and are often consulted by the men in important matters. However, this is not very common, and in decision-making, women mostly have a marginal role.

India is principally an agricultural country and, despite their contribution of effort and labour for economic production, the lot of women is far from being equal to that of men. From childhood, they are brought up in a fashion that makes them economically dependent on men. In childhood, the girl remains constantly under her father or elder brother, after marriage she is dependent on her husband.

Thus, women grow up imbibing and adjusting to their secondary economic role under a traditional process. Marriage brings about a radical change in the woman's role and duties. In the house of her husband, her position depends on the status of her husband in the family, the economic and social status of her own parents and, above all, her own behaviour in the husband's joint family in the context of traditions and customs.

So far as men's attitude towards women is concerned, it is undeniable that women, at large, were not granted parity either at home or in society. Unfortunately, in the traditional Indian society, woman was misunderstood and often wronged as well. The hangover of the pre-19th century period is very much in existence even today and is often used to exploit a girl and extract dowry. Even today, married women are required to observe fasts on different occasions and pray for the welfare of their husbands, whereas there is no such obligation on the part of the husband. The paradox is that Hinduism also presents the woman as endowed with qualities of self-sacrifice as a mother which places her at par with divinity, as held by the Tantrik Shakti cult in which she is elevated to the position of the divine mother, Durga.

The main problem before an educated Indian woman relates to adjustment to the environment in her secondary position and how she can free herself from that position. This requires her to establish her identity at home and outside. With the development of intellectual and spiritual parity, women have to pick up courage to assert their rights. In the first stage, she might have to substantiate her economic independence by taking up employment. The material advantages of an employed wife is obvious, leading to better harmony in married life as a result of lesser friction over money matters.

In the case of working wives, normally husbands assist in domestic work. However, despite all the assistance a wife gets from her husband or children, the ultimate responsibility of household management rests with her.

In India, the problem of reconciling the duties of wife and mother with that of breadwinner has not so far assumed as much significance as in the West. Normally, working wives and mothers in India yield to the attraction of a career, while her counterpart in the West is now tending towards home and motherhood. Today, woman is not the submissive person she used to be, depending on others for her very right to exist. She is no more an embodiment based on the ideal of Sita or Savitri. She is aggressive if circumstances demand and does not refrain from using religious traditions to suit her interests.

In these circumstances, the educated woman, conscious of her rights and obligations finds it difficult to merge her personality with that of her husband and the husband's family. However, without economic security, she cannot assert her social rights. Thus, she dangles between two aspects of Indian society which often kills her potential to expand her personality. She is educated and appreciates and contributes to society in a broader capacity than just as a wife and mother.

She also wants to be a good wife and mother, and participate in social and other activities outside the home. She wants the love and affection of her husband and children and the shared responsibility of bringing up the children while at the same time she is conscious of her capacity and ability which cry out for exercise.

The main problem is how to be a good mother, wife and housekeeper and still retain a job. Until the children are grown up, it is quite difficult for the woman to do so. Further, different religious traditions and customs of the household sometimes force women to sacrifice their desires and aspirations in favour of family traditions. In her favour is the fact that the greater her self-effacement, the higher the esteem in which she is held in traditional society.

The demand of women for increasing opportunities outside the home should, at best, be seen as a transitory stage in the history of her emancipation. There is a rapid shift from the traditional role of the woman as subservient to men to that of revolt against exploitation and striving for equality with men in all professional and work areas.

There has been considerable impact of various constitutional, legal and administrative provisions in the post-independence period on the social status of women, their education and employment avenues. The Constitution of India guarantees equality of status and opportunity and forbids discrimination or denial of equal protection on the ground of sex. It empowers the State to make "any special provision for women and children," even in violation of the fundamental obligation of non-discrimination on the basis of sex. On the basis of this provision, the State has made certain special provisions in favour of women in the field of labour legislation. These special provisions are both beneficial and protective as well. For example, in the case of adultery, a man is punished, but not a woman, and this is not regarded as discriminatory (Yusuf vs. State of Bombay, 1954, S. C. 398).

The traditional concept of the woman's role being restricted to domestic chores is changing; they increasingly take up jobs in commercial and industrial establishments as well as in the administration. This state of affairs has made a profound impact on the attitude of the educated middle class woman in three areas:

1. Higher education,
2. Employment and all levels of industry, commerce and administration, and
3. Politics.

They have achieved success even in occupations that had hitherto been the monopoly of men. In sum, woman has laid the foundation for a radical attitudinal change in society.

WOMEN IN THE HINDU FAMILY

Before considering various aspects of the position of women in Hindu society, it would be appropriate to consider family structure in India with particular reference to its historical and cultural setting.

The term 'family' is defined as a standard social unit, which has been observed in one form or the other in societies at almost all stages of cultural development. The most common units are matriarchal and patriarchal, polygamous and polyandrous. There are even families resulting from voluntary and involuntary monogamy and from group and trial marriages. It is doubtful if any other social institution has raised more problems than the family (D. N. Majumdar. *Races and Cultures of India*. Mumbai: Asia Publishing House).

In the moral and sociological sense, the family consisting of husband, wife and children is observed in all societies with varying degrees of importance assigned to the following functions as the basis of the development of the family:

1. Reproduction of population;
2. Protection and care of the child;
3. Economic production and consumption of family goods and services;
4. Socialisation of the child;
5. Education of the child;
6. Recreation;
7. Giving affection, love and a sense of security to all members of the family; and
8. Emotional satisfaction through intimate personal relations.

In the course of time and with the development of society, economic, educational, recreational and socialisation functions have been taken up by other institutions. Further, modern labour-saving devices and the introduction of social insurance have evidently released the family from many other burdens and it can concentrate on implementing its duties.

In India, the structure of the family is characterised by certain special attitudes, for example, the sanctity of domestic life, a well-defined and traditionally followed code of conduct and relationship between husband and wife, father and son, brother and sister, between brothers, etc. Thus, the Indian concept of family has been somewhat distinct from that in Western countries where the family has been restricted to an elementary or nuclear type comprising a man, his wife and their children. Due to the prevalence of an extremely liberalised attitude towards divorce, the family in the West has a comparatively lesser element of permanency. As against this, in India, marriage is considered an indissoluble union despite the legal provisions of separation and divorce and goes a long way in strengthening the family. This relationship is elaborately depicted in the Hindu epics, the *Ramayana* and the *Mahabharata*.

The *Ramayana* may rightly be called a compendium of Hindu codes of behaviour expected of the individual in his different capacities in the family as well as in society, for example, Rama's obedience and respect for his father, affection for the other members of the family, etc. may be called the ideal code of behaviour of an Indian family. For a realistic appraisal of the dynamic character of the Indian family structure, it is necessary to study the past, the present and the projected trends of the family. The family plays the most important role in the process of development of society. The structure of the family depends not merely on meeting sexual needs and childcare but also, on the intellectual level, a spirit of adaptation and acceptance of change as circumstances alter.

The distinguishing feature of the Indian family is its joint structure; that is, three generations normally live together and share accommodation under the same roof. Usually, an Indian family consists of a man, his wife, their children, the man's parents, uncles and aunts, male cousins and their wives and children. Thus, a joint Indian family comprises members of three generations. A similar type of joint family existed earlier in certain parts of Europe, for example, the Russian *bretsvo,* the southern Slavic *Zadruga,* the French *maisonee,* etc.

Sociologists sometimes comment that a joint family is nothing but a conglomeration of several nuclear families having the senior-most male member functioning as paterfamilias. In such a joint family, the ownership of land and homestead, the responsibility for parental care and economic authority, etc. were vested in the eldest living male member. The Indian family structure presents striking divergence. In most parts of the country, the family is patrilineal and patrilocal, tracing descent from father to son; matrilineal and matrilocal families tracing descent from mother to daughter can also be found. A matrilineal and matrilocal family consists of a woman, her brothers and sisters, her own and her sisters' sons and daughters. In such families which existed in certain parts of south India until quite recently, no relation by marriage lived in the same house. Instead, the married women were visited occasionally by their husbands (A. K. Sur. *Sex and Marriage in India*. New Delhi: Allied Publishers).

In the matrilineal family, the mother's brother acted *in loco parentis* not only to his own children but also to the children of his sisters. Thus, whereas in a patrilineal family we observe a sense of companionship between father and children and husband and wife, in a matrilineal family this is absent.

Although the patrilineal and patrilocal types of family have been dominant in most parts of India, certain castes and communities in south India, Nairs and Tiyans of Malabar and Bants of Kanara as well as some Telugu-speaking castes in Karnataka, have been matrilineal and matrilocal. In northern India, the matrilineal pattern of family is observed only in the Khasi tribe of the North-East.

This structure has been continuing for millennia, but in the present century, particularly during the post-independence period, there has been a progressive disintegration of the joint family due to social and economic changes in life at large. The causes of this change are varied, for example, some family members who had to contribute more than their proportionate share for running the family began to protest.

Also playing a role has been disparity in income of the different family members and consequently more respect and authority being reposed in members who earn more. Of course, family pride and prestige in society sometimes acts as a brake to the disintegration of the joint family.

The general histriographic problem in studying family change over a span of several centuries is that certain types of data are missing which resulted in historians not being able to deal with this institution adequately. Whatever sources are available to us from the past refer only to the literate and upper classes. Data regarding the illiterate, the young and women of the lower strata of society are missing completely.

Further, it would be unjust to apply to the Indian family the hypotheses that satisfactorily explain contemporary Western industrial, middle class and urban family life. Certain family behaviour patterns have no parallel in any other society, for example, the peculiar marriage customs of the Nairs in south India.

The tradition-bound Indian still finds it difficult to believe that the structure of the family in the West has undergone such radical change that parents have no expectation from their children. They care for the children up to adulthood. Immediately after school education, the children become eligible to an adult's wage and this economic independence, coupled with weak emotional attachment to the family, makes them choose to go their own way. The parents find economic security in their old age in the compulsory social insurance system.

There is a belief that industrialisation undermines the large family system and moves it generally towards some type of conjugal system as in the Western countries (William J. Goode. *World Revolution and Family Patterns.* Introduction). However, we find that classes that are industrially prominent have larger households; there is more discipline, parents have more control over their children and the head of the family enjoys more authority.

Most modern countries were industrialised late in the 19th century but changes in the family structure were evident even before that. Thus, industrialisation is not a necessary antecedent to the disintegration of the family. The absence of reliable data, adequate census information and credible demographic materials does not lend authenticity to sociologists in this field.

Three millennia ago, Plato saw the family as the keystone of the stratification system and felt it was necessary to abolish the institution of family to ensure equal opportunity to all. Plato further pleaded for the abolition of the class system. He said that the parents of lower quality or class might produce a potential 'gold' child and golden parents might produce an untalented child. Thus, parents should not be allowed to rear their own children.

Plato's concept was the subject of various experiments, but it was realised that it was not possible to abolish either the family or social stratification. Both these institutions, endowed as they were with considerable mobility, could stand the test of time.

Concerning the *inter se* behaviour of different members of the family, one might even maintain that husband-wife relations are less important to society than socialisation practices in determining personality dynamics, achievement motivation and normative commitment of the next generation. As for parent-child behaviour, both sociologists and psychologists are aware that parents have used the two socialising techniques, namely, physical punishment and affection for centuries without the slightest change.

Thus, one can well imagine to what extent the statements made by Jesus, Locke, Rousseau, St. Augustine, etc. on parent-child relationship have a bearing in this regard. Relations between social structures, as also family life, undergo change at a very slow pace if at all.

In modern India, there exist different patterns of family:

1. the old joint family, sharing the same house and kitchen or with different kitchens,

2. the nuclear families living apart, but owning land and property in common and tilling the soil together, and

3. the entirely independent nuclear families, all of which are found in our rural society (D. N. Majumdar. *Races and Cultures of India.* Mumbai Asia Publishing House, 1973).

A typical Indian joint family is somewhat like a commune where all the property and earnings of the different members are collected in a common pool. Generally, the eldest member is entrusted with the responsibility of being the head of the family. Indian family systems are not static, nor have they been so in the past. Both polyandrous and matrilineal systems have been declining; they began to disappear with the dawn of the 20th century. Legal changes, which have been substantial, show a gradual evolution over the 20th century. Although these legal measures are clearly ahead of public opinion, even when we consider the attitudes and values of only the better-educated strata, they show a steady direction, without regression, towards some form of the conjugal system of the family.

Further, there are many changes other than the legal ones. The gradual shift in the family network's focus is the most important of these. Further, the increasing approval of remarriage of both divorcees and widows may be seen as a change in the position of women and also as an alternation in the traditional family structure. The discarded or widowed wife is no longer relegated to a shameful position in the family, but is permitted to resume a normal life, and even some property rights are given to her.

It may be noted that these changes have been taking place in the face of relatively little industrialisation. The changes have been too many, and in too many different parts of the family structure, to be attributed either to industrialisation or urbanisation. We must recognise the extent to which many indigenous Indian ideological forces have been at work, perhaps in the same direction as the forces whose origin was essentially Western.

All forms of these familial groupings are evidently interdependent as the individuals belonging to a family are linked together by emotional as well as economic ties. There are cases where, despite lack of economic co-operation between the members of a family, prayers to the deity are performed jointly. Even seemingly disintegrated families retain emotional ties and, in case of emergency or crisis, the affinity comes forward. Even after separation from the family, each member cherishes the family honour and takes pride in adhering to the family code.

The reluctance with which Indians are giving up some older family patterns is due to the failure of emerging social systems to provide viable and fruitful alternatives as yet. For example, the opposition to a woman doing a paid job has been great, but until lately, her opportunities were few. Moreover, since marriage still occurs at a relatively young age, if the educated girl attempts to establish herself in a genuine career, she may miss her only chance at marriage.

Similarly, the industrial and urban systems have not yet developed all the co-operative services, aids and solutions for the individual that were and, to some extent, still are furnished by the large family network. Consequently, the reluctance of most Indians to move towards the new family set up seems understandable. Though the movement is slow in some areas, for example, real freedom to choose one's own spouse, in others it is more rapid and there is no evidence of any important movement towards traditional family patterns.

The only exception may be found in the actions of a few castes seeking to move upwards in social standing, which imitates one or the other pattern of the older Brahmins (for example, the prohibition against divorce, demanding a groom price, etc.). These are numerically few, however.

It has often been asserted that since the attainment of independence, India has undergone rapid changes and the family with its social pattern evolved in this period of change may be quite different from that in the West. Admittedly, India has a peculiar cultural heritage. For millennia, the tribal, rural and urban societies have been developing their own cultures. Almost all the religions of the world have prospered in this country, which in turn is divided in States having their own distinct social, linguistic and cultural patterns.

Another unique feature of Indian society is the caste system, and the whole Hindu society is divided into hundreds of endogamous castes and thousands of exogamous sub-castes, each with their distinct values and ideals. Above all, it cannot be said with certainty to what extent the standard of values and behaviour gathered from literary, philosophical and religious sources were actually accepted and followed in practice by the 'average' Hindu.

In the West, the significant change in family patterns took place after the First World War, indicating that industrialisation and urbanisation were major contributors to this change. However, they are not the only factors bringing about a change in family structure. India's family patterns have not changed as rapidly as those of Japan or China during the past decade, although they have changed faster than in the West. Whatever change the Indian family pattern has undergone can be attributed less to industrialisation and urbanisation alone than to certain ideological influences resulting out of the natural internal changes or from an increasing contact with the West.

As regards urbanisation, in India cities were built long before any were founded in the West. The excavations of Harappa and Mohenjodaro have proved beyond doubt that India had highly developed urban settlements even in 3000-2500 B.C. However, the overwhelming love for tradition did not allow rural migrants to the cities to change their way of life to a great extent. The rural population migrating to the cities even today for employment keeps interests of a permanent nature in the village and continues clinging to traditional rural values and standards of behaviour. Actually, this is a fundamental difference in the Indian and Western city life.

Contacts with the West, coupled with fast growing urbanisation during the post-independence period have initiated a tendency to free oneself from family traditions. Although there is still an overwhelming adherence to orthodoxy and convention, there is a simultaneous process of transformation from the past to the present and from the present to a freer future. This structure of the joint family in India is facing a grave challenge in the wake of developing communications, which makes emigration easier. Growing urbanisation has further contributed to the breaking up of the joint family. Consequently, the absolute authority that the eldest male member of a joint family enjoyed in the past is wanting. In this process, the disintegration of the authority of age was initiated by the development of a tendency among the individual members of the family claiming respect and authority in proportion to their individual income, which later gave way to an almost total neglect of the elders. They are mostly remembered during social ceremonies.

With all its far-reaching restrictive influence on the younger generation, the old system suffered from certain shortcomings. The new generation was subject to control by outmoded ideas and this manifested itself throughout the world. Today the head of the family continues to command traditional respect, but the son is not blind to the justifiable appeal and merit of modernity. Thus, he is facing a situation of conflict, whereas his children, the youth of today, are outright modern in their convictions and behaviour. Owing to the breakdown of the family and the decay of faith, the individual is swayed by violence, lawlessness and crime, which is evident from the fact that despite affluence in the modern industrial societies, crime rates continue to rise. The young are prone to take lightly heinous and brutal acts and glorify violence. The history of the family structure presents a study of growth, of strain and stress of change, rather than of survival. Whereas one group of sociologists considers the family to be sacred, unyielding, restrictive and outmoded, another group considers it to be unstable, disorganised and highly vulnerable, exposed to all sorts of crises.

This state of affairs calls for serious thought as to which direction the family structure should take to meet rapid social changes of modern times. Strictly speaking, there is nothing wrong with the family today; it is simply different from that of yesterday and may, at best, be taken as being in a stage of transition facing a challenge which is natural for any developing institution. All those living in a society which is changing from the old traditions to the newly developing concepts have to mediate between the two moralities, between tradition and modernity.

With the present speed of change in the structure of the family, it can be assumed that in a few decades human society may take to living in communities. The West seems to be trying to evolve a rationalised form of joint family system, in which the pattern of life will consist of living near each other in a kind of village community where the men and women would be involved in the task of bringing up the children. There would be no gender bar to any type of employment. However, this does not touch even the fringe of the problem that the family institution is facing today.

Admittedly, family structure has not been able to keep pace with rapid social change, but this does not provide justification for abandoning the institution. It is a fact that the pioneers who struggled for establishing new norms had to pay heavily for the privilege as the intermediate stage of choice between the old and the new is always difficult. Of course, some amount of confusion precedes reorganisation, but it is bound to develop the structure of the family in a form most suited to the present needs, as also a brighter future.

ROLE OF WOMEN IN THE FAMILY

The status of an individual or group of individuals in a society represents a composite concept comprising a mass of values and standards of behaviour and the different roles one has to play in society at large. For determining status one has to take cognisance of the possessions of the individual, coupled with the values attached to those possessions. Thus, it involves both institutional and attitudinal study.

Institutional change can be brought about, although slowly, by means of legislative measures, but attitudinal change is a long and arduous process. Further, institutional change is profoundly dependent on attitudinal support. This explains the delay in bringing about improvement in the status of the Indian woman in society, despite the effort of our legislators to introduce institutional changes.

The normal role of a woman in an Indian family is confined to the performance of household chores and bearing and looking after children, with varying degrees of participation in the decision-making process in the family on matters of collective interest. The degree of difference depends mainly on the class of society to which the women belong, tribal, rural or urban.

At home, there are a variety of jobs to be performed collectively or separately by members of the family. Some items of work are attended to mainly by men, others by women, where certain others may be in the hands of both men and women according to the exigencies of the case. At the socio-psychological level, the different items of work normally attended to by women, that is, household chores, are generally given low value in comparison to the work attended to by the men.

This state of affairs is comparable to the basic idea behind the wage structure in most of the countries in the so-called Third World which have suffered centuries of foreign dominance and where the people engaged in domestic service, industry, trade and administration are paid almost 10 to 15 times more than others making an equal contribution in terms of service and production.

The next point for consideration is the extent of authority given to women deciding matters of importance in the family, for example, the educational career of the children, their marriage, etc. Despite all the claims of equality for women in Hindu religious scriptures, the actual behaviour pattern in this regard is that the female members of the family have had very little authority in matters of significance.

The conclusion that one comes to is that it is fundamentally a problem of attitude. It may be mentioned here that the treatment meted out to the male and female members of the family, right from childhood, clearly reflects the prevailing attitude towards the sexes. As stated earlier, there is no denying the fact that in Indian society, people react differently to the birth of a boy and a girl. The birth of a boy is preferred.

Further, there is a custom that meals are served in the family first to the male members and then to the women.

In the ancient Hindu scriptures, we find great emphasis on the development of a faithful and uncomplaining attitude in the wife. The idealisation of the austerities and negation for the welfare of the husband is well borne out by various characters in Hindu mythology such as Sita, Savitri, Ahilya, Damayanti, Mandodri, Gandhari, Draupadi, etc. The ideal of a woman's role as wife is based on loyalty to her husband, faithfulness and chastity. This involves absolute identification with the husband's personality.

In a joint Hindu family, a young daughter-in-law is at a very low rung of the social ladder. Only in course of time, after having made necessary adjustments with the mother-in-law by means of undergoing prolonged trials and tribulations, and partly on the basis of the amount of dowry and gifts received from her parents and the social position and earning capacity of her husband and after giving birth to a son, the status of the wife starts improving.

However, authority to women is mainly restricted to the mother-in-law and the elder sister-in-law (husband's sister) and hence the young wife can hardly be expected to evoke a balanced relationship with the husband or to have a role in decision-making. So much so that she has hardly any control even on certain important aspects of her life such as planning one's family, taking up or continuing a job, education, etc.

In a nuclear family, which is developing in the wake of urbanisation and industrialisation in the post-independence period, the woman plays a more important role in the management of family affairs. This is because, in a nuclear family, the wife is not subordinate to any other elderly woman. The husband is virtually dependent on her for the management of domestic affairs, rearing the children and maintenance of social relations. In these circumstances, an educated wife with a developed personality becomes the true mistress of the house.

With increasing employment opportunities for women and consequent economic freedom and disintegration of the joint family, women of the urban middle classes are acquiring a better status in the family. In the rural, small scale agricultural and artisan communities also, there exists a similar situation, as their women make an equal contribution to the income of the family.

With fast increasing urbanisation, social isolation of the urban housewife has occurred. They remain alone at home, with their children, while the menfolk are out all day. They have no sound basis of interaction with neighbours and this restricts their social contacts. Housewives are now seeking gainful employment or social work to break their isolation.

Unfortunately, there is hardly any basis of identification of the housewives with one another. They constitute a social category rather than a group and hence it is difficult to organise themselves in order to contribute to social welfare. Further, they are isolated from their relatives and friends by distances of modern cities.

The desire to take up employment to escape from these restrictions has created two distinct categories among married women—those employed outside their homes and those doing only domestic work. Working married women are often criticised for being trouble-makers in the family, leading to increase in matrimonial disharmony and juvenile delinquency, while those engaged only in domestic work are often said to be under-employed and parasites on society.

A working wife evidently needs more assistance from the husband who, traditionally, dislikes domestic chores. Thus, it is often argued that couples where the husband and wife are both employed are more susceptible to marital discord than those in which only the husband works. This is, perhaps, a clear indicator that human society still clings, although unconsciously, to the traditional attitude of exploitation of women by restricting them to domestic chores which, in the scale of values for different jobs, is still rated very low. A fundamental change in the system of values in this respect is necessary to avoid growing marital discord in society.

WOMAN AS MOTHER

It is clear that Hindu scriptures do not present a comprehensive appraisal of the woman's personality. As against this, their specific roles, that is, those of mother and wife, have been considered in detail.

The cult of the mother-goddess, which is often attributed to pre-Aryan matrilineal or tribal cultures has greatly influenced the status of women in Hindu society. Hindu religious literature has elevated the mother's role to a very high position. There are innumerable laudatory references in Hindu scriptures commenting on women on the one hand as the embodiment of purity and spiritual power and, on the other, as being fundamentally weak and dependent on the constant protection of men. However, the images of women as young virgins before puberty and as mothers of sons, evoke heavy veneration.

The *Mahabharata* states that the mother in her greatness, excels 10 fathers (P. V. Kane. *History of Dharmasastras*). There is no *guru* (spiritual teacher) like the mother. Thus, the mother came to be the symbol of sacrifice which although endowing her with respect and veneration, restricted her to the house.

There is a famous Sanskrit saying: "Where women are worshipped, there live the gods." (*Yatra nariman Poojiante, Ramante, Tatra Devata*) From earliest times, Indian society has given a highly esteemed position to women, as witness the prevalence of worship of the mother-goddess and the fertility cult. Through its varied manifestations, whether in its crude form of the Harappa culture (c. 3500-1500 B.C.) or as the consorts of various gods, both benign or malevolent, or the more esoteric *Shakti* of the *Tantriks,* the mother-goddess is the dominant deity, for she is implicit even in the worship of the *Lingam.*

The fact that in the early cultures of Mohenjodaro and Harappa, the goddess was worshipped as mother is evident from archaeological excavations. Worship of the mother-goddess has been traditionally prevalent among Indian tribal as well as rural societies. However, in the *Rigvedic* period, the mother-goddess is conspicuously absent. Under the patriarchal conquerors from the north, the earlier mother-goddess was subjected to the secondary position of Brahma's wife. The imposed superiority of Brahma was not totally accepted by the people and, in course of time with the fusion of the pre-Vedic and Vedic cultures and traditions, generally woman regained her godhood as Kali, Durga, Chandi, Chamundi, Uma, Sati, Shakti, etc.

The goddess as mother is the greatest power in the East. Similarly, the Indian woman as mother wields tremendous moral authority. The respect in which the mother is held by an earning son and the daughter-in-law in the traditional Indian family vouchsafes this. The mother is virtually the central figure to decide on affairs of the house. In all religious ceremonies in the house, the mother's presence is considered indispensable. The famous song *Bande Mataram* by Bankim Chandra was sung to the mother-goddess (Mother India) who is conceived to be the spirit of Indian mothers in her various manifestations, demanding devotion and sacrifice of her millions of sons and daughters. The ideal of Indian womanhood is the mother, godlike in her unlimited love and devotion, with no expectation of return or recompense. The female sculptures in our temples, whether Halebid or Konarak or Khajuraho, are not of maidens or virgins, but of full-breasted women. No marriage ceremony was concluded without a prayer for offspring and the blessing given by priests and elders at the marriage is: "May you have ten children and your husband be the eleventh." (Devaki Jain. *Indian Woman*, 1975).

Indian history provides evidence that during the Vedic age, women were regarded with respect in every sphere of life. Societal laws unsympathetic to women did not exist at that time. However, in course of time with the development of eschatological ideas, anxiety about the next world necessitated the development of an elaborate system of rituals for the salvation of the soul. The imperative of a son who could offer oblation to his dead parents was a consequence with this preoccupation with the after-life. Thus, woman who had so far enjoyed respect and veneration, was reduced to the position of a medium for giving birth to sons. In this fashion, she lost her right to participate in intellectual and social activity.

It needs to be clarified that the hard life of women referred to elsewhere in this book, applied normally to women with no sons. This again was a consequence of the religious need of a son. Immediately on begetting a son, the woman was considered as highly auspicious and an omen for the prosperity of the whole family. The role of the mother in the emotional integration of the family and the psychological development of the children does not need to be stressed. The rapid change in the position of women during the last five to six decades was accompanied by a change in the structure of the family. The need of a mother's care for developing the personality of the children, which is inadequate due to her preoccupation in her profession is being increasingly felt.

Love and affection make economic hardships more bearable. Thus, even the austere life enjoined by religion on a widow was mitigated by the respect and affection of her sons and daughters-in-law. The respect given to a person is in recognition of his/her contribution to the welfare of others, be it a family or society at large. This was, however, reduced to a formality and women came to be deprived of their economic rights. The position is now changing and the modern Indian woman is neither a symbol of the mother-goddess of ancient India nor the object of exploitation of feudal India. She is no more dependent on man in her struggle for emancipation.

Normally, the function of looking after the household and bringing up the children is under-valued and does not take account of development that takes place in the character and mind of growing children. In recent times, the importance of upbringing is being appreciated both from the economic and cultural points of view. Experiments of bringing up children away from the parents resulted in the development of various psychological distortions and emphasised the fundamental importance of the mother's role. Traits of character such as integrity, punctuality, discipline, initiative, dignity of labour, etc. are the result of basic training at home.

DIMINISHING PARENTAL AUTHORITY

It is worth considering the changes that have taken place in the family structure, mainly in the West and, generally, throughout the world. Contemporary literature in different Western countries indicates that these changes have varied in degree in different countries. Husbands can no longer command the unquestioning obedience of their wives. Similarly, parents seem to have lost a great deal of authority over their children. Children are less willing to comply with parental orders. Parents and especially grandparents often complain about the decadence in children's behaviour towards the parents and elderly members of the family.

The concept that members of the modern nuclear family should love one another and that permissive love is psychologically healthy for the child has provided children ideological support to exercise greater choice in all matters. The positive effect has been the increasing amount of affection between parents and children and a corresponding decrease in formal terms and gestures of respect by the young. This trend towards informality leads to intensification of the emotional relationship between parents and children, leading to healthier, friendly and more equality in family behaviour. Smaller family norms and more people living to a ripe old age, has had its impact on children's care for their ageing parents. There is a widespread feeling that young people are revolting against traditional values and standards of behaviour especially in respect of their parents. However, in the broader perspective, it is clear that the wide difference in the values and attitudes between the two generations is due to the progress of science and technology leading to rapid industrialisation and urbanisation. Admittedly, some conflict is bound to occur between the generations. First, parents' behaviour towards their children normally combines affection with authority while society leads them to be pragmatic. Also, there is always some psychological difference between two generations brought about by the forces of religio-socio-economic evolution.

Although India is now seeing the spread of old age homes and economic security of senior citizens through social and individual insurance, the psychological needs of the elderly have not been fulfilled. A field survey indicated that 90 per cent of parents and their adult children said that after marriage a person's loyalty was to his own family and only secondarily to his parents. Although about half the parents lived with their children at some time or another, 94 per cent of the parents said this was not a good idea. The concept of parents living with their married children appears to have been rejected by a majority of both parents and children.

It is clear that the increasing tendency towards the conjugal family pattern and the challenge to feudal values and standards of behaviour by the young are often wrongly dubbed as rebellion by the youth. Studies of attitudes among modern youth and their parents do not show great differences in values between the two generations. Yesterday's rebels usually succumb to parental relationship and the revolt of adolescence is discarded in adulthood after marriage.

—oo(O)oo—

21

LEGAL STATUS OF WOMEN

MODERN society gives great importance to legislative measures for bringing about social change to eliminate inequality and exploitation. The social reconstruction of the country that suffered centuries of foreign rule and various forms of social and religious exploitation, saw legislation as a potent instrument.

Thus, legislative measures were taken during the post-independence period to protect the interests of those weaker sections of society that suffered from prolonged social and political disability. The guiding principle of these legislative measures was to remove various social, legal and political bias based on caste, creed or sex. This was strictly in conformity with the concept that in order to achieve liberty, "all legislative traces of inequality of women without exception must be removed."

The position of Indian women during the earlier periods has been discussed in previous chapters. During the British period, the Government's policy of *laissez-faire* was to let the Hindus and Muslims be guided by their traditional laws in family relations. Their declared policy was of non-interference in family law. This resulted in social tension to such an extent that modernisation of the personal laws of these two major communities of India was delayed. However, there have been certain marginal adjustments on humanitarian considerations because of the effort of social reformers. This, in a way, proved to be the background for legislative measures. With the dawn of the 20th century, as the national movement gained momentum, the legislature was activated. To ameliorate the plight of widows who were without economic security and entirely dependent on the family of the deceased husband, the Hindu Women's Right to Property Act was passed in 1929.

Later, under the leadership of Mahatma Gandhi, women were enlisted in the national struggle for freedom on an equal footing with men. This resulted in a growing demand for bringing about improvement and modernisation of the law to protect women from discrimination and removal of unjust legal provisions pertaining to guardianship, marriage, divorce, inheritance, etc. The matter of inheritance needs to be considered with reference to the Hindu law relating to the joint Hindu family, in which succession was intimately related to the coparcenary properties. In such property, the right of succession was acquired by a son, son's son and son's grandson by virtue of birth. The most important features of the coparcenary system were community of interests, unity of possession as also the right of survivorship among the coparceners. Besides, there were some other systems of succession in different parts of the country, in most of which women were given little property rights. Even when such rights were given it was restricted to their lifetime. Although the systems which deprived women of their rights enjoyed social approval earlier, there has been increasing social resentment in the post-independence period of this state of affairs, especially in view of the guarantees of equality and non-discrimination incorporated in the Constitution of India.

This led to the passage of the Hindu Succession Act of 1956 which introduced certain fundamental changes by granting equal rights of succession to the male and female heirs. Section 14 of the Act provided that the property of a female Hindu is her absolute property as against her restricted life interest under the earlier systems.

Social change in a society with deep-rooted prejudices and traditions cannot be achieved merely through legislation. Both the judiciary and executive need to be simultaneously involved. If the judiciary interprets new legislation strictly in terms of the letter of the law, ignoring the principle underlying the legislation, it will not help in ensuring social justice. The executive branch of the Government must also develop machinery to educate the people about the need for socio-economic change in conformity with the needs of the times.

The actual practice and mode of behaviour is guided more by the traditional concept of the woman's role in society than by legal and official provisions. Various studies of this situation have revealed fundamental differences between the two sexes in various spheres, personal relations, religious behaviour as well as in social activities. Right from childhood, boys and girls are made to believe that different modes of behaviour are appropriate for them.

An explanation for this situation lies, perhaps, in the fact that a sense of distinction of sex roles is infused right from childhood and the deep self-image thus developed cannot be easily changed by ideologies encountered in later life, however rational and convincing they may be. Further, the traditional concept of sex roles has certain other aspects: it satisfies the ego and gives a sense of security; men assume a feeling of superiority and women feel free from certain worries while gaining a degree of protection and comfort.

Furthermore, most of the spheres of family and social life are regulated by traditional and psychological norms as are beyond the reach of legal provisions. Various economic, educational, administrative and legal provisions for bringing about a change in social behaviour and individual conduct are bound to take long to show results.

The principle of equality between the sexes is so vague that it has led to different interpretations and social and psychological problems. Most of the present day patterns of behaviour seem to be based neither on traditional principles nor on the modern concept of equality.

PRESENT SCENARIO

The Constitution of India directs the State that women shall not only have equal rights and privileges with men, but also that the State shall make provisions—both general and special—for the welfare of women. The legal status of women has to be considered from various points of view, particularly with reference to marriage, divorce, abortion, guardianship of children, maintenance and inheritance, matrimonial property and criminal law for the protection of women. While it is not possible to bring about a change in the status of women through legislative action alone, the importance of an effective legislative policy cannot be under-estimated.

CALL FOR SOCIAL CHANGE

It was observed that the "tasks of social reconstruction, development and nation building all call for major changes in the social order to achieve which legislation is one of the main instruments." This was particularly true in the case of removing gender inequality, which has been prevalent in Indian society across generations based on a complex system of social institutions, norms of behaviour and religious prescriptions, some of which were enshrined as statutory laws. It was also noted that "stress on the removal of discrimination and special protective legislation for women was necessary because British policy in the field of family law had a crippling effect on women."

After reviewing the role of the law in bringing about the desired transformation in women's status through nearly 25 years, the following persistent issues that had constrained that role were identified:

1. The continued lacunae and the differences in the various systems of personal law in the absence of a uniform civil code;

2. Continuation of certain outdated provisions in criminal law which bore little relationship either to the Constitutional directives or the emerging social reality;

3. The absence of adequate enforcement mechanisms which had made many of the laws ineffective; and

4. Inadequate efforts of social organisations to educate women regarding their legal rights. While literacy and poverty constitute the major obstacles to women benefiting from progressive laws, it was the absence of any alternative methods to deliver such information and assistance to women that was regretted.

The National Plan of Action stated:

> "Legislation represents national intent and policy and it is necessary that existing legislation of personal laws be reviewed, properly amended or new laws formulated to ensure equality before the law among the sexes. Equally important is the need to provide free legal services to weaker sections, including women in need. Legislation in itself cannot achieve results unless it is supported by socio-economic changes, an awareness of rights and responsibilities by the weaker sections, effective legal implementation and follow-up machinery."

The plan included specific recommendations for reforms in personal law, labour laws, criminal law, nationality laws and social security provisions.

SIGNIFICANT TRENDS

A review of developments in the field of law during the last quarter of the 20th century reveals significant trends. There have been legislative enactments to reduce some of the lacunae in personal, criminal and labour laws. Some of the important enactments affecting women, which have been amended from time to time, are:

1. Hindu Marriage Act;
2. Special Marriage Act;
3. Child Marriage Restraint Act;
4. Code of Civil Procedure—insertion of new order laying down the procedure in family matters;
5. Dowry Prohibition Act;
6. Equal Remuneration Act.
7. Factories Act;
8. Maternity Benefit Act;
9. Criminal Law (Amendment) Act (Act 43); and
10. Criminal Law (Amendment) Act (Act 46).

The amendments in personal law have, however, been concentrated in laws relating to the majority community—the Hindus. This has contributed to a widening of the differences between different systems of personal law. There are five systems of personal law that govern five religious communities—Hindu, Muslim, Parsi, Christian and Jewish. In addition, there are some secular laws, for example, the Special Marriages Act, 1954, which can be invoked by citizens belonging to any community.

The National Plan of Action had hoped for the elimination of polygamy (which persists under one system) and disparities between different communities in their right to divorce. This has not been possible as the laws relating to non-Hindu communities have not been amended. However, a great deal of publicity is being given to the need for amendment of personal law in the interest of women. Some women's voluntary groups have also advocated the need for a common civil code. The Government, however, does not want to ride roughshod over the feelings of the minority communities and would like to take up the matter when the minorities themselves are convinced of the need for amendment.

The review and amendment of criminal law has been markedly influenced by a rising rate of crime against women and the increasing articulation of public reaction against this trend. This reaction has been expressed by social action groups, including women's organisations and civil rights groups, professional bodies and the media. In response to this public demand, the Government referred the laws relating to the protection of women to the Law Commission for review in 1980. The consequent enactments seek to make the laws more relevant to the current situation.

In the process of consultation between the Law Commission, other legal professionals and social action groups, a new legal concept has evolved which underlines and emphasises the role of the State in ensuring the protection of women. This is the concept of custodial rape. The Act provides that in the case of rape by a police officer or by a group of persons or by a person having custodial control of the victim, the onus of proving that sexual intercourse (if proved that it did take place) was with the consent of the woman, should be on the accused. The amendment thus introduces a distinction in punishment and rules of evidence for the same crime committed by an ordinary citizen and public servant who violates his custodial responsibility. The right of social organisations concerned with women's rights to initiate cognisance of such crimes has also been admitted.

The most significant development is the revival of the social debate on women's rights to equality and fuller participation in national development. The debate has been reflected in the emergence of new organisations and reorientation of older women's organisations that are performing a new function of vigilance and articulation of women's rights. They have identified new issues and trends in social change, have controlled the support of a section of the media, academia and the legal profession and have engaged in a dialogue with the various wings of the Government, including the judiciary. An analysis of the more significant legislation and judgements indicates that there is a new trend in the judiciary to interpret laws and deliver judgements in favour of women.

LEGAL AID SCHEMES

Some measures have been initiated to improve the effectiveness of the existing laws. The report of the National Committee of Legal Aid (NCLA) which preceded the Committee on Status of Women in India, had already recommended special measures for providing legal aid services to women as one of the most vulnerable groups. The National Committee for Implementing Legal Aid Schemes was constituted by a Central Government resolution of September 26, 1980. The Committee evolved a model scheme on legal aid programmes for adoption by State Governments.

The State Boards envisaged under this model were to be constituted so as to give due representation to lawyers, legislators, State officials and representatives of the weaker sections including women. The normal eligibility condition for free legal aid will not apply to cases where a woman, child or member of the weaker sections is involved. A woman would, thus, be entitled to legal aid irrespective of her economical position.

The NCLA was also engaged in promotion of legal literature among women through publication of booklets and pamphlets by various voluntary organisations and professional bodies. It framed a National Plan for Legal Literacy and initiated measures to incorporate the legal rights of women into Adult Education Programmes, Workers' Education Programmes and National Social Programmes. Legal aid camps emerged as a new instrument to serve a double purpose—one, to identify people requiring legal aid and, two, to inform them of their rights under the law.

Recognising woman "as a class who have been subjected to deprivation, brutality and extortion," the Committee also initiated a programme for training women social workers on the use of law in various subjects. Several women's organisations and one women's university have assisted this scheme by organising such training programmes with the assistance of the NCLA. The Committee also supported the efforts of both professional and social organisations to promote the needed research in legal issues through seminars, workshops and conferences. There is a growing demand for better knowledge of the law being voiced by women's groups from different parts of the country. In Delhi, this was also articulated by students of some educational institutions.

The demand for family courts with simplified procedures was voiced repeatedly by both women's and professional organisations following the CSWI's recommendations. In response to this demand, the Family Courts Act, which enables the Government to establish such courts, was passed in 1984. The principle of associating social organisations with women's welfare and the right to initiate certain types of criminal cases, such as those relating to dowry and rape, has been accepted and built into the legal amendments.

PERSONAL LAW

Commending the provision of mutual consent as a ground for divorce in the Special Marriage Act (1954), the recognition of this principle in all personal laws was recommended. Though it was incorporated into Hindu Law by an amendment in 1976, similar amendments in other systems of personal law have not been introduced.

The right to exercise the 'option of puberty' to obtain a divorce (available earlier only to Muslim women who were married while still minors) was extended to Hindu women with the difference that while this right in Muslim law is limited to unconsummated marriages, in Hindu law it can be exercised whether the marriage has been consummated or not. The amendment was particularly welcomed by women's rights advocates.

Cruelty as a ground for divorce has also been added to Hindu Law. The period of waiting for a decree of judicial separation or restitution of conjugal rights has been reduced from two years to one year. While adding cruelty to the grounds for divorce, the legislature did not enumerate situations that would constitute cruelty. Here, the judiciary stepped in and interpreted it to include mental cruelty. Since the amendment, high courts have also consistently held that a false allegation of adultery by the husband or wife should be construed as mental cruelty.

A debate was initiated in the latter part of the last century within the judiciary regarding the judicial and constitutional validity of matrimonial relief symbolised in the restitution of conjugal rights available to either husband or wife in case one spouse withdraws from the matrimonial home without a reasonable cause. The law confers the right on the spouse in whose favour the decree is given to approach the court in case of non-compliance of the decree by the other spouse. In such cases, the court may order the attachment of the property of the erring spouse or order that a certain sum of money should be paid regularly. The remedy does not offend the equality clause of the Constitution as it is available to both husband and wife.

In 1963, the Andhra Pradesh High Court stated categorically that this relief was unconstitutional as it was "a savage and barbarous remedy violating the right to privacy and human dignity guaranteed by Article 21." The Delhi High Court, however, took a different view. It opined that "sexual relations constitute a most important attribute of the conception of marriage. But it is also true that they do not constitute its whole content." The Supreme Court supported this point of view and regarded the decree for restitution of conjugal rights as serving a social purpose.

The Supreme Court's idea of offering an inducement in the hope of bringing about an amicable settlement was followed in a unique manner by Justice Krishna Iyer in a divorce case. Instead of directly giving any matrimonial relief, the judge directed that the young couple should live separately from the parents and the grandparents for a month and only then decide whether they really wanted to end their marriage. He also requested a retired judge to visit the couple occasionally in case they needed advice, and he requested the husband's employer to permit him to proceed on leave for a short term.

While legal orthodoxy may hold that it is not the function of the judiciary to act as a marriage counsellor, the question could be raised that if the object in a matrimonial case is to try to preserve the marriage, then perhaps the humane approach adopted by the judge is preferable to a decree by the court compelling an unwilling party to return to the matrimonial home.

The suggestion of restricting the right of a testator to will away his entire property without providing for his dependants was reiterated by the Working Group on Woman and Development constituted by the Government. The rights of inheritance conceded to daughters under the Hindu Succession Act were restricted through the continuation of the Mitakshara coparcenary and its abolition was recommended.

In coparcenary properties, a son, son's son and a son's grandson acquire the right to property by birth. No female can be a member of the coparcenary and, as such, it has contributed to continuing the inequality between sons and daughters. A significant development was the lead taken by the Andhra Pradesh Government in introducing a bill giving coparcenary rights to both sons and daughters, thus linking the measure squarely to constitutional equality of men and women and the national policy of eradicating "the socially pernicious dowry system."

JOINT FAMILY

Before the amendment to the Special Marriage Act enacted in 1976, the law was that anyone marrying under the Special Marriage Act, irrespective of the community he or she belonged to, would be governed for purposes of succession by the Indian Succession Act. A special provision for Hindus was that it would bring about severance with the joint family and separation of his share. The present amendment provides that when the two parties to a marriage under the Special

Marriage Act are both Hindus, then this provision will not apply; instead the provisions of the Hindu Succession Act will continue to apply to them and there will be no severance from the joint family. The amendment makes no such provision for members of other communities.

The daughter's right to the family dwelling house is of residence only. Even for this, daughters are not treated on par and the right is denied to a married woman unless she is judicially separated or divorced. With the growing increase in domestic violence, the Government is attempting to set up short-stay homes for women in distress, the majority of whom are likely to be married women who can no longer endure harassment in the matrimonial home. Yet they may not, as of right, seek shelter in their ancestral homes. Even an unmarried daughter or a widow entitled to reside in the family house cannot demand partition to get her share. But no such restriction has been placed on a son's demand for partition. This disparity in rights has been supported by the judiciary out of a desire to prevent "fragmentation or disintegration of a family dwelling house at the instance of the female heirs and the hardships and difficulties to which the male heirs may be put." The rights of women to adoption and guardianship are based on their status and concern as mothers. The Hindu Law of Adoption made radical changes and introduced equal rights between men and women. It also legitimised the rights of a girl to be adopted, which was not recognised in pre-independence India. But there is no law of adoption for other communities. The Adoption Bill—a secular law which would have enabled any citizen to adopt a child—was introduced in Parliament in 1972.

The judiciary has played a progressive role on the issue of mothers' rights over the custody and guardianship of a minor child when the marriage is dissolved. It was recommended that the sole criterion for deciding this question should be the child's interest. According to the Hindu Minority and Guardianship Act, the father is the natural guardian of all minors, the mother coming only after him. The judiciary has, however, constantly held that the statutory requirements cannot take precedence over the interests of the child. In one case, the Bombay High Court decided that even the conversion of the mother did not disqualify her for guardianship of her child. Thus, while the law as it stands makes the father the natural guardian even of a minor daughter, the judiciary has been guided by the interest of the child in such cases.

CRIMINAL LAW

The rights of a wife to be maintained by her husband even when she is separated is recognised in all systems of personal law. But the right is essentially a civil one and civil suits take an inordinately long time. To prevent hardship to wives who may have no means of support, there is a special remedy in Indian law—the right given under the Criminal Procedure Code. This provides "a remedy far more speedy and economical than that available in civil court," the purpose of which is to prevent "starvation and vagrancy leading to the commission of crime." This right was earlier available only to a wife. It is now available to a 'divorced wife' as well. This addition brought distinct relief to Muslim women who could be divorced by their husbands at will without recourse to any legal procedure.

The pressure from a section of Muslims that this provision introduced a change in their personal law resulted in the addition of a provision that stated that if the personal law of the couple required payment of a lump sum of money to the wife, she would not get the benefit of this provision under the revised maintenance law. Since the objective of this provision was social justice—to prevent destitution of the divorced wife, the judiciary has taken over the role of interpreting the law to fulfil this aim. The Supreme Court had a case before it where the husband had paid his wife the *mehr* which was due at the time of divorce. She claimed later that she was unable to maintain herself in Mumbai where she was living. The husband's plea that the payment of *mehr* absolved him of all future obligations was rejected. Because of the untiring efforts of the judiciary, the law today is that payment of *mehr* or a lumpsum under the customary law will relieve the husband from further payment of maintenance only if the amount paid could be considered as adequate for maintenance of the divorced wife.

SHIFT TOWARDS DOWRY

The Dowry Prevention Act was passed in 1961. Certain States even passed amendments to this Act. However, the implementation of this Act was not effective; and in 1984, another amendment was made by Parliament which made the provisions of the law more stringent and also changed the definition to include dowry demands before, during and after marriage. As far as the personal enactments are concerned, a legal umbrella is necessary; as also the effectiveness of the implementation of the enactment. What is equally, if not more, important is the growing awareness in society about the social evils inherent in the dowry system. This awareness is the result of the publicity given to the problem by the official media, school curricula and the efforts of voluntary organisations. The Government Servants' Conduct Rules have been amended to prohibit the display of gifts and the taking and giving of gifts as well.

Ever since focus was placed on this social evil, there has been a qualitative change in the situation. It is not only that dowry deaths have decreased but that public concern has been increasingly voiced in the Press, inside Parliament and in other forums. Another qualitative change is in the whole attitude towards dowry. It is no longer regarded as a gift extracted at the time of marriage but as a continuing demand made by the bridegroom and/or his parents.

Dowry cases which have gone to court clearly reveal two distinct trends: (i) reluctance to use the law as a means of changing social norms to promote social justice; and (ii) to regard the judge's role in interpreting the law in the spirit of the times where the language of the legislation does not debar it. By this it is evident that the courts have accepted the fact that judges also can influence public opinion. The second noticeable factor has been that in many cases the lower judiciary—being perhaps closer to the people and societal reaction—has taken a bold stand in giving deterrent punishment.

DETERRENT PUNISHMENT

The Additional Sessions Judge in North Delhi, for instance, sentenced to life imprisonment the brothers and two sisters of a groom for having killed the bride for dowry. Similarly, the Sessions Judge in Dhanbad sentenced the father-in-law, the husband and two others for torturing and killing a young bride. Such convictions indicate a new trend in the judiciary's attitude and this has been recognised as a response to the women's movement.

As a result of the increase, in certain regions, in what are euphemistically called dowry deaths but are, in reality, murder or cases of women driven to suicide, women's organisations and members of Parliament demanded that a stringent law be passed to fight the "growing dowry menace." In August 1982, and again in November of the same year, Parliament debated the question of dowry and was assured by the Home Minister that stringent measures would be taken against police officers found guilty of dereliction of duty in registration and investigation of dowry deaths and a bill to make the Dowry Prohibition Act more effective would be introduced at the earliest. This was done in August 1984.

As a result of the growing anger of the public and the demands of social organisations for drastic amendments to the Dowry Prohibition Act, Parliament appointed a Joint Committee of both Houses to review the working of the Act in early 1981. The Committee's report, submitted in August 1982, focused its recommendations in four directions:

1. The need to widen the definition of dowry;
2. To make the offence cognizable with a minimum punishment;
3. To impose ceilings on all marriage expenditure as well as on gifts; and
4. To establish rigorous enforcement through the appointment of Dowry Prevention Officers in all States and an annual system of reporting to State Legislatures and Parliament.

The Dowry Prevention (Amendment) Act, 1984, has defined dowry by substituting 'in connection with the marriage' for 'in consideration of the marriage', because it used to be difficult to prove that gifts were given 'in consideration of' the marriage and not 'out of love and affection'. The amendment also extended to the right to women's organisations to initiate proceedings in court instead of limiting it only to the aggrieved party as in the original law.

CRIMINAL LAW (SECOND AMENDMENT) ACT, 1983

The Law Commission had suggested an amendment of the Indian Penal Code, Criminal Procedure Code and the Evidence Act to deal effectively with the growing menace of dowry deaths. The amended law, as enacted, lays down that when a woman commits suicide within seven years of her marriage *and* when it can be shown that her husband or his relatives had subjected her to cruelty, then the suicide will be presumed to have been abetted by the husband. Also, when a woman dies within seven years of marriage "raising a reasonable suspicion that some other person has committed an offence", there will be a post-mortem. It further provides that "no court shall take cognizance of the offence except upon a police report or a complaint made by the victim's family."

Apart from dowry deaths and cruelty, another form of violence against women which has increased, is rape. Since 1869, rape has featured as an offence in the Indian Penal Code. What is of concern today is the increase in its incidence, both in rural and urban areas, and the fact that many of them are committed by persons in authority or by groups of people. A report by a Supreme Court lawyer estimated that 15 per cent of rapes committed in rural areas and 20 per cent in tribal areas were by officials.

The Criminal Law Amendment Act, 1983, provides for the crime of rape being punished with a minimum of seven years imprisonment and for the "protection of the victim of rape from the glare of embarrassing publicity during the investigation as well..." The Act also amends the definition of rape to remove certain loopholes and inadequacies. 'Custodial' means rape by a person in authority in an institution where the woman is. This includes not only a police station but also a hospital or a protective home for women in distress. As the victim is in a weak position, the onus of proof has been shifted and it will be for the alleged rapist to prove there was consent. In cases of gang rape, the woman is in a still more vulnerable position and the law prescribes a more severe punishment.

DISCRIMINATION IN EMPLOYMENT

While the Indian Constitution guaranteed equality of opportunity for women in matters relating to employment, the impact of transition to a modern economy had meant the exclusion of an increasing proportion of women from active participation in the productive process. A very large number of women are subjected to exploitation of various kinds with no protection from society or the State. Constitutional guarantees should be made meaningful and the trend towards gradual exclusion of women from their right to a fuller participation in the economic process should be arrested.

Certain revisions are necessary in the Maternity Benefits Act, 1961, and it should be extended to all working women—industrial and agricultural; There should also be legislative enactment of Article 39(d) of the Constitution—equal pay for equal work—and the incorporation of this principle in the Minimum Wages Act and some amendments in the existing labour laws to make them more effective *vis-à-vis* women workers. The Equal Remuneration Act, 1976, provided for (a) the payment of equal remuneration to men and women workers; and (b) prevention of discrimination on grounds of sex against women in the matter of employment and for matters connected therewith or incidental thereto. The Act required the setting up of advisory committees to review recruitment, promotion and other personal practices to ensure that there is no discrimination against women candidates and to identify measures necessary to expand women's access to employment.

The recommendation to reduce the number of women workers from 50 to 20 for purpose of restrooms, creches and other facilities under the Factories Act was accepted partially. An amendment to this effect was made in 1976 reducing the qualifying number to 30. The suggestion to extend hours of work for women from 7 a.m. to 10 p.m. and to provide transport and other security measures was also accepted in principle.

It was pointed out that the rules governing appointments in the Judge Advocate General's Office excluded women and the rules in the Foreign Service requiring a woman to resign on her marriage were violative of the Constitutional guarantees. Though the latter rule had been struck down, a writ petition filed by the senior-most woman in the Foreign Service who, along with other women, had been denied promotion, revealed continuing discrimination in some of the rules. However, adverse criticism from the Press and the judiciary, and the possibility of pressure from women's organisations and civil rights groups, persuaded the Government to delete the rules and to appoint the petitioner as she was "meritorious enough for promotion." The judgement ended with a plea that all service rules should be overhauled to remove the stain of gender discrimination.

While Articles 14 to 16 of the Constitution ensure equality of status and opportunity and clearly prohibit discrimination, *inter alia,* on the ground of sex, a specific provision [Article 15(3)] permits the State to make special provision for women. 'Special provision' has been interpreted by the Court not to be confined to measures which are beneficial to women, but may be any which is not applicable to men. As noticed earlier, the provision of punishment to men for adultery but not women is not violative of the Constitution according to the judiciary on the ground of this discriminative clause. The special provisions have, however, in most cases been relied upon for measures beneficial to women, like prohibition of night work or carrying of heavy loads.

Finally, in addition to the various legislative changes, a constitutional amendment was also made in 1976 by adding a Chapter—Fundamental Duties. This enjoins all citizens to renounce all "practices derogatory to the dignity of women."

—oo(O)oo—

22

POLITICAL STATUS OF WOMEN

THE political status of women in a nation is reflected by the extent of freedom granted to women to participate in political activity. Article 15 of the Constitution of India guarantees political equality through the institution of universal adult franchise, a revolutionary departure from the socio-cultural norms of tradition-bound Indian society and a major step towards political evolution. However, the right to vote for women can, at best, be a starting point in the struggle for their political equality.

The forces that worked for this revolutionary first step can be traced back to the 19th century reform movement, when a process was initiated for improving the status of women. In the beginning, the movement was based on an elitist approach and all efforts in this direction were concentrated on the acceptance of women's right to formal education, thereby improving her status in domestic life then considered to be women's sole occupation. During this period, efforts were made to improve women's rights to property, allow widow remarriage, abolish child marriage, etc. With the dawn of the 20th century, some progress was observed in the field of women's education, leading to heightened awareness among women. This manifested itself in the emergence of women's organisations such as the All-India Women's Conference, the National Council for Women, etc. In 1917, a demand for women's franchise was presented to the British Parliament by a women's delegation headed by Sarojini Naidu.

The demand for women's franchise received specific support under the leadership of Mahatma Gandhi who appraised women's potential for *Satyagraha* and for social reconstruction as higher than that of men. This provided widespread inspiration to women of all sections of society to join the freedom struggle. As the modern age is characterised by political equality and casting votes is an individual's own decision, the Government of India Act of 1935 increased the number of enfranchised Indians by granting proportional suffrage rights to women relaxing certain earlier conditions of property and education.

With the advent of independence, Indian women were guaranteed political equality with men. However, it is a general comment that in a country where large sections of the population are poor and illiterate, social status depends on the caste hierarchy and women are regarded as inferior to men both physically and intellectually, political equality is virtually meaningless. This argument ignores the fact that equal legal and political rights serve as a starting point in the process of transformation of a society from exploitation to social justice based on increasing opportunities for women.

Participation of women in the political activity of the country has improved in consonance with the rights conferred by the Constitution. Though the number of women reaching the highest levels is not very high, their capacity and capability in administrative and organisational matters have been recognised and accepted. Since 1952, women have become ministers in the Central Government and even held the prime ministership. There has been a woman vice-chairman of the Rajya Sabha, and they have also been governors, chief ministers of States and speakers and deputy speakers of Assemblies. In proportion to their overall number in the legislatures, the number of women holding high political office has been commendably high.

Generally speaking, women legislators have done exceedingly well compared to their male counterparts. However, although their number in politics has increased and they have made a mark in problems relating to women, they have had little impact on mainstream political decisions, probably because, politically, they are not fully mature. Even their approach to resolving the basic problem of women's inequality shows sharp contradictions. Thus, despite their almost equal number in population, Indian women are a minority community in three aspects, inequality of class based on economic structure, inequality of status on account of their peculiar social position, as also inequality of political power. These contrasts in the standard of values and norms of behaviour (evidently traditional) and the objective of the new social order contained in the Constitution of India still need to be resolved.

PRESENT SCENARIO

The most significant event in the movement for women's political rights in India has been the demand for equal political rights made by a delegation of distinguished women led by Mrs. Sarojini Naidu in the British Parliament in 1917. This demand paved the way for a series of concessions to women in India and by 1937 women had acquired not only limited franchise rights, but they could also contest elections to the legislatures. Furthermore, a policy of reservation of seats for women guaranteed for the first time the election of a sizeable number of women to different legislatures in 1937. During this period, the national movement also was at its peak and under the stewardship of Mahatma Gandhi, it allowed women to play a significant role.

The political consciousness of women was not an isolated phenomenon, the seed having been implanted in the 19th century renaissance in India. Largely, because of their involvement, Indian women were able to get education and thus could participate in activities beyond the narrow spheres of immediate family and kinship. A number of urban, educated women began taking part in social welfare activities. Their participation in these activities raised their level of consciousness.

However, there were some cultural barriers to political participation of women. A large number of them in rural areas, for instance, continued to be guided by considerations which dictated that their role outside the family circle was neither 'respectable' nor 'healthy'. So, in reality, only a few urban women who were educated and those few from rural families who had taken part in the freedom movement could participate in public life.

As far as consciousness with regard to women's plight in society is concerned, in India it has a history of over a century—a unique case for any developing country. Many of the earlier reform movements, while questioning the prevailing social mores, assailed the culturally defined social roles of women. The spread of education among women and later of Western education, created a new awareness in them. Several voluntary organisations sprang up from 1860 onwards. Subsequently, the formation of the Congress Party, the freedom movement and the emergence of Mahatma Gandhi by the turn of the 20th century, created a favourable climate for public participation of women. And by the time India attained independence, women's participation in public life was an accepted fact. The constitutional provision of equality furthered this by legitimising their roles for public life participation in the formal-legal framework. It is against this background that women's political participation in the post-independence phase in India should be assessed and evaluated.

Participation can be viewed from different angles—right from within the family (decision-making in the family) to decision-making in different positions of power and authority; office holders in different political parties and interest groups, voluntary organisations and the highest office of the nation. But two levels are of concern here:

1. The level of representation in legislatures and the extent of participation; and
2. The level of ordinary citizens and voters and the extent and nature of their participation in the polity.

For this purpose, two national representative sample surveys will be analysed. One of these was undertaken by the Centre for the Study of Developing Societies in 1971 soon after Parliamentary elections were held (a post-election survey) and the other was undertaken in 1980 soon after the elections were announced (a pre-election survey).

Women throughout British India started participating in legislatures of different provinces a decade before independence. In the 1937 elections, 41 women were elected against seats reserved for women. There were another five women who were nominated in the provincial councils. Across the different provinces, their representation varied from one to four per cent. The policy of reservation was done away with after independence.

The first general election in independent India was held in 1952 on the basis of adult franchise and women have continued to participate since then in this and other subsequent elections to the Lok Sabha and different State legislatures. It is, however, the Lok Sabha which, as a legislative body, is supreme in its scope of power and authority.

As regards the cross-section of the people who exercise their franchise to elect their representatives, it has been observed that over the years the voting turnout has been increasing both for males and females.

In each election less women than men have voted. This gap, however, has narrowed down from a 17 per cent difference in 1957 to 11 per cent in 1990 at the all-India level. Between 1957 and 1990, the women turnout has gone up by about 12 per cent, while for men by only six per cent. Unmistakably, there is a uniform relationship between structural factors and turnout levels. By an analysis of the aggressive district level socio-economic and electoral data, it has been observed that turnout is 'positively' related with literacy and urban population and 'negatively' with Scheduled Tribe population. This was, however, on the basis of three Assembly elections in 1957, 1962 and 1967. Interestingly, no significant relation of voter turnout with sex ratio (females per thousand males) was found.

POLITICAL PARTICIPATION OF CITIZENS

Political participation has attracted a great deal of attention of the theorists of political development. It is argued that for a healthy and responsive government, an actively involved citizenry is a must, especially in a representative democracy. Social scientists have attempted to look into the nature and extent of participation of the citizens. It is the citizen's skill and ability to participate in the given institutional framework that has greater relevance in the new democracies, for without the development of citizenship, the institutional structure of new democracies will continue to remain fragile.

It has been argued that in developing societies like India, the focus should be on the citizen's 'political capacity'. The political capacity of people grows as and when they are able to transform their traditionally submissive attitude to political authority and forge new political relationships with their rulers based on the principle of periodic conditional mandate given to govern and continuing obligation on the part of the elected deputies to be accountable for their professional policy and performance.

Political participation, thus viewed, is a process of growth of citizenship. The central issue in women's participation is how far they have assumed the role of citizens beyond their traditional roles in the family and kinship groups, and to what extent such a role has been legitimised in the political system. Political participation is not simply voting. Besides voting, there are many of the acts in which people take part. These are: campaign-related acts (membership of parties, working for a party during elections, attending rallies and meetings); contacting officials and leaders for community-related needs and lastly, contacting them for personal needs. All these acts are conceptualised as different dimensions of political participation.

NATURE OF POLITICAL PARTICIPATION

An examination of different political acts (such as organising meetings and rallies, canvassing for candidates, distributing campaign literature, etc.) by men and women, shows that expectedly voting is the only act in which people most often engage themselves. The next most frequently engaged in act is that of attending meetings, a reasonably good indicator of interest, if not active involvement in political matters. In all the other acts, the participation of the general population is low and of women particularly, lower than that of men. For assessing the political participation of women, therefore, the primary focus would be on the act of voting—a decisive factor influencing the fortunes of political parties. In fact, as is revealed by election after election, the Indian voter has shown shrewd political sense. But voting by itself can be a ritual act, a consequence of a herd-type mobilisation of voters by political parties. It is, therefore, important to see how informed is the act and how consciously women engage in it. The act of voting should, therefore, be assessed in conjunction with levels of information and interest exhibited by women voters.

Accordingly, an index of political participation is created by using the three items of (a) voting; (b) level of political information; and

(c) level of political interest. An examination of relationships of voting with interest and information in the data is now made.

Information of political events is likely to be positively related with voting. Among those who vote, a substantial number would be aware of political events in society. This is seen to be so in both the studies of 1971 and 1980. Political involvement is a psychological feeling of interest and concern with politics pre-disposing and motivating people to take part in politics. The electorate has been divided into five types: non-voters; passive participants; informed participants; involved participants and active participants. Those who vote without any information and involvement are the 'passive' voters, while the 'active' voters have both information and a high level of interest. The 'informed' participants are likewise those with knowledge alone; whereas 'involved' voters have interest but no information.

The socio-economic characteristics that determine the male-female differences in political participation may be listed as under:

1. Age,
2. Education,
3. Family income,
4. Caste,
5. Religion,
6. Occupation,
7. Land holding, and
8. Urbanity.

AGE

The relationship between age and nature of participation is non-linear in both the sexes. With active participation, it is negatively related. Lower age groups show greater active participation both in men and women. In the highest age group (56 and above) there is a greater tendency of men to be either passive or non-voters. In females, this trend is reflected earlier than in males, however, that is, after they cross

45 years. Active voting starts falling sharply thereafter and on-voting increases. Women are also likely to enter much earlier than males, a stage of life when their involvement in family is more intimate and demanding.

EDUCATION

Education is positively related with participation. Active participants are more in the literate group while either passive or non-voters are more in the illiterate group both among men and women. The difference in active participation is about 21 per cent for both men and women between the illiterate and the primary-educated electorate. Once literate, the proportion of activists is substantially more than the averages of 56.3 and 29.5 per cent in men and women, respectively. This upward trend in active participation is maintained in higher levels of education, too. However, the most significant difference is seen once they cross illiteracy.

In women, education is more strongly related to participation than in men. Education enables them to increase their participation uniformly. In the highest category of education (high school and more), in women, an increase of over 11 per cent in active participation is seen while in men there is a fall of six per cent. It is, therefore, clear that while women in general suffer from low literacy, once they are educated, a meaningful change in participation takes place and from being passive and non-voters, they begin to vote with information and awareness. In a predominantly rural society like India, education opens up a new horizon of awareness and also allows the individual to get linked in a network of relationships at different levels. For women, it also enhances her understanding and awareness of the political environment.

FAMILY INCOME

Income is of special significance in India which is still bedevilled by the problem of poverty. Active participation goes up with income in both men and women. However, as in education, it falls a little in the highest category of 51 and over in men, though it still remains much above the simple average. Passive participation is again lowest in this group of men and non-voting is slightly more than in the sample.

In women, active participation increases with higher income levels but as dramatically as was seen with education. Unlike in men, there is no fall in active participation in the highest income category.

Passive participation is seen mostly in the lower-income levels both in men and women. However, it is to be noted that unlike in males, there is no substantial fall in passive voting in women. Thus, while income does explain active and passive participation in men just as education does, in women income has a limited explanatory power. Passive participation decreases but not to the extent as in men, and so also for active voting the impact of income is muted in women. While literacy and education enhance one's understanding and comprehension of politics, family income can at best be indicative of a favourable social setting, aside from signifying social and economic status.

CASTE

Caste has been a symbol of status in India and has continued to have a very high positive relationship with other indicators of socio-economic status. Caste has also been operative in a complex way in politics in India and most of the political scientists working on India have explored its salience. At one level, caste status behaves in the same way as other variables of socio-economic status. The Brahmins and other upper castes register higher active participation than the rest. This is true for upper caste women, too. In this sense, traditional social status is related with participation as are income and education.

Among women, the worst sufferers of low traditional social status are the Harijans, the lower castes and the middle castes within whom are vast majorities of non-voters and passive participants. Compared to a respective sample norm of activities in men and women, Brahmin women participate actively at a much higher level than the men (16.3 per cent in women and 7.1 per cent in men). Also, Brahmin women are more active participants than the women of other upper castes. Among men, such a difference is no more than one per cent.

To understand this anomaly seen in the participation levels in some of the caste groups, the educational levels of both men and women in each caste group were examined. It was found that men invariably were more educated than women as reflected by their mean education levels. Moreover, the mean values were ordered in the same way as the caste hierarchy, both in men and women. (Except for Harijans and Adivasis: while Adivasi men have a little higher mean education than Harijans, Adivasi women have a little lower mean education than Harijan women).

Interestingly, tribal women tend to be active participants. Men, too, are not so low in active participation in comparison to the average. Tribals are no longer as isolated as they used to be. Their political consciousness has increased and this is reflected in their higher levels of active participation. Though Harijans have a low status, the men among them are not among the most mobilised groups. The women, however, are not so mobilised and a large number do not vote.

Though caste behaves like a status variable at the upper levels, the experience of competitive electoral politics is changing this matrix of status relationships for some of the low status and peripheral groups that are participating much more than would be expected given their low positions in the status hierarchy.

RELIGION

Next to Hindus, Muslims are the most significant religious community in India. Among men there are substantial voters in this community. The maximum proportion of active participants is found in the residual category of other religions which comprise Sikhs and Christians only.

Among women, the lowest level of active participation is in the Muslim community. Though a large number of Muslim women vote, most do so as passive participants.

OCCUPATION

Men in white collar jobs, other professions, skilled and unskilled occupations, business or those who are cultivators are likely to be informed and involved voters. It has been observed that those in the highest education and income category do not participate passively. Such participation is lowest in this group. Within the unskilled, followed by skilled job holders, some participate passively. Among women, there are very few who are active voters in the work force. Notably among those, the few who are in white collar skilled occupations do show a marked tendency to participate as active voters. From among the unemployed (some of whom are likely to be students) there is above average active participation. They are likely to be from the better socio-economic strata. Most of the women are housewives in the study sample and show similar distribution as the overall distribution.

Farm areas and rural areas are the most deprived group and thus their distribution across various participation types, both in men and women, show a slightly higher level of non-participation than the average. Among those who vote, a sizeable number do so as passive voters. The women seem to be particularly mobilised as indicated by their passive voting. The same seems to be the case with women belonging to the cultivator families, a number of whom do not vote or vote passively, and active voting is slightly lower than that of the farm labourers.

A re-grouping of these occupations in terms of non-farm (modern) and farm sector, further divided into manual and non-manual occupations, show that both in men and women non-manual and non-farm sectors show more of active participation. Within the non-farm sector, the non-manual job holders have a higher proportion of 'actives' than those with manual occupations. Thus, both the nature of the economy and type of occupation seem to be related to participation.

LAND HOLDING

Land holding in a predominantly rural society is one of the best indicators of status and viability. However, for many urbanites it is not true and they are shown here as having no land. As with income and education, active participation goes up with land holding to fall again in the highest category in men. These people are likely to be enjoying a high status and social standing and to that extent behave in a fashion similar to that of high income and educated groups. There is a similarity in the incidence of non-voting also in this group. The women behave otherwise; among them there is a stronger relationship of land holding (and thus social status) with active participation in keeping with the trends seen so far while examining occupations with participation; women are more likely to be passive voters in the middle level land holding classes. And this is especially so with those possessing up to two acres of land. Women with no land tend to be active participants. Though some very likely would be from the urban areas, the other landless are active participants because of participation in movements of late.

URBANITY

A positive relationship between urbanity and voting was found when the aggregate turnout was examined. Those who are located in an urban setting would be better informed and interested in politics. They are the ones who are exposed to media and communication networks which allows them to be contacted relatively easily by political parties. Those in urban areas are at the centre of events which is conducive to meaningful participation. The nature of participation reflects this. Both men and women vote more in urban areas. However, with active participation, this relationship is stronger than with simply voting. In women, the urban environment has still greater impact on active participation.

The above analysis so far shows that men in general and across all categories of socio-economic background register significantly higher rates of political participation. This is not a surprising finding in view of the fact that politics is still perceived as a male domain. What is interesting to note is that in comparative terms, participation of Indian women is not significantly lower than their counterparts in other democracies if one accounts for overall depressing levels of education and income on the one hand and the traditional role concept of women on the other.

More significant is the fact that with the increase in education, income and employment in white collar and skilled jobs, women consistently improve their rates of active participation in politics. In fact, among the white collar skilled groups, the proportion of women participating actively is almost as high as that of men in these groups. It can safely be concluded that with increasing levels of education buttressed by increasingly equal opportunities in employment, political participation of women can improve further.

POLITICAL MOBILISATION: MASS MEDIA

Turning to the role of the mass media in political mobilisation, we find that the communication network plays an important catalytic role. To that extent, today's world has been ushered into the 'age of information' and its flow to the citizens is vital for any political behaviour. Exposure to the mass media is of tremendous educative value in today's society. Most of the Third World countries realise this and despite their resources have been investing substantially in this area.

While listening to the radio does not necessarily need any literacy, reading a newspaper does require that. It has been observed that the greater the exposure to the mass media, the greater is the active participation for both men and women. But compared to men, women are much less exposed. As many as 57 per cent men and 82 per cent women are unexposed to the media. With mass media exposure, women tend to participate actively at a rate much higher than men (a difference of 53 per cent in women to that of 43 per cent in men). As with education and employment, women benefit much more than men in improving their rates of political participation through exposure to the mass media.

CAMPAIGN EXPOSURE

The elite in India, immediately in the post-independence phase, addressed themselves to the twin tasks of economic development and a deliberate policy of extending citizenship rights to hitherto peripheral groups in Indian society. This task was greatly facilitated by the institutional structure it adopted with its periodic elections at different levels and its relatively open competitive party system and consequent mobilisation strategies adopted by the various political parties competing for support.

The role of mobilisation has to be seen in this perspective. It has already been observed while examining individual characteristics that there are groups that participate more than their socio-economic and educational levels would suggest and the reason appears to be that they were mobilised by parties. When the extent of such mobilisation and its impact on participation was studied, it was found that women were contacted less than men—a difference of 12.6 per cent among those who are not contacted at all. Greater political mobilisation through campaign exposure leads to greater active participation and lesser passive participation and non-voting. The impact is also sharper in females—a sector which suffers from cumulative disadvantage as a group in Indian society—than in males.

Both in men and women, the voting in earlier elections increases active participation and decreases non-voting in subsequent elections. However, passive voting is also somewhat weakly related with past voting. Those who had voted in the earlier two national elections tend to vote passively more than those who had voted in only one election. Probably with elected experience, some are likely to form loyalties and thus vote without being aware of issues.

The question now arises whether factors like exposure to mass media and mobilisation through campaigns and experience of voting in elections, help citizens, especially women, to overcome their handicap of their illiteracy and low economic and social status. It is seen that when education is 'controlled', the impact of campaign exposure, past voting and mass media on participation for both men and women remained substantial if not constant, showing independent contribution of political mobilisation on participation.

It was suggested that if political parties and other institutions take women voters seriously and mobilise them independently rather than approach them as adjuncts to their male counterparts as they seem to be doing now, women will register a much higher rate of active participation than expected by their low level of literacy and socio-economic status.

GROUP ORIENTATION AND POLITICAL PARTICIPATION

So far, the social and political context of participation has been examined in general and women's participation in particular. It is argued that an orientation or attachment to a group larger than one's family can boost participation to an extent not explained only by the given socio-economic characteristics of the individual. The role of local, regional and sub-regional identities as well as that of caste and religion as group motivational forces operating on the individual voters have helped in bringing them into the mainstream of Indian politics. It is to be seen whether citizens with orientation to public and community problems show higher rates of political participation than those whose primary orientation is to their family and are least concerned with issues pertaining to communities to which they belong. With respect to women's political participation, this is particularly important. Women being generally confined to their role in the family are least prone to be involved and interested in issues of their community and hence will be less involved in active participation.

Holding opinions on group-related issues and voting is very strongly related both in men and women. Those holding 'no opinion' tend to be overwhelmingly non-voters or passive voters. Those who hold opinions and feel strongly for the community tend to participate actively. A not so intense concern is related with passive voting. However, among women, such a relationship with active participation is not that clear. Tough opinion holders tend to vote actively, those who show a lot of concern and those who do not are equally likely to be active participants among women.

Both among men and women, those who feel their interests are similar to the interests of a larger community than their own tend to vote more as active voters. Among women, however, those who view their interests to be other than their own community's are proportionately less than in men (a difference of 11.7 per cent). It seems that group orientation is not that well-structured in women as in men.

The most significant factor that emerges is that irrespective of gender, out of those who do not hold an opinion on community-related issues, about 43 per cent are unlikely to vote, and as women are more with no opinion, they vote less often than men. Secondly, active voting is more among those who find self interests as similar to larger community interests.

That there is a stronger relationship of involved and active voting with identification of interests beyond one's immediate group is undeniable and is further clarified when the strength of party identification with voting is considered. It has been found to be one of the most stable predictors of party vote. Here, however, its relationship with the nature of participation is being looked into.

People tend to look at parties as closest representatives of their interests intervening on their behalf in politics. Feeling of closeness to parties, therefore, is likely to promote more informed and involved participation.

As in all other variables, men identify themselves with parties more subjectively than women—a difference of about 12 per cent. Similarly, subjectively, they feel much closer to one or the other party than women—such men are double the proportion of women. Those who do not identify themselves with any party tend to be non-voters whether among men or women, and if they vote, they do so as passive voters. Those who feel very close to a party tend to be active voters, irrespective of gender.

However, within women, mere identification with a party is sufficient for voting with information and interest to go up markedly. While in men the difference is 22 per cent, in women it is 32.8 per cent between those who do not identify and those who identify themselves with a party somewhat closely. There is a uniform strong relationship of party identification with participation both in men and women. In fact, in women it is a little stronger than in men.

Individualisation in the voting decision is conducive to the growth of citizenship and responsible participation. In both the genders, the maximum number of active voters is from those who believe voting with the community to be unimportant. They are the people who are for more individualisation in voting and they form the most numerous response category in both sexes, forming 57.1 per cent of males and 42.2 per cent of females.

Again, those with no opinion are more among females and only a few of them are active voters (19.2 per cent of females and 29.7 per cent of males) A little less than half of those who do not have an opinion are non-voters. Among women, while the maximum active participants are from those who are for individualisation in voting, the passive participants are mainly from the other response category—those who endorse the importance of voting with the community. These women are guided by consideration of conformity, though such women are less in number than those who feel it is unimportant.

AWARENESS OF ISSUES AND PARTICIPATION

While group orientation and political mobilisation do motivate some people to vote, quite a few are motivated by their own understanding of issues thrown up during the elections. Both in men and women, the rates of political participation go up with awareness of issues (such as: what is the elector's view on the stability of a government formed by several parties; which national leader can solve the problem of rising prices; who can solve the question of law and order, corruption, etc.). Those having lesser awareness tend to be either non-voters or passive voters. There is, however, an important difference. While in general, voting goes up with greater awareness of issues, in men there is also less of passive voting, but in women initially only passive voting increases with a fall in non-voting. Women tend to utilise opportunities of politicisation more efficiently than men once they cross the structural barriers to their participation.

The awareness of electoral issues is expected to be related with education. That is, among literate men and women, the awareness of issues is likely to be greater and hence the impact of awareness will be more among the literate than among the illiterate. Relationship of participation and opinionation has, therefore, to be seen by 'controlling' education to find out whether the impact of participation is due to literacy or is independent of literacy. An examination indicated that both in men and women, opinionation has a greater effect on literates, while with illiterates a similar relationship with nature of participation is also equally visible but in a muted fashion. The likelihood of illiterate women developing awareness is low. However, if they are aware of political issues, they tend to be more active than literate men and women who are unaware of these issues.

MEMBERSHIP OF VOLUNTARY ORGANISATIONS

There is a difference of about 13 per cent in organisational affiliation between men and women. Men invariably more often seek membership of voluntary associations than women. But then the overall socio-economic status of men is higher than that of women which leads to greater electoral participation. An interesting question, therefore, is whether women who are already electorally active are equally prone to join voluntary organisations as the men or are they less inclined to utilise their electoral participation to enhance their role as citizens in public life. The differences in men and women in the degree of participation and voluntary affiliation shows that the relationship between electoral participation and membership of voluntary organisations is stronger in women than in men. For instance, in active participation, within men the difference is 23.8 per cent as contrasted with 32.5 per cent in women. This means that women, once out of the shell of the traditional role, utilise political inputs more effectively than men for participation in public life.

The sense of political efficacy is a subjective feeling of competence and understanding of happenings in the political arena and a feeling that the individual, if desirous, can affect the decision making process. Such political efficacy has been found to be positively related with electoral participation. Marginal distributions show that men have a greater sense of efficacy in politics than women. This is in keeping with the higher rates of voting and participation among men.

While active participation is related with a sense of efficacy among women, a 'little' sense of efficacy is associated more strongly with active participation than among men. Those feeling non-efficacious are either non-voters or passive voters. The differences between those who are highly efficacious and those who are non-efficacious indicate that the impact of participation in generating a 'high' sense of efficacy is similar in both men and women—those who are active participants are most likely to feel highly efficacious among both men and women. Organisational affiliation and sense of efficacy are expected to be related to education.

DEGREE OF PARTICIPATION

Available data affirms the finding that because of their higher socio-economic status, especially with higher rates of literacy, men tend to be more active in politics than women, whereas women suffering from a dual handicap of confinement to a traditional role within the family and kin-group and of literacy, are less participative in politics. At another level, the data suggests that women, once they cross the formidable barrier of literacy, are unable to transcend the limitations of their traditional social role and tend to participate almost equally, if not more actively, in politics. Further, they use their experience of electoral participation a little more effectively than men in achieving a higher sense of political efficacy and a tendency to join voluntary associations. In so far as women, including the illiterate ones and those belonging to the lower socio-economic status (the tribals, Harijans, the landless) are concerned, they can use political participation for improving their social status collectively. Thus, political participation has a dual role for women: firstly, to collectively elevate their social status and secondly, to help them acquire effective citizenship.

PROGRESS AND FUTURE THRUST

Women, who are nearly half the population, suffer from many social and economic disadvantages. Culturally also, their roles are ill-defined for public participation. However, universal adult franchise has allowed them to participate in politics ever since the first general elections of 1952, and women have generally been increasing their participation over the years, though still not as much as men. This has been no mean achievement given their low level of literacy leading to limited participation in other spheres of activity in society.

Detailed examination of participation shows that to a great extent women have been able to outgrow these structural constraints even when in the immediate political and social contexts, no significant women-related issue has been thrown up over the years. In this sense, woman power has remained largely under-mobilised in India by the polity in general and by the political parties in particular. Whatever political mobilisation has taken place lately has been through the mainstream of politics. Thus, there is greater possibility of collectivisation and articulation of their demands in Indian politics.

Although constitutionally women enjoy equal political status with men, in reality women have not had many elected positions proportionate to their number in society. A 33 per cent reservation has been made in all elected bodies. The policy of reservation, though seeming to ameliorate the situation in the short run, may very well turn out to be counter-productive in the long run. A policy of positive discrimination may prove to be counter-productive to the process of conscientising the people of inequalities and may hide the reality of discrimination. It may also give rise to a particular class of women, through whose co-operation the leadership of the movement may be alienated from the masses and from the real issues affecting them. Besides, the very nature of reservation with its patronising undertones may harm the individual's own sense of autonomy and dignity.

Instead, although slow and arduous, the process of electoral participation, issue-oriented protests and larger movement may prove to be a more effective means for launching the second battle (universal franchise being the first) for political equality and effective citizenship for Indian women.

—oo(O)oo—

23

HEALTH STATUS OF WOMEN

INDIAN planners have always accepted health as an important area for women's development. The First Five Year Plan recognised the need for adequate services for women's welfare to 'enable women to play their legitimate role in the family and the community' and also recognised high infant and maternal mortality as major problems to be solved through the provision of maternity and child health services (MCH) and family planning.

Reviewing the status of women's health after several Five Year Plans, several persistent problems which were responsible for women's lower health status were identified. In order of priority, these were:

1. Malnutrition—caused by poverty, over-work, repeated pregnancies and the "result of her dependence and lower educational and social position;
2. High gender differentials in access to health care services, even when available;
3. Inadequate development of primary health care and preventive health services, particularly in rural areas;
4. Inadequate development of maternity and child health services; and
5. Poor availability of women health personnel, especially in rural areas.

The development of family planning as a major thrust in Government policy from the Third Five Year Plan had been expected to improve the health status of women radically but it was felt that women's access to such services depended more on the overall status that they enjoyed within the family and the community. While commending the developments in the field of family planning and the legislation liberalising abortions, it was observed that inadequate development in public health services, especially MCH services, through over-concentration on the provision of contraceptive services, had created an imbalance and defeated the objectives of the population policy. Integration of contraceptive services with MCH, nutrition and programmes for the improvement of the life expectancy of children and mothers could help the success of the population policy.

Other problems identified were regional imbalances in the provision of various services, the alienation and status barrier that separated medical personnel—both men and women—from poor women and the absence of adequate data on women's morbidity and access to health services of different types. In the absence of specific studies on women's health, demographic trends were used as an indicator of women's health and used whatever data was available was used with regard to provision and utilisation of health care services.

DEMOGRAPHIC TRENDS

The major demographic trends used as indicators of the health status of women are the sex ratio in the population, life expectancy and mortality rates, fertility and infant mortality rates, maternal mortality and female morbidity patterns. The analysis, however, related these to women's status in economic participation, literacy, education, nutrition, migration, etc.

Concern was expressed at the steadily declining trend in this ratio for over a 100-year period. Announcing the provisional results of the 1981 Census, the Registrar-General observed that one of the most positive findings of the Census was the improvement in the sex ratio at the national level for the first time in a hundred years.

There has been a steady decline in the overall death rate from 16.1 per thousand population in 1970-71 to 9.1 per thousand population in 2000-2001. This makes an impact on the life expectancy of the population. The following table presents decadal variations in the life expectancy of men and women in the last three decades. While the gender differential in life expectancy continues, there has been a reduction in the difference between male and female life expectancy between the quinquenniums 1971-1975 to 1976-1981. The crude death rate in 2001 was 9 per thousand people.

Expectation of Life at Birth 1951-2000

Year	Male	Female	Difference in Life Expectancy
1951-61	41.9	40.6	1.3
1961-71	46.4	44.7	1.7
1971-75	50.1	48.8	1.3
1976-81	52.6	51.6	1
1997	62.1	62.7	–
2000	6.4 (overall)	61-8	–

There has been a general reduction in female mortality as well as the gender differential in the death rate in both rural and urban areas. The significant variations, however, come in the appearance of a gender differential adverse to females in the 0-4 and 10-14 age groups in urban areas, where none existed before. The second significant difference is in the rise in both male and female death rates in the age groups 50-59, 65-69 and 70+. In the 60-64 age group, while there has been a reduction in the male death rate, the female death rate increased from 28 to 30.1. In comparison, in rural areas there has been a substantial reduction in the death rate of both sexes in the 0-4 age group from 55.3 to 48.9 in the case of males and 61.0 to 57.9 in the case of females. This also shows a reduction in the gender differential. In all other age groups, there has been a reduction in the death rate, mostly for both the sexes but in some cases only for females.

It is generally assumed that the health status of women is always worse in the rural than in urban areas and the neglect of female infants is also higher in rural areas because of ignorance, superstition and anti-daughter bias. However, available data indicates that in the 5-9, 10-14 and 15-19 age groups, more girls died per day for every thousand boys in urban areas than in the rural areas. In the reproductive age groups (20-24 and 25-29), however, the ratio is higher in rural areas. In the 30-34 age group, the rural-urban differential becomes negligible. In the next two age groups (35-39 and 40-44), urban women have an edge over their rural sisters, which they lose in the 45-49 and 50-54 age groups. In the 55-59 and 65-69 age groups again, urban women appear to be doing better but in the 60-64 age group and the 70+ age group, they lose this advantage.

In fact, it appears that women over 70 in rural areas have a substantially higher chance of survival than their counterparts in urban areas. Considering the fact that the total death rate for all persons in rural areas was 15.3 as against 9.4 for urban areas, the near parity in the sex ratio between rural and urban areas raises serious issues regarding the health status of women in urban areas.

INFANT MORTALITY

Between 1970 and 2001, while the combined infant mortality rate declined from 129 to 67, in rural areas it declined from 136 to 124 and in urban areas from 90 to 65. Data on infant mortality rates by sex in rural and urban areas from 1970 to 2001 shows that the female infant mortality rate increased in rural areas from 134 in 1970 to 142 in 2001. The increase was extremely sharp in 1972 (161) since when it has declined gradually. During the same period, the male infant mortality rate in rural areas increased from 138 in 1970 to 141 in 1972 and declined to 131 in 2001. In urban areas, the female infant mortality rate (85) was lower than the male rate (94) in 1970. In 1972 the two were at par at 85.

From 1973, however, the female infant mortality rate in urban areas has been higher than that of the male. While the male rate has declined from 88 in 1973 to 64 in 2001, the female rate has come down from 90 to 71. In rural areas, the sex ratio (female deaths per thousand male deaths) increased from 971 in 1970 to 1044 in 2001. In the urban areas, the ratio increased from 904 in 1970 to 1029 in 1979. The highest figure in rural areas was in 1972 (1142) while in the urban areas it was in 1976 (1050). The reduction in infant mortality does not seem to have resulted in any improvement in the health status of female infants. In 2001, the infant mortality rate was 67 per 1000 live births. Children dying before the age of 5 were 98 per 1000 live births and the maternal mortality rate was 41 per 1000 live births.

Data on selected indicators of infant mortality by socio-economic groups for 2001 suggests that far greater investigation is needed before we can generalise about the causes of infant mortality. Any assumption that higher infant mortality goes with a particular region is demolished by the difference seen between rural and urban areas in this sphere. An assumption that the infant mortality rate has an inverse relationship with the educational level also cannot be maintained.

The educational level is an index of economic position as well. Illiteracy and lower educational level is usually the lot of poor women. The higher infant mortality rate with a lower educational level should not, therefore, be interpreted as a consequence only of lack of education since it is in most cases the result of malnutrition and lack of care of the mother and child. Infant mortality because of the mother's age at marriage is the only sound index for an analysis of infant mortality. The lower the age of motherhood, the higher seems to be the mortality rate in both rural and urban infants.

Within infant mortality, neo-natal mortality (death of infants of less than 28 days) is considered to be directly a consequence of the mother's health. The percentage of neo-natal deaths to total infant deaths has registered some increase over the period 1970 to 2001—in rural areas from 53 to 62. In urban areas, the increase was from 51 in 1970 to 61 in 1976, and a decline since then to 51 in 1978.

The rate of peri-natal deaths (infant deaths within seven days of birth) per thousand live births has also registered a sharp increase from 28 in 1970 to 52 in 1978 in rural areas and from 20 to 23 in urban areas.

These statistics should cause grave concern with regard to the health status of mothers and infants. They also point to the necessity of concentrated effort to improve the health of mothers as the most important strategy to ensure the survival of infants. In the absence of any data by which women's access to nutrition can be assessed, the data on maternal and infant mortality provides the most telling indicators of increased malnutrition among a large section of women in the reproductive age group.

According to the Census of 2001, the mean age of marriage for males and females during the decade rose to 24.1 and 18.9, respectively, from 22.2 and 17.2 during 1961-1971.

The 2001 Census revealed a decline in the percentage of population in the age groups below 10 from 14.5 in 1971 to 12.4 in 2001. In spite of this reduction, the "young structure of the population holds the potential for rapid population growth in future years unless special measures for more accelerated reduction in fertility are taken." These special measures are primarily in the field of socio-economic development, poverty alleviation and the development of health programmes including family welfare which means provision of contraceptive devices. A variation in the birth rate is seen also because of the availability/non-availability of some basic facilities in rural areas.

ACCESS TO HEALTH CARE SERVICES

To improve women's access to health services and the level of the knowledge and awareness of women's health needs within the health establishment, along with expansion of general facilities, a separate and visible thrust for provision of MCH services was recommended. The specific measures recommended to correct neglect of this branch of health care and to deepen its functions were:

1. Separation of MCH budget from the general health budget—for better administrative supervision, increased allocation and adequate provision of personnel;

2. Separation of the MCH unit at the PHC level to "limit the clientele to women and children and make the services more accessible to these weaker groups," to "co-ordinate nutrition and immunisation measures" under the Integrated Child Development Services (ICDS) Programme and to collect fertility and morbidity statistics for women and children; and

3. Establishment of a health statistics section at the district level to collate and evaluate the data.

Health services for women also include ante-natal care of expectant and post-natal care of nursing mothers. A study by the Planning Commission revealed that about 59 per cent of the pregnant women had no routine check up—about 23 per cent had two check ups and the remaining 18 per cent three or four. The percentage of pregnant women who had no check up at all was the highest among the Scheduled Tribes (77 per cent) and lowest (52 per cent) among "others". The study also showed that only 27 per cent of pregnant women in the selected *anganwadi* areas had received any health check up. Only about 25 per cent of the pregnant women were provided with treatment for specific disorders during their course of pregnancy. Also, 18.5 per cent of the total pregnant women received treatment for obstetric complaints and 7 per cent of pregnant women received immunisation against tetanus during the repeat survey as compared to only 7.5 per cent at the base line (1976).

NUTRITION INTERVENTION

The Sixth Five Year Plan initiated a new approach to the problem of nutrition among women. In previous plans, women had been viewed as targets for only health, education and welfare services. For the first time, the Plan Document included a chapter on Women and Development and acknowledged women's need for employment and economic independence. While the basic approach of the plan was to accept the family as the unit of development, special attention was given to the most vulnerable members.

> "The most vulnerable members may change from family to family and within the family from time to time. But for some time in the future, women will continue to be one of the most vulnerable members of the family. Hence, the economic emancipation of the family with special attention to women, education of children and family planning will constitute the three major operational aspects of the family-centred poverty alleviation strategy... The long term approach to solving

> the problem of malnutrition in women would be to generate employment among them as it would provide better purchasing power to women, which will have an impact on her as well as her family's nutritional status. Along with this, basic services like health, creche-cum-*balwadis* (child care centres), etc. would be provided to enable their employment retention. Till the long-term programme effectively builds up, nutrition intervention to most vulnerable groups of women, namely, pregnant and nursing mothers from the weakest sections of society would continue to get nutrition supplement under the Supplementary Nutrition Programme. Education will also be imparted on the production and consumption of nutritious food and on the adoption of small horticultural remedies involving kitchen gardening for the major nutritional maladies of the large block."

The evaluation report made by the Planning Commission on the ICDS Programme showed that though the percentage coverage of pregnant women and nursing mothers by Supplementary Nutrition had gone up at the time of the repeat survey (1977-1998) as compared to the Baseline Survey (1976), 70 and 62 per cent, respectively, of the eligible women yet remained to be covered. About 30 per cent of the pregnant women and 37 per cent of the lactating mothers benefited from the Supplementary Nutrition Programme. The coverage of pregnant women is the highest in the case of the Scheduled Tribes and lowest in the communities grouped as "others".

The average coverage of pregnant and lactating mothers in the rural project did not record much increase (only from 18 to 20); in the Tribal Project it increased from 13 to 18. The Urban Project, however, showed a large increase—from 3 to 24.

Health and nutrition education to expectant women, nursing mothers and all the other women in the age group 15-44 years was one of the important objectives of the ICDS to lay the foundation for proper psychological, physical and social development of the child. But the same study conducted by the Planning Commission showed that "the coverage of health and nutrition education programmes was weakest, being only 13 per cent in case of women other than pregnant ones and lactating mothers"—about 41 per cent in the case of pregnant women and 36.4 per cent for lactating mothers. Rural *anganwadis* have done much better that tribal ones.

IMPACT OF FAMILY PLANNING PROGRAMME

An increase in the number of the family planning acceptors has been indicated and births averted in consequence. There has been a reduction of dependence on sterilisations from the peak figure of 65.9 per cent in 1976-1977 to 28.2 per cent in 2001-2002. It is significant that the percentage of tubectomy to total sterilisations has shown an extremely interesting trend. In the earlier years, that is, up to 1959, they made up the major share of sterilisations. During the period 1960 to 1975-1976, except for a variation between 1972-1973 and 1974-1975, the percentage of tubectomies constituted less than 35 per cent of the total sterilisations. In 1977-1978, this proportion jumped to 80.2 per cent even though the number of sterilisations declined very sharply during that year from 8.26 million in the previous year to less than 0.94 million. Of these, as high as 0.76 million were tubectomies. In 2001, the Couple Protection Rate was 46.2 per cent or 74.2 million persons and MTPs totalled 6.14 lakh.

A close interplay was noted between the issue of population growth, developmental trends and problems of women's status. It was found that an improvement in women's status through education, employment, access to health services and increased age of marriage had a direct impact on their fertility behaviour. Some studies in the acceptability of family planning had arrived at the conclusion that women's education or employment often influenced their decision to accept contraceptive services. It was, however, felt that establishing such a one-to-one co-relationship between education or employment overlooked the overwhelming influence of the economic factor and the class position of the women. The most employed women in the country were the poorest, assetless labourers who often found it impossible to obtain access to contraceptive services. The access to education, particularly higher levels of education, was also by and large an indication of their higher class position. It was also felt that decisions regarding contraception and fertility behaviour were the result of a composite set of factors which affected the overall status of women within the family and the community.

MAJOR BREAKTHROUGH

A major breakthrough during the decade has been the growing recognition among some population experts of this interlinkage between women's status and population and development trends leading to a suggestion that for any breakthrough on the population front there has to be "an all out assault on the transformation of women from productive workers to reproductive machines." The Working Group on National Population Policy (1977-78) came to the conclusion that one of the new strategies that needed to be added to the existing population measures was improvement in the status of women. The Draft Sixth Five Year Plan (1978-1983) acknowledged the interlinkage between these two issues.

> "No worthwhile population policy can succeed if it does not focus on change in the economic conditions and social status of women...It is after all the women who have to bear the brunt not only of bearing children but also of rearing them...An integral part of the national population policy should be measures to improve the status of women. It is generally accepted that low female participation in work is a barrier to changing their values about family norms, but it may not be true to assume that high female participation in work by itself will change the economic conditions of women. A large number of Indian rural women work for long hours. This impairs their health but not their fertility rate. A change in their social and dependency conditions is necessary to improve women's position in society and their attitude to family norms...The experience of Kerala and Gujarat proves, however, that women's role is crucial in changing fertility rates and attitudes to family norms."

In the way of specific measures, the Draft Plan recommended increasing the age of marriage through better enforcement of :

1. Child Marriage Restraint Act and introduction of registration of marriage;

2. Direct involvement of women in the family planning programme through their own organisations like Mahila Mandals; and

3. Measures to improve women's employment opportunities and status and particularly directing adult education programmes towards women.

The Sixth Five Year Plan (1980-1985) maintains this approach:

> "The family planning programme has to be re-activised by education and persuasion of people, avoiding any form of coercion. The small family norm has to be built into the social and cultural ethos of the people. A multi-pronged but integrated approach comprising education and employment, particularly of women; eradication of poverty; maternal and child care services including immunising, prophylaxis and nutrition; and building up of health care facilities in the rural areas with due attention to control over communicable diseases, promotion and preventive health, water supply, sanitation, etc. is called for."

MAIN DRAWBACKS

In the chapter on Women and Development, which appeared for the first time in India's planning history in 1980, the main drawbacks in women's development were identified as:

1. Preoccupation with repeated pregnancies;

2. Physical workload;

3. Lack of education; and

4. Lack of independent economic status.

The strategy for women's development, therefore, has to be three-fold:

1. Promotion of economic independence;
2. Education; and
3. Family planning.

This three-fold strategy, it is expected, would help to overcome the negative demographic features, namely, excess child mortality, declining sex ratio and low rate of literacy, particularly of women.

The chapter on Health, Family Planning and Nutrition states:

> "The family planning programme has to be made a part of the total national effort for providing a better life to the people. The Plan seeks to make a massive attack on the problem of unemployment and poverty through specific programmes directed towards target groups such as the small and marginal farmers, rural artisans, landless labourers, women, Scheduled Castes and Scheduled Tribes...Economic emancipation will enable children from poor families to attend school to receive adequate education and develop into useful citizens. Special attention will be paid to the education and employment of women to liberate them from dependence and insecurity and improve their social status."

The implication of this demographic profile is that the birth rate is likely to show rising trends even if the age specific fertility rate remains static. An effective strategy for fertility control is, therefore, necessary if the long-term population goal is to be achieved. Social pressures have to be built up against early marriages and large-size families and women's organisations are identified as having an important role to play in this context.

Some population experts have pointed out that the great divide of the 20s age-group is characterised by certain significant demographic trends. Women's economic participation rate began to decline from the same decade. In fact, the changes in the sex ratio in the population and the sex ratio among workers follow a somewhat similar trend. A close connection was inferred from this between the decline in women's economic opportunities and the increase in the number of women who were victims of poverty and malnutrition and consequently the higher female death rate.

LONG TERM EFFECT

It will be useful to study the long-term effect of health measures on the life of the people. For this purpose, six decades were chosen ending 1981 as, according to demographers, the census data from 1921 onwards are amenable to long-term analysis, earlier censuses not being very accurate. Moreover, only since 1921 has there been a steady growth in population as a result of improvement and extension of health services, particularly after the country achieved independence.

It can be seen that the rise in population is mainly the result of the dramatic decline in death rates which fell by more than two-thirds during this period. As against this, the birth rate in six decades fell by even less than one fourth. The impact of such major demographic changes has, however, been adverse to women. Thus, while the sex ratio in the population has changed only marginally (a little over two per cent), the sex ratio for workers has fallen by almost one half. This is more clearly brought out by an almost 60 per cent decline in the work participation rate of women.

The decade 1971-1981 had thus registered several shifts in demographic trends that had followed a pattern over several decades.

1. The acceleration in the population growth rate witnessed in 1921 has been arrested; and
2. The implied trend in fertility is one of decline.

There has been a universal decline in the fertility rate in both urban and rural areas and in all age groups between 15-49. Total marital fertility rates for rural areas declined from 6.8 in 1972 to 5.2 in 1998 and for urban areas from 6 to 4.1. The distribution of births by birth order also showed a reduction in the percentage of higher order births both in rural and urban areas. Between 1972 and 1998, the percentage of births of order four and above declined from 47 to 35.2 in the rural areas and from 44 to 31 in urban areas.

Two other shifts observed in the demographic trends were:

1. Relative improvement in the sex ratio in favour of women and in female expectancy of life at birth, both of which are suggestive of the improved status of women; and

2. Relative improvement in the economic participation rate of women between 1971 and 1981.

Soon after the Bucharest Population Conference, a comprehensive policy was formulated as part of a "frontal attack" on the problem of population. In pursuance of this policy, the Minimum Age of Marriage was raised by law in 1978 to 18 years for girls and 21 for boys. There was increased emphasis, backed by financial allocation, on providing population education for all children in the middle and secondary schools. Representation to Parliament from each State was frozen up to 2001 A.D. at levels based on the 1971 population figures. This assured the States with lower population growth rates that they would not be put to any disadvantage in regard to their representation in the national Parliament. There was also a scheme for community incentives to villages and towns which achieved high levels of contraceptive protection. The policy placed particular stress on the logistics of the family planning services delivery system.

Summing up the perspectives for India's population policy, the Country Statement prepared by the Government of India for the International Conference on Population stated that

> "the grimness of the situation cannot be denied but there are hopeful signs...Fertility decline has been firmly established in many parts of the country...family planning has picked up...and there is evidence that a large measure of latent demand for improvement in the status of women and planning has accorded a special importance to upgrade the role of women in the development process."

—oo(O)oo—

24

WOMEN'S EDUCATION

CONCEPTS pertaining to the value and necessity of education from the point of view of the individual as well as society have varied from society to society in different stages of their evolution. Education is considered as a value in itself because it leads to the development of the overall personality of the individual. The Indian concept of education is that of a potential medium for attaining *Mukti* (salvation) from the trials and tribulations of life. The function of education is to widen the horizon of our experience, as our direct contact with reality is always limited. If education expands the mental horizon, it is obvious that the higher the level of education, the wider is the horizon it opens to us. Conscious of this innate value of education, society has always granted high status to the educated.

Another category comprises those who emphasise the utilitarian aspect of education to society at large for fulfilling economic, political and cultural functions necessary for socio-economic activity. This category sees education in the service of economic development and social change, thereby eliminating inequalities and ensuring social justice.

However, although learning has always been honoured in India, as evidenced from the respect accorded to the Brahmins because of their knowledge of philosophy and literature, there was inadequate motivation to learn to read and write on account of lack of reward for such learning either in social status (which was regulated by the rules of caste hierarchy) or in enhancing the earning capacity of the individual, as jobs beyond the caste profession could not be accessed.

The history of the women's liberation movement all over the world shows that, right from the beginning, the importance of women's education was recognised as the most potent agent for improving their status in society. As stated elsewhere, during the 19th century, various social reformers and liberals, took up the cause of women's education. However, the idea of motivating these reformers to break away from the then prevalent tradition was evidently the development of the personality of women. There was no idea of mobilising the women's force in the wider social context. Education is one of the biggest potential processes of modernisation for generating new forces to bring about fundamental changes in the standard of values and norms of behaviour. Besides ensuring development of the personality of the individual, education provides opportunities for acquiring economic independence. Further, education provided for upward mobility in modern society, raising the status of an individual in the family and in society at large.

During the post-independence period, the whole idea of the purpose of women's education underwent a radical change based on the belief that in a democratic society where all citizens have to discharge their civil and social obligations, differences which may lead to different standards of intellectual development in men and women cannot be envisaged. The consciousness of the indispensable necessity to equip women for taking up multiple roles of homemakers (as wives and mothers) as well as equal partners of men in all social, industrial and administrative activity is a new development.

Social, economic and industrial development can be achieved only through expansion of education. Although formal, institutionalised education may not be either fruitful or feasible, educational programmes to suit different environments and requirements must be devised, or the existing programmes adapted. Further, education must aid national development, not only by developing skills and leadership but also by preparing people for social change covering all instruments of education.

Admittedly, economic development leads to disparity in income and social status. In order to avert both these aspects, it is necessary to take up programmes that ensure economic growth coupled with social justice. Women in rural areas, especially those belonging to the backward classes and tribal areas need special attention in this regard. Strictly speaking, they need non-formal education linked with economic activity of the area, including training for the development of local handicrafts.

The problem of fulfilling the constitutional directive that enjoins upon the State "to endeavour to provide within a period of ten years from the commencement of the Constitution, free and compulsory education for all children until they complete the age of 14 years," is mainly in regard to the education of girls. This problem was examined by the National Committee on Women's Education in 1958-59, which observed that the problem of providing universal primary education in India was practically identical with that of expanding the education of girls.

Some people assert that the education of women should be differently oriented. They ignore the fact that any system of education based on the difference of sex is bound to lead to discrimination against women in the field of employment. The point to be kept in mind in this connection is their additional function of domestic responsibilities and motherhood. In quite a number of cases, women abandon their profession after marriage.

It is unarguable that no social change can be effected without the active participation of women. Jawaharlal Nehru once said: "In order to awaken the people, it is women who have to be awakened. Once they are on the move, the household moves, the village moves, the country moves." Women constitute the most important psychic factor in all cultures and civilisations. All traditions and religious beliefs, actually the whole pattern of life of a society, draw inspiration from this factor. Further, refinements of civilisation, gracious living and compassionate behaviour are all transmitted to succeeding generations through women.

In urban areas in India, women's education has made remarkable progress during the post-independence period, reducing the gap between the elementary education of boys and girls. Further, in the rural areas, education of girls in the upper middle class families has also been encouraging. However, among the low-income groups, the gap continues, partly due to certain traditional prejudices and partly because of sustained poverty.

A major part of the wasted potential of human resources in India is due to the poor economic condition of the masses. A child is willingly sent to school between the ages of 6 to 9 because, at this stage, the child is of little help at home. Later, the child becomes an economic asset as it can work at home and add to the family income.

This applies particularly to girls who can assist their over-worked mothers at home. The child is, therefore, withdrawn from school. The only solution is to improve the general economic condition of the masses. An immediate step could be providing part-time education to children so that they could earn and learn simultaneously.

Other major obstacles in the development of the girl-child's education that need to be taken in hand are: traditional prejudice against sending girls to schools, especially co-educational schools; lack of women teachers; poverty of rural parents who need the children to work at home or in the fields or outside the home and the tradition of early marriage.

The Government is aware of these problems and has taken some measures to remove them. Among them, intense educational propaganda to break the prejudice against co-education and provision of incentives to women teachers, especially in rural areas.

PRESENT SCENARIO

From the beginning of the movement for women's status, education had been identified as the major instrument for this change. With the acceptance of gender equality in the Constitution, the principle of equality of access to education for men and women was accepted by the national planners. Reviewing women's educational development till the early 1970s, though marked improvement can be found, yet several problems were identified. In order of priority, these were:

a. Illiteracy;

b. Widening gap in access to elementary education through problems of non-enrolment, wastage and dropout;

c. Imbalances in educational development; and

d. Ideological imbalances among educational planners and administrators regarding the objectives of women's education.

FEMALE LITERACY RATE

During the decade 1991 to 2001, the female literacy rate rose to 54.16 per cent. The number of literate females was 226,745,947. The highest was in Kerala (90.92 per cent), Mizoram (88.49 per cent) and Lakshadweep (87.52 per cent) and the lowest was in Bihar (47.53 per cent). To a large extent, the literacy problem is a female literacy problem and overall literacy will not improve until female literacy improves. Among major States, female literacy is still remarkably low in Chhatisgarh, Andhra Pradesh, Orissa, Madhya Pradesh, Rajasthan, Uttar Pradesh, Jharkhand and Bihar. In Jharkhand and Bihar, this figure is lower than 40 per cent. District-wise figures are not available as yet, but don't be surprised when these figures are available if the female literacy rate in some districts is lower than 10 per cent.

An analysis of illiteracy data is an important indicator of changes in women's access to the educational process and the reduction of the gender gap because it helps to prevent any attitude of complacency and identifies a new problem of a widening gender gap among the illiterate population. In the early decades of the 20th century, gender differential among illiterates was negligible since the large mass of the population was illiterate, but with the progress of education, the sex ratio among illiterates changed to 1055 women for every 1000 men in 1911 to 1138 in 1951 to 1250 in 1961 to 1248 in 1971 and 1322 in 1981 and 933 in 2001.

Recognition of this widening gap has resulted in some special efforts to increase the enrolment of women in adult education centres during the last few years. According to the Monitoring Report of the Directorate of Adult Education, the enrolment of women in adult education centres in the first quarter of 1983 showed a marked improvement over the situation reviewed in 1980 when women constituted only 35.7 per cent of the total number enrolled in such centres. The position has improved further and by the end of December 2001, the percentage coverage of adult women in these centres was 52.53 of the total coverage.

ACCESS TO ELEMENTARY EDUCATION

On the basis of estimated data for the mid-1970s, only two out of every three girls in the relevant age group (6-11) were in school in the primary stage (classes I-V) and only one out of every five in the middle stage (classes VI to VIII; age range 11-14). There has been progress in the enrolment of boys and girls of the relevant age group in the primary, middle and secondary schools.

There has also been a general rise in the proportion of enrolment in all the three age groups (or educational levels). While this is generally true, there has been a marginal decline in some cases (one to two per cent in enrolment ratios). However, a sharp fall in enrolment percentage at the primary level for girls is found in Uttar Pradesh, a major State in India. This is certainly a cause for concern.

At the all India level, the gender gap in enrolment has remained stationary in the case of the primary and middle levels. But in the case of the secondary level, a slight worsening of the situation is observed. Coming to the States, the widening of this gap is discerned in Haryana and Rajasthan at the primary level, Madhya Pradesh at the middle level and Andhra Pradesh, Madhya Pradesh and Rajasthan at the secondary level. The States where noticeable improvement has taken place are Himachal Pradesh, Maharashtra, Manipur and Tamil Nadu at the primary level; Rajasthan and Uttar Pradesh at the middle level and Bihar and Jammu & Kashmir at the secondary level.

Taking the entire intercensul period (1971-1981), it is found that more girls are in school at all levels of education in 2001 than in 1999. In other words, the gender gap as indicated by the sex ratio of children of school-going age on the one hand and enrolment on the other is narrowing down. The rate of narrowing down is, however, different in different States.

OBSTACLES

Prior to 1975, the high rate of dropout and non-enrolment of girls was generally attributed to social attitudes and early marriage that did not favour the education of girls. Some of the factors identified were involvement in labour—paid or unpaid, distance of the school and the consequent problems of security faced by girls and the absence of women teachers as concrete obstacles affecting different sections of the target groups. It was observed that except in the case of particular communities whose cultural taboos might prevent girls from going to school at the middle and secondary stage, the availability of women teachers would certainly help to improve enrolment and reduce dropouts.

The Indian Education Commission (1964-66) had reported that the rate of wastage and dropout at the lower primary stage was 62 per cent for girls as compared to 56 per cent for boys. A study undertaken by the National Council of Educational Research and Training (NCERT) in 1971 on the problem of wastage and stagnation in primary and middle schools reported that the rate was 71.36 per cent for girls and 62.3 per cent for boys. It was found that of every 100 girls enrolled in class I, only about 30 reached class V, that is, the last class in the primary stage.

Calculating dropout and wastage requires class-wise enrolment data which is not always available An exercise was undertaken—using the enrolment data of the 3rd and 4th Educational Surveys (1973 and 1978)—to calculate the dropout and wastage rate among children enrolled in schools during this period. Of the children enrolled in schools during this period in 1999, it was found that 65.73 per cent of girls and 56.81 per cent of boys did not reach the middle class stage and 61.77 per cent of girls and 51.01 per cent of boys did not reach the secondary stage. At the all India level, there has been a marginal reduction in the dropout/wastage rate for both boys and girls.

IMBALANCES IN EDUCATIONAL DEVELOPMENT

At the national level, while 29.65 per cent of the rural population was literate in 1981 the literacy rate in urban areas was 57.4 per cent. Except for Kerala, all the States have very high variations between rural and urban literacy. Among these, the States of Andhra Pradesh, Bihar, Jammu & Kashmir, Madhya Pradesh and Rajasthan stand out for very sharp rural-urban differentials in literacy.

The rural-urban differential is highly significant in the case of female literacy. The States of Madhya Pradesh, Rajasthan and Uttar Pradesh have a female literacy rate below 10 per cent in rural areas whereas their corresponding figure in urban areas is 34 per cent and above. In the States of Bihar, Haryana, Jammu & Kashmir, Madhya Pradesh, Orissa, Rajasthan and Uttar Pradesh, female literacy rates constituted half or less than half the male literacy rate.

Persistence of these regional imbalances in women's education has resulted in the recognition of nine States as specially backward in women's education by the Government of India. A major study to identify reasons for this backwardness was undertaken by the NCERT.

According to the Census of 1981, the literacy rate among Scheduled Castes and Tribes continued to be still substantially lower (21.38 per cent for Scheduled Castes and 16.35 per cent for Scheduled Tribes as compared to 31.22 per cent for the rest of the population). The female literacy rates in these communities are 10.93 per cent in Scheduled Castes and 3.46 in case of Scheduled Tribes. The enrolment rates in primary schools for girls of these communities are 57.8 per cent and 45.9 per cent. "The gap between educational development of Scheduled Castes and Scheduled Tribes and other communities goes on increasing as we ascend to higher stages of education and this gap is more pronounced in the case of females." Comparing the female literacy rate among Scheduled Castes and Scheduled Tribes with 1971 figures, however, it is noted that there has been a substantial improvement during the decade since the female literacy rate among the Scheduled Castes in 1971 was only 6.44 per cent and that amongst Scheduled Tribes was only 4.85 per cent.

HIGHER EDUCATION

The sex ratio in enrolment in major faculties in higher education during the decade 1970-71 and 1980-81 shows that the percentage in the faculties of arts and science education has steadily increased over the decades and stood at 782 girls for every 1000 boys in 2001. In commerce, in which women were barely represented until the beginning of the decade, their enrolment has increased rapidly to 22.8 per cent in 2001-2002. In the faculties of agriculture, veterinary science and law, women's participation was marginal in 1970-71 but there was a slight improvement over the years standing at 32 per cent in 2001. The one faculty in which the women's enrolment trend raises some concern is that of medicine but more and more women are enrolling in medical colleges now..

Along with teaching, this is the profession which women entered even before independence and the representation of women in this faculty in the post-independence period has been substantial. Not only has their enrolment not expanded adequately during the decade, but there has been a remarkable drop in the mid-1970s from which women appear to be struggling out in the 1980s. The sex ratio in medicine in 1970-71 was 296. In 1975-76, it dropped to 223 but it has registered an improvement since 1979-80. The sex ratio shows a steady improvement in the faculties of arts, science, commerce, engineering, law, etc. where women entered much later. In education, the improvement in the sex ratio indicates that within a few years women will be on a par with men. In terms of the total enrolment in higher education the sex ratio has registered a steady improvement.

Though the national policy does not advocate separate institutions at the higher education level, the increase in the number of women's colleges has continued. The number of such colleges increased steadily from 430 in 1971-1972 to 624 in 1981-1982. The States of Tamil Nadu and Andhra Pradesh also decided to establish women's universities. The other women's university in the country was the SNDT Women's University at Mumbai which was established in 1916 by a group of social reformers. The establishment of these universities, however, does not mean that women are being excluded from other institutions of higher education.

The most important problems in the field of education in India are:

1. Spread of literacy; and
2. Universalisation of elementary education.

The Sixth Plan lays emphasis on minimum essential education for all citizens, irrespective of their age, sex and residence. The highest priority has, therefore, been assigned to the programme of universalisation of elementary education for children of the age group 6-14 and literacy for adults in the age group 15-35. These programmes are included in the 20-Point Programme which had set a target date of 1990 for the realisation of these objectives.

ADULT EDUCATION PROGRAMMES

The National Adult Education Programme (NAEP) initiated on October 2, 1978, placed special emphasis on enrolling women as students, instructors and decision-makers, as women constituted more than two-thirds of the target population. A special Working Group on Adult Education Programmes for Women was appointed by the Ministry of Education in 1977-78. The group identified the urgent necessity of recognising the productive and economic roles which the large majority of adult illiterate women played in society, particularly in the case of rural women. In the Group's opinion, the adult education programme should aim to make women and men more conscious of their rights and responsibilities and laws governing women's status; assist women to improve their economic conditions through literacy and other skills; provide women access to knowledge in other areas including health, child care, family planning, etc. and "assist women to form their own groups for learning and productive activity and to strengthen their participation and voice in the development process."

The Review Committee on NAEP reported in 1980 that only 35 per cent of the population covered up to January 31 that year were women. The Committee identified certain special problems for this slow progress in women's access to this programme. These were—resistance among men and the community, lack of time and energy among poor women, difficulties in finding common time for men and women to attend classes, inadequate number of women instructors and supervisors and absence of child care facilities. The Committee recommended more meaningful efforts to relate educational content to the characteristics and need of the women's groups, provision of child care facilities with each adult education centre for women and organising classes during and as a part of women's working time by reorganising work schedules of government, development agencies and other employers in the organised and semi-organised sectors. The Committee also advised stronger efforts to involve women and women's institutions (schools, colleges, etc.) in the programme and the promotion of grassroot level women's organisations (Mahila Mandals) along with education centres.

According to a report up to December, 2001 total enrolment under Adult Education was 62.21 lakh, out of which 29.13 lakh were men and 33.08 lakh were women, coverage of women being 53.22 per cent of the total. In addition, 7.21 lakh were covered under the Functional Literacy for Adult Women (FLAW) programme for literacy learning.

It may be noted that the second National Conference on Women's Studies (Thiruvananthapuram, April 1984) adopted a resolution that female illiteracy should be reduced to 50 per cent by the end of the Seventh Five Year Plan and to zero per cent by the year 2000 and called on the Government, voluntary organisations and educational institutions to harness all their resources into a massive movement for this purpose. The ground reality today is totally different.

To encourage voluntary organisations working in the field of Adult Education to run adult education centres exclusively for women, the Government of India has liberalised grants-in-aid rules and has given them enhanced grants.

SPECIAL AWARDS

A scheme of special awards was introduced by the Government of India to promote adult literacy among women in the 15-35 age group. There are three categories of awards for adult education centres—District, State and Union Territories—level awards. To encourage competition among equals for the State level award, the States have been grouped in four categories:

a. Those with a female literacy rate up to 16 per cent;

b. Those between 20 to 26 per cent;

c. Those between 27 to 37 per cent; and

d. Those above 32 per cent.

In each of these categories, the State which has shown the best performance was awarded a prize of Rs. 25 lakh during the year.

SCHOOL ENROLMENT

The Committee on Status of Women in India had recommended a whole package of measures to increase enrolment in schools. These included provision of schools within walking distance, provision of child care centres with schools (to enable older sisters—who are denied schooling because they have to look after their siblings while their mothers are at work—to attend classes), abolition of single-teacher schools and provision of women teachers in all schools, free education up to the end of the secondary stage for girls and the launching of an active propaganda campaign to persuade the community of the value and importance of education of girls. It had also recommended several incentives in the way of midday meals, free uniforms, scholarships/ stipends and enrolment awards.

According to the Fourth All-India Educational Survey (1978), in the country as a whole, 77.31 per cent and 93.05 per cent of the habitations with a population of 300 or more served by primary schools within the habitation or within a distance of one kilometre, respectively and 66.94 per cent and 90.05 per cent of habitations with a population of 300 or more, predominantly of Scheduled Castes, were served within the habitation or within a distance of one kilometre. For habitations predominantly populated by Scheduled Tribes, the corresponding percentages were 76.78 and 90.84. The Ministry of Education reports efforts to cover the rest of the habitations with primary schools within one kilometre and middle schools within three kilometres.

As regards the provision of child care centres along with schools, the debate took an unexpected trend. Administrative agencies concerned with child welfare regarded child care centres as a child welfare measure. Labour welfare agencies claimed that since most labour laws demand provision of creches as an essential protective measure for women workers, it is a labour welfare measure. The demand for child care facilities to be attached to educational and training institutions as an essential measure for women's development has come from women's rights groups.

While at the policy level, there is no disagreement on the importance and the validity of this measure both as an instrument for women's development and as an essential measure for the protection and welfare of children, the problem has been in finding the implementing agencies. Educational administrators appear to be reluctant to accept this additional responsibility and state that it should be the responsibility of social welfare and/or voluntary agencies. At the National Conference on Women and Development (May 1979), these differences provoked sharp debate in the Working Group on Education with educational administrators from States pleading that it would be difficult for them to implement this measure.

CHILDHOOD EDUCATION CENTRES

For the first time, the Sixth Five Year Plan included setting up of early childhood education centres as adjuncts of primary schools. The centres would provide for educational development of this age group and also creche facilities to enable girls to attend schools by leaving their younger siblings in such centres. The Ministry of Education formulated a scheme of financial assistance to voluntary organisations for running these centres as adjuncts of primary or middle schools run either by the government, local body or private management in the nine educationally backward States.

The National Plan of Action for Women stated that in all two-teacher schools, at least one teacher should be a woman. The Plan also suggested recruitment or posting of husband-wife teams and the use of locally-educated women wherever possible. The data available on this issue is the Fourth Educational Survey, according to which 34.74 per cent of primary schools in the country were still under single teachers. The Ministry of Education suggested to the States that they should either convert all single-teacher schools into two-teacher ones or provide an additional teacher as a leave reserve for a cluster of 3-4 schools. Efforts are being made to recruit women teachers from the local population. Since 1983-1984, the Government of India has sponsored a new scheme of financial assistance for appointment of women teachers in primary schools for the nine educationally backward States. The assistance is given on an 80:20 Centre-State sharing basis. Assistance for 2,000 such teachers was sanctioned. It may be noted that the objective of the scheme is "to increase the enrolment of girls."

An increase was seen in the proportion of women teachers at the primary, middle and secondary levels. While the percentage of women teachers at the primary level declined to 20.7 per cent in 1970-1971, it had increased to 25 per cent in 1980-1981. At the middle level, the peak was reached in 1965-1966. There was a drop in 1970-1971 and then a gradual increase to 30.3 per cent. At the secondary level, the peak was reached in 1965-1966, followed by a sharp decline in 1970-1971 and a slight improvement since that year. In 2000-2001, it stood at 37.4 per cent.

A Statewise picture in percentage distribution of women teachers at different school stages of school education obtained from the Fourth All India Educational Survey shows that there has been a reduction in the percentage of women teachers between 1978 when the survey was conducted and 1980-1981 from 27.37 per cent to 25 per cent, whereas there has been an improvement at the middle and secondary stages from 27.76 per cent to 30.3 per cent and from 24.57 per cent to 28.3 per cent, respectively.

Education in the elementary stage, that is, classes I to VIII, is free in all government, local body and aided schools in all the States and Union Territories except in Uttar Pradesh where there is positive discrimination. Girls' education has been made free up to class VII but boys' education is free only up to class VI. Sixteen States and three Union Territories have enacted legislation making primary education compulsory. However, the Government of India recognises that the penal provisions of these enactments cannot be enforced immediately.

All these recommendations were built into the National Plan of Action for Women. The Sixth Five Year Plan incorporated these measures. The mid-term appraisal stated that school-going girls were being provided incentives like uniform, free text books, stationery and attendance scholarships. These are programmes in the State sector and data on implementation is inadequate. According to data supplied by the Ministry of Education, the coverage under this programme was 136.48 lakh in free books and stationery, 88.97 lakh in free uniforms, 1.16 lakh in attendance scholarships and 179.81 lakh in mid-day meals. However, gender-wise beneficiary data is not available. To promote enrolment of girls at the primary stage, incentive awards have been instituted by the Government of India. There are five categories of awards, that is, Panchayat, Community Development Block, Tribal Development Block, District and State/UT level awards. In addition, three State level awards have been set apart for nine educationally backward States for promoting enrolment of girls through non-formal education. An allocation of Rs. 70 million has been made for this scheme.

NON-FORMAL EDUCATION

The ongoing centrally sponsored scheme of non-formal education for girls in the 6-14 age group who failed to enter school was liberalised during 1983-1984. Financial assistance is now provided to the nine educationally backward States on a 90:10 sharing basis for establishment of these centres. Seven States were sanctioned assistance for establishing 10,000 such centres. It may be noted that the National Committee on Women's Education which submitted its report in 1959 and had recommended a scheme of special central assistance to States to speed up progress in girls' education, had also recommended the appointment of special officers as Joint Directors for promotion of women's education in the States.

As a result of these measures, a sudden spurt in the progress of women's education was noticed in many areas of the country during the late 1960s. It was agreed that without special assistance from the Centre it would be difficult to expect much improvement by the States as their resources were fully committed. The schemes of special assistance to the nine educationally backward States for various measures to promote girls' education is thus a resumption of an earlier strategy. It is also an acknowledgement of the strategy recommended by various working groups as well as non-official organisations that unless funds for women's development were earmarked within the overall sectoral allocations, the chances of women's developmental needs receiving adequate attention from the States would be meagre as there were also competing priorities and pressures on State administrations. The principle of earmarking was not accepted in the initial period of the Sixth Five Year Plan but mid-term appraisals and the recommendations of the Parliamentary Consultative Committee on Education resulted in this positive change in government strategy.

THREE MAJOR THRUSTS

During the decade, the need for the transformation of content and quality has developed into three major thrusts:

1. Review of school text books to remove sexist bias, developing at the same time approaches to promoting the value of equality through school curricula;
2. Orientation of teachers to promote gender equality through their teaching; and
3. Increasing the coverage of women and women's issues in the research and teaching activities of higher education.

The NCERT sponsored a few studies to identify sexist bias in school text books and began a round of seminars across the country to identify "values commensurate within the status of women" for incorporation in school text books. The national seminar which took place at the end of several regional seminars identified the following objectives in the light of which school text books should be reviewed and new literature produced to reflect these values:

1. In the educational system, areas of home management should be promoted as a joint responsibility of all the members.
2. Dignity of labour must find reflection while taking care of the roles performed so that men and women develop respect for the roles performed inside and outside the house.
3. Dependence of girls and women as a traditional value must be rejected, from which it follows that emphasis has to be laid on equal commitment for work at home and outside by both the sexes.
4. Equality of opportunity in all walks of life must lead to the realisation of the responsibility for equal participation in the development of the nation.
5. Women should become conscious of their rights and abilities.
6. Decision-making process at all levels from family to society being shared by both sexes must be emphasised.
7. Women should not be projected as sex symbols and the dignity of persons is to be promoted so that women become

self-reliant, self-propelled and self-directed instead of being continuously protected.

The seminar also gave some specific directions for revising text-books in social studies, science and languages.

Following these seminars, the NCERT produced a series of teachers' hand books for improving the curricula. The NCERT's Women's Education Unit has evolved a methodology for removing sexist bias in existing text books. It may be noted, however, that school curriculum and production of text books is a State subject. Except in areas where text books published by the NCERT have been adopted, a very large number of text books used in different languages in different States has yet to be reviewed from this perspective and sexist bias continues in a large number of text books. The NCERT has also initiated orientation of teacher trainers from this perspective since 1982. Over 120 trainers at the elementary stage and 130 at the secondary and higher secondary stage received this orientation.

WOMEN'S STUDIES

The year 1975 was celebrated by many agencies with special programmes of publications or seminars on women's issues. The Indian Council of Social Science Research (ICSSR) decided (a) to publish a summary of the CSWI's report with a view to reaching a wider reading public; and (b) to publish a series of volumes using selected papers from the studies commissioned for the CSWI. For this purpose, the ICSSR sponsored a long-term research programme on Women's Studies which developed rapidly under the guidance of an Advisory Committee of eminent social scientists, jurists and civil servants in charge of policies for women with the Government of India. The objectives of the programme of women's studies were as follows:

1. To improve policies for women's socio-economic development;

2. To increase public consciousness and revive the debate on women's problems; and

3. To develop new perspectives in the social sciences—

through examining basic assumptions, methodological approaches and concepts, for example, the family household, women's work, productivity, economic activity, etc.—to remedy the neglect and under-assessment of women's contribution to society.

The SNDT Women's University at Mumbai established a research unit on women's studies in 1974. Forty-one universities, eight advanced centres of research and nine institutions of national importance reported that they had undertaken research on women. Such studies included 181 projects and 57 doctoral dissertations, indicating a marked increase in research interest in women since before 1975. In the period since 1980, three out of seven central universities and at least 10 of the State universities had initiated some activities in research and teaching on women. In 1983, the University Grants Commission (UGC) requested Vice-Chancellors of all universities to consider ways of integrating women's issues and concerns in the teaching and research programmes of different disciplines. The Commission invited proposals for restructuring of courses, curriculum development, research projects and extension type of activities. An advisory committee had also been formed to examine such proposals.

Side by side with the efforts to develop institutional bases for women's studies within the higher education system, there has been a growing movement among a section of academic professionals to develop new perspective and conceptual approaches to the study of women's roles and problems. The startling findings and the explosion of new empirical data on women of different classes, particularly the poorer working women in rural and urban areas, has re-opened the analysis of roles and position of women, questioned earlier assumptions and the conceptual framework of previous studies. The movements for re-conceptualisation and institutionalisation of studies on women have gained momentum from the organisation of the National Conferences on Women's Studies and the formation of an Indian Association for Women's Studies.

In spite of substantial policy support, the progress of educational development for women's equality reveals the persistence of very major problems. The basic obstacles have their roots in the social structure and its values as well as deficiencies in some of the instruments created for change. The educational system has problems of its own, apart from tending to reflect the inequalities in society. Being an extremely vast and complex system, with multiple authorities responsible for different aspects and sectors of its growth and development, bringing about reforms within the system has always posed one of the most difficult challenges of nation building. The resources available for educational development have also never been adequate. While the overall structure of education has expanded enormously in the decades since independence, the share of plan allocations available for its development has shrunk.

These broad constraints of socio-cultural resistance, inadequate resources and multiplicity of authorities, however, do not complete the list of obstacles. Without a massive movement to ensure adequate attention and priority, neither the quantitative nor the qualitative transformations that are required can take place. Such a movement requires some institutionalisation of the effort within the educational machinery and the growth of public opinion in this direction.

One of the positive developments of this decade is the renewal of public concern for women's oppression and deprivation. In the development of this concern, the growth of new information through researchers and activists has made a distinct contribution. Within the agencies responsible for the implementation of educational development, however, the mechanism to respond to changes in public opinion or to harness it for bringing about positive changes has not been adequate. Even monitoring the implementation of existing policy directives has been difficult in the absence of special units within the Education Ministry or the Departments of Education in the States. The principle of earmarking resources for investment in educational programmes for women has been adopted only recently and it is not possible to evaluate its impact at this stage. However, the experience of the late Sixties suggests grounds for some hope, provided State administrations respond adequately with human and other resources.

Lastly, among the groups spearheading movements for women's rights there has not been that much emphasis on educational issues unlike the women's movement during the freedom struggle. Economic justice and the prevention of crimes of violence against women have received much greater concern from these sections during the present, new wave of women's movement. The formation of a National Committee of Women's Organisations to initiate a movement for eradication of women's illiteracy must be welcomed as a positive step in creating an appropriate social climate for tackling this major problem.

—oo(O)oo—

25

WOMEN'S RIGHT TO WORK

THROUGHOUT history, society has assigned the role of breadwinner to man and expected him to provide for himself and for his family. Woman has all along been assigned the role of a helpmate, to look after the family and contribute wherever possible, to the earnings of the family. Her role as an economic contributor to the family has varied over time and from society to society. As in other nations of the world, women's role in Indian society has not been static and has all the characteristics of a society in transition from tradition to modernity. A great majority of tribal women have been engaged in the production and marketing of their handicrafts. They still supplement the earnings of the family by working on construction sites and agricultural areas. Women of the urban middle and upper classes normally did not do paid labour at home or outside, because of the feudal concept that the status of the family depended on whether the women engaged in paid work or not.

Some supporters of women's liberation feel that the emancipation of women is closely associated with their right to work. Obviously, they referred to paid work as in agrarian societies work is more often a hardship to be borne than an income earning activity. Rural Indian women are not confined to their homes and most of them work in the fields as agricultural labour to help their menfolk. In some parts of south India, women workers actually outnumber men among agricultural labourers.

The feudal tendency to disapprove of women who do paid work outside the home has a direct bearing on the attitude towards work, especially manual labour. Manual labourers are paid very low wages despite government measures to ensure a minimum wage for them. In agricultural economies, certain jobs were traditionally performed only be men and others exclusively by women. There were only a few tasks in which both men and women participated. In justification of this division of labour, it was claimed to be the natural result of the physiological and psychic differences between men and women. However, an appraisal of the different tasks assigned to the men and women does not substantiate this contention. For example, in India as well as in Europe, farming is considered to be principally a male occupation, whereas in Africa farming is normally done by women even up to the stage of marketing their produce. In many African countries, most of the retail trade is in female hands. In India, many tribes have a similar set up, but the Hindu set up (rural as well as urban) assigns trade related activities only to men.

Another typical trait of Indian society is the custom of engaging women labour for building construction, which is rarely seen in other parts of the world. Similarly, secretarial help such as typists, stenographers, etc. is normally considered to be a female task, but in India, men outnumber women in this profession.

In these circumstances, the concept of specialisation based on the physiological and psychic differences between the sexes cannot be justified. In fact, the assignment of tasks based on gender seems to be rooted in the development of the cultural traditions of each society. In primitive times, when each family produced all the goods and services required by it, there developed a sharp distinction between male and female tasks. The fathers taught their sons to perform their jobs and mothers taught their daughters the tasks that they did.

When society progressed from traditional agriculture and household industry to organised industry and services and the urban sector began to grow rapidly, the traditional division of labour between the sexes ceased to operate. In an industrial economy, most of the work traditionally assigned to men can be done by women and *vice versa*. The unit of labour under the industrial economy is the individual against the household in the agricultural economy.

India is mainly still an agricultural country. The traditional village community comprises cultivators, artisans and those doing labour, and the village women play a distinct role in the family's effort to earn a livelihood by contributing their labour. In the present socio-economic set up, this contribution of labour by women is not adequately recognised. A great majority of Indian women participate in the family's earning effort as unpaid family workers. Women's efforts in running the household, freeing the husband to pursue his vocation, remains unrecognised even by law.

Quite a number of women who were employed before marriage give up their jobs after marriage in order to be able to devote their time to family obligations. This renders them economically dependent on their husbands and discredits the concept of the economic status of women as being an indicator of the stage of development of a society.

The various development activities of post-independence India, and the expansion of women's education and their training in various trades and crafts, as also the social changes that have taken place in society, have gone a long way to enable women (tribal, rural and urban) to avail of the new opportunities of earning provided by industrialisation. They are now entering new professions and occupations that were closed to them earlier. With the shift over from cottage to modern and organised industry, a majority of the female labour force, apart from those in agriculture, suffered a set back as they were illiterate and not trained to meet the needs of organised industry.

Before the development of the modern marketing system, most traditional occupations open to women were divided according to caste; for example, spinning, weaving, basket-making, midwifery, etc. were all, more or less, monopolies of different castes. With the introduction of organised production and marketing, earnings from caste-monopoly occupations were minimised. The government is undertaking various programmes to provide training and credit facilities through women's polytechnics and rural credit banks to enable the affected women to go in for alternative employment and ensure their economic emancipation.

Besides, the unorganised sector comprising agriculture, construction and village and small-scale industries, the organised sector of India's economy provides employment to women in services under the Central and State governments and non-agricultural private establishments. The latter sector, which is governed by laws, rules and regulations, is increasing rapidly.

Article 16(1) of the Constitution of India guarantees equality of opportunity for all citizens in matters relating to employment and appointment to any office under the State. In the wake of the growing awareness of their rights, the Indian woman can today enter any profession, old or new, that she chooses and is restricted only by her own predilections and prejudices. Nothing stands in her way to meet the exacting demands of a profession except the demands of marriage and a private life of her own. It may still be that, to some extent, marriage stands between a woman and her total commitment to a profession at the highest level in India (Promilla Kapur. *Marriage and the Working Women in India*. Vikas Publications, 1970, Conclusions).

Increasing opportunities for employment of women as a result of expanding education, urbanisation and industrialisation is significant of the emerging new India. Once limited to household chores and farm labour, the scope for women has widened tremendously. In ever increasing numbers, they are entering the fields of education, industry, administration, legal and political activity. This has particularly benefited the urban middle class woman.

PRESENT SCENARIO

One of the major thrusts in Mexico in 1975 was on women's employment and this was seen as the critical entry point for women's integration into development. This expression came from the assembled women's knowledge that women needed income for survival; it also came from the knowledge that women in any case were *working* for survival.

DATA BASE

A worldwide problem in statistical measurement and analysis is the difficulty in pinpointing the statistical economic profile of women. This has been the drawback in India as well.

However, the decennial population census gives some indicative information of the trend. The national Sample Survey, the Labour Bureau and other sectoral data sets provide further supplementary data. Some of the important facts are briefly presented below:

In 2001, the women labour force was 90 million. Between 1971 and 1981 the overall Work Participation Rate (WPR) for males declined by one point from 52.61 per cent in 1971 to 51.62 per cent in 1981. For females, the WPR increased from 12.06 per cent in 1971 to 13.99 per cent in 1981. The increase in the WPR among females is shared by all age groups except the age group 60 and above.

In the primary sector, the proportion of both male and female main workers has declined, while in the secondary and tertiary sectors, it has increased. A sectoral shift is taking place with males moving away from the primary to the secondary and tertiary sectors. Females are also shifting, though in a smaller way.

Both in rural and urban areas, more females than males were reported as marginal workers, who form a substantial proportion in all age groups among females. Among males, this proportion tapers off rapidly above the age of 25. The female WPR in urban areas has not increased much between 1971 and 1981, specially when compared to rural areas.

SECONDARY DATA REVIEW

Studies undertaken in India and other countries, as well as special analysis on the 32nd Round of the NSSO, as also data collected from the Agro-Economic Research centre reveal that the female WPR varies in direct proportion to increase in poverty. The greater the poverty, the higher the WPR.

Evidence provided by the larger number of women than men on public works sites reveals the pressure on women to take up any employment offer, whatever be the arduousness or however small the wage. Among the poor and resourceless, the pressure to find work for survival is great. While there is an upward trend in employment figures among educated classes, there is a decline in employment among the poorest.

CHANGES IN POLICY AND PROGRAMME

It should be borne in mind that the Constitution of India provides several safeguards for women workers. It guarantees equal opportunity for all citizens in matters relating to employment or appointment to any office under the State and forbids discrimination in respect of any employment or office on grounds of sex, race, caste, colour and creed. It also includes stipulations that women workers be saved from exploitation and given just and humane conditions of work; that their educational and economic interests, as part of the weaker sections of society be taken care of; and it empowers the State to make special provision for women and children.

Besides these, several legal measures have also been provided to ensure that the constitutional rights of women are enforced. The Factories Act of 1948, the Plantation Labour Act of 1951 and the Mines Act of 1952 provide for the welfare and protection of women in these sectors of industry.

The Employees State Insurance Act, 1948 (ESI Act) ensures financial help for medical facilities during pregnancy for women workers. Women workers not covered by the ESI Act can obtain benefits under the Maternity Benefit Act, 1961. Section 48 of the Factories Act also provides for creches to be maintained for children below six years in every factory employing more than 30 women.

Until 1974, very little work had been done to monitor the effectiveness of the policy and legal measures provided for women workers. The first comprehensive insight into the actual conditions of working women and women in need of paid employment was provided and after a detailed study, several suggestions were put up to the Government of India. Among them were the following recommendations:

1. Policy resolution to see that women are not debarred from any occupation without reason and such a refusal being clearly specified.

2. Creation of a women's cell in the Ministry of Labour at the Centre and in all the States to consider and solve women workers' problems.

3. Extension of maternity benefits to all types of women workers including agricultural workers, the self-employed and home-based workers. This also included a suggestion that maternity benefits should be given periodically rather than in a lump sum.

4. The limit of 30 women workers in a factory for creche facilities should be provided for casual and contract labour as well; as far as possible, such facilities should be near the residence of workers.

5. Working time for women should be extended from 7 p.m. to 10 p.m. with adequate transport and security arrangements.

6. Training for employment needed strengthening; specially apprentice training based on need. Self-employment should be promoted and training-cum-production centres set up.

Besides these, several other recommendations were also made including part-time employment for women, employment information and assistance to women, provision of special leave without pay, more effective enforcement of laws for women and unionisation in agriculture and industry.

In 1976 itself, a women's cell was formed in the Ministry of Labour which has since been working on the problem of women workers. The Equal Remuneration Act was also passed in Parliament the same year. This Act provided for equal wages for the same work or work of a similar nature. The Act also stipulates that committees may be constituted to advise the appropriate government for the purpose of providing increasing employment opportunities for women.

NATIONAL PLAN OF ACTION

Simultaneously, an exercise in formulating a National Plan of Action (NPA) for Women was taken up by the Department of Social Welfare in consultation with other ministries. The 'blueprint of action points' presented a situational analysis of women workers in wage employment and self-employment and identified their problems. The

Action Plan for Women in wage employment stipulated that besides the implementation of the Equal Remuneration Act:

1. The Central and State Government departments would determine the direction and the method by which the participation of women could be increased in different occupations.

2. Village and women-intensive industries which provide employment to women would be promoted in economic development plans. Increased participation of women in promotion and management of such enterprises would be stepped up.

3. The maximum age of entering service for women in government and the public sector should be raised to 35.

4. Each establishment—public and private—should ensure that there is no discrimination against women, identify jobs with part-time work possibility, give preference to women for temporary and daily wage employment and set up creches, family planning education programmes and career-counselling centres.

5. Improvement in employment exchange services for women was needed.

6. Creches and child-care centres would have to be provided by the State through voluntary and State agencies for agriculture labourers and women working in small establishments.

7. The need for better data on employment in the unorganised sector should be looked into.

8. The advisory committee envisaged by the Equal Remuneration Act would advise and oversee specific action taken on the plans listed above.

A review of the progress of the Action Plan was carried out in March 1977.

For the Self-Employed, the Plan included identification of occupations for the self-employed, publicity about the facilities available for self-employment; development of special training; motivational programmes for women, special assistance for credit facilities, etc.; support for voluntary agencies promoting self-employment; training services organised for women; providing credit facilities and developing specific plans of action to encourage women's participation in self-employment activities.

For the Sixth Five Year Plan (1980-1985) a working group was constituted by the Planning Commission on the employment of women. It was the first such body to be instituted by the Central Government. As a result, for the first time, the draft Sixth Five Year Plan (1978-1983) recognised that women's employment and income opportunities should be greatly accelerated. To achieve this, there was need for expansion and diversification of education and training opportunities for women. To increase employment in rural areas, the Plan recommended a conscious increase in the share of benefits to women in rural economic programmes like the Small Farmers' Development Agency (SFDA), Operation Flood II, Integrated Rural Development Programme (IRDP), National Rural Employment Programme (NREP), etc.

For the Sixth Five Year Plan (1980-1985), a working group on women's employment was constituted by the Planning Commission for the first time.

The recommendations made for increasing employment opportunities for women in rural areas were:

1. A conscious increase in the share of benefits to women in rural economic programmes like SFDA, Operation Flood II, IRDP, NREP, etc.;
2. Women should be full and equal participants in the entire spectrum of economic development;
3. A credit policy for self-employed and home-based workers;
4. The areas and sectors where women's employment is low or on the decline should be identified and corrective measures indicated to promote additional avenues of employment.

A special chapter on the self-employed was a feature of the Plan. This was an important step since the majority of these workers are women; also, the task force to draw up this chapter came from self-employed workers. As an outcome of the special emphasis on the developmental activities for women, a new scheme entitled 'Science and Technology for Women' was initiated by the Department of Science and Technology.

WOMEN'S CELLS AND BUREAU

The Women's Bureau was set up by the Ministry of Social Welfare. The Ministry of Rural Development has a special Women's Programme Officer who maintains almost 50,000 women's clubs or mahila mandals sponsored by the State. Considering the critical need of economic participation by women and women's organisations, a working group on the Development of Village Level Organisations was set up by the Ministry of Agriculture. Many of the ideas and recommendations made by these groups were incorporated into the Development of Women and Children in Rural Areas (DWCRA) in 1982, a joint venture to organise women around occupations, to be used as an entry point to reach development programmes to poor women. The programme was begun as a sub-scheme of the IRDP and its objective is to help rural women and children benefit from existing development programmes.

Another development in 1978 was the setting up of the Inter-Commodity Board representing all the sectors which provided mass-scale employment such as handlooms, handicrafts, khadi and village industries, coir, silk, etc. as well as the Central Social Welfare Board. The objective of the Board was to safeguard the interests of workers, especially women, and give a linkage to women's projects with the economic development boards.

The Women's Cell in the Ministry of Labour which was set up in 1976 has addressed itself to various problems relating to the employment of women. Various studies have been initiated by the Cell, for example, research on the women migratory workers of Kerala engaged in fish processing in Gujarat. The Cell has also encouraged non-government schemes for women workers. One instance of this was financial assistance to a project set up to employ women from low income groups through the production of cardboard boxes, file boards, etc.

The Women's Cell is responsible for monitoring the administration of the Equal Remuneration Act. The Central Advisory Committee set up under this Act was reconstituted in 1983 by the Ministry of Labour with representatives of grassroot organisations, women's research organisations, trade unions and different ministries.

The Women's Labour Cell of the Ministry of Labour constituted a Group of Women Workers where persons with scholarship and experience in the sphere of women's development have been associated. The group reviewed the status of women's employment and women workers and also deliberated on the role of the Ministry of Labour in this area. The group indicated the following priority areas where action would be initiated by the Ministry of Labour.

1. Employment

It was decided that the Ministry of Labour in cooperation with the Ministry of Social Welfare should monitor women's access to employment but special emphasis in the Ministry of Labour should be given to the study of impact of technology on women's employment and to identify areas which hindered women's employment. The Ministry of Labour should also make persistent efforts to move towards equal employment opportunities between men and women.

2. Access to Means of Production

The group felt that there was a need to insist on creation of economic assets in the name of women members of the household and to give rights over land, forest, etc. to women. The group also felt that there was a need to treat technology as a means of production and to extend it increasingly to women.

3. Review and Implementation of Labour Laws

The group felt that there is a need to review the laws which affect women workers. For example, it needs to be examined whether equal remuneration under the Equal Remuneration Act is related to 'work of a similar value' rather than 'work of a similar nature'. Provisions for maternity benefit is available to women only if they work for 160 days in a year. The group recommended that it should be examined as to why pro-rata benefit cannot be given. The group felt that there may be several other provisions which affect women workers and in respect of which there is need for re-examination. The group felt that the matter regarding enforcement of laws which affect women needs to be gone into in greater detail and the setting up of a separate enforcement machinery or induction of a large number of women employees in the existing enforcement machinery needs to be examined.

4. **Organising Women Workers**

The group felt that organisation of women workers in the vast semi-organised or unorganised sectors is one of the most important issues in respect of women workers. The group made a number of suggestions regarding organisation of such workers.

5. **Home-Based Workers**

The group discussed in detail the various characteristics of home-based workers and suggested that the question of setting up of a commission on self-employment of women should be considered by the Ministry of Labour.

6. **Maternity and Child-Care Arrangements**

There was insistence by the participants for maternity benefits and child care arrangements for women workers throughout the country for all categories of women workers. A suggestion was also made that it should be examined whether a levy or cess on all employers and workers for provision of these services should be made.

In its first deliberations, the Advisory Committee set up two sub-committees to focus attention on statistics on women workers and women in the unorganised labour sector—particularly women in the handloom, powerloom and construction industries. The recommendations of both the sub-committees were endorsed by the Committee.

The Women's Vocational Training Cell of the Directorate General of Employment and Training conducted a nation-wide survey of women's needs for vocational training with the help of the International Labour Organisation (ILO) and the Swedish International Development Agency (SIDA). On the basis of this survey, three vocational training institutes were set up in Delhi, Bangalore and Mumbai to give training in basic, advanced and instructional skills in the trade of electronics, instrument mechanics, electronic measuring instruments, TV service, secretarial practice, dress making, embroidery and needlecraft, etc.

To help improve the data base on women workers, the Planning Commission formed a steering committee in 1982 which recommended the use of the time allocation method to gather data on women and children's work in the rural areas more accurately. The committee commissioned the National Council of Applied Economic Research (NCAER) to apply the time allocation method on a sub-sample of the National Sample Survey (NSS), which they felt would help to assess whether the profile on women workers and employment patterns that emerged by the usual household survey could be improved upon. The fourth institute was set up in 1983 at Thiruvananthapuram.

INCREASE IN WORK PARTICIPATION RATE

Between 1972-1973 and 1977-1978, an increase in Work Participation Rate (WPR) among urban females was evident. The rates for rural females also showed a marginal increase, which was largely due to the increase in the rate of the casual labour category. In the case of males, too, the casual labour participation rates indicated a clear increase in both rural and urban areas—the increase in rural areas was almost offset by reduced rates in workers who were self-employed in agriculture and regular salaried/wage employees in agriculture. The urban casual labour rate increase was roughly compensated by the decrease in the rate of regular salaried/wage employees in non-agricultural sectors.

Between 1977 and 1982, the public sector accounted for 74 and 70 per cent increase in women's employment, the bulk of the increase being in the service sector. Manufacturing, transport and communication recorded only a fair amount of increase, while in agriculture and allied sectors a reduction was registered.

The average earnings of a regular woman worker improved between 1972-1973 and 1977-1978, but there was still a "feeling that women continue to be discriminated against" and that the gains were confined to a small section.

The Labour Bureau's study on employment aspects in selected organised industries like cotton, jute, silk textiles, mica and food processing revealed the adverse impact of rationalisation, automation and modernisation on women's employment.

During 1976-1977, the Labour Bureau conducted a study of working and living conditions of women workers in mines. It found that:

1. There was no appreciable change in the occupational pattern of women employed in mines between 1971 and 1976. Most were shifted from one unskilled job to another, without prospects of their graduating to supervisory jobs.

2. A majority of the women workers in mines, other than in coal or manganese, were either temporary or casual.

3. In a few occupations, wage rates for women for identical work were significantly lower than for men, even after the promulgation of the Equal Remuneration Act. Otherwise, the average rates for both were identical or almost so.

4. A large number of the sampled units were not complying with statutory provisions regarding separate toilet facilities for women.

EMPLOYMENT EXCHANGE STATISTICS

The total size of the live register figure for both men and women has been increasing steadily from 9.3 million at the end of 1975 to 26 million at the end of 2003. The educated component (matric (or tenth) and above) also increased from 4.8 million to above 13.4 million during the same period. Around 6 million people, of whom nearly half were educated, register with the employment exchanges each year. But the annual placement situation has been less than 5 lakh, one-third of whom are educated.

Regarding work preference of women engaged in household and marginally allied activities, a sample survey indicated that 23.1 (rural, aged five and above) and 19.8 (urban) per cent were willing to accept certain specified activities like dairy, weaving, tailoring, etc. at their household site. Nearly 94 per cent of those who wished to accept such gainful activities wanted them regularly either on a full-time or part-time basis. A majority reported possession of the necessary skill, but had little finance to carry out the activities; while those lacking in skill asked for training facilities and access to finances.

REASONS FOR UNEMPLOYMENT

The decline in employment among the poorest could be due to various policy measures such as redistribution of land which reduces the need for hired labour; technological changes in agriculture including introduction of cash crops and mechanisation and the declining number of non-farm activities in rural areas such as hand-based activities.

A study noted a rise in the incidence of rural female agriculture labourers in at least 91 districts of India during 1961-1971. The progressive shift from cultivator to labourer status during the last decade is a disturbing trend in women's participation in agriculture. This rise in the ranks of women agricultural labourers (from less than one-third of the female work force in 1951 to more than two-thirds in 2003) points to shrinking employment opportunities in family farms and growing pressure on women to resort to wage labour, often under exploitative conditions.

A similar shrinking seems to be taking place in the non-farm sector in rural areas due to technology changes, competition from machine-made goods, changes in consumer taste, pressures of export competition, distortion of the domestic consumption pattern, shortage of raw material, etc. Women appearing in large numbers at public work sites (which concentrate on road building and tank desilting and similar earth work); and the figures of long distance, inter-State migration for employment (2001 Census) reveal that the rate of absorption in agriculture does not match the growth rate of women seeking work.

Case studies of women workers in milk production underline the physical burden faced by them and the lack of attention paid to their needs such as easy access to water and fuel, child care and health facilities. The problem of overwork for underfed women seems to be responsible for female mortality. Studies on bidi workers, stone workers and cart-pullers reveal the hazardous nature of women's work. Facts related to women's employment reveal the special linkages between the work and infrastructure for women.

DISCRIMINATION IN LABOUR MARKET

A systematic difference in male and female earnings in agriculture and related activities has been revealed by some micro studies, according to which operations that fetch higher wages like ploughing are male preserves whereas transplanting (an area where women are a higher proportion of the work force) brings lower wages. The same is the case in small-scale industries like bidi-making, construction work, cashew and coir. Here, women are assigned unskilled work and are paid less even in skilled operations.

Even in the organised sector, professional and skilled workers report lower remuneration for equal work. Another facet of discrimination is the crowding of women in certain types of jobs. The females are much more concentrated in agricultural operations than males; and that forced idleness is higher among women are phenomena borne out by numerous studies.

In the informal sector, some of the lowest paid occupations have a disproportionately high percentage of women. In the organised sector, 90 per cent of the women are found in unskilled and semi-skilled jobs. Scheduled Caste women have a higher WPR (different in different regions) than women belonging to other castes. Studies also reveal that the female WPR varies much more than the Male Participation Rate (MPR) due to the marginalisation of the female work force and the strong "discouraged worker" effect in the slack season.

WOMEN IN THE UNORGANISED SECTOR

Some problems of women in unorganised labour were discussed at the National Seminar on Rural Unorganised Labour held in New Delhi in 1984 organised by the Ministry of Labour. The issues taken up included:

1. The problem of displacement of women from work due to technological innovations and inadequacy of organisations;
2. The need to organise women around occupational tasks; and
3. The need for extending the Employment Guarantee Scheme.

In the field of organising self-employed women, there has been commendable effort by voluntary organisations. Thus far, however, these organisations have been more successful in reaching urban self-employed women than rural women.

The methodology has been surveys of occupational clusters, identification of wage rates as well as economic and social problems and needs; and organising poor self-employed women to uplift their socio-economic conditions through the joint action of struggle and development strategies. Arrangements have been developing with banks and the wage-negotiating clout of women workers has increased by developing an alternative production and marketing system.

Among special employment programmes, Maharashtra's extensive and sustained Employment Guarantee Scheme (MEGS) has provided rare employment opportunities to vast sections of the rural population. MEGS may well be one of the factors for a comparatively lower extent of employment among rural women and men in Maharashtra than in Andhra Pradesh or Tamil Nadu. Thus, the discussions and recommendations could broadly be classified under seven general categories:

1. Equal remuneration and fixation of minimum wages;
2. Creche and maternity benefit facilities;
3. Training and education to increase the number of occupations in which women are engaged;

4. Improvement in database;
5. Special problems and needs of self-employed women workers;
6. Displacement of women workers due to technology; and
7. The organisation of women workers.

ISSUES AND OBSTACLES

One issue that has been causing concern in India is that opportunities for women in the labour market are declining, not increasing. Marginal improvements in sectors like electronics have been observed yet, from available data, it is obvious that women are not only in need of employment, but are also going all out to bring home a subsistence earning. A review of the situation brings out the following implications:

> That the provision of small micro opportunities for women which are usually classified as income generating projects can only make a marginal dent on the widespread need of women for gainful employment. Thus, it is in the mainstream of agriculture and non-farm rural employment, including construction, industry and the services sector, especially as self-employed workers, that women have the basic opportunity for earning income. In these sectors, however, changes in policy change the capacity to absorb certain types of skills.

Thus a strong recommendation made by those who are involved in this field is for a scrutiny of the existing employment picture; anticipation of possible negative consequences of change and built-in safeguards either to prevent dislocation or to re-absorb in another avenue.

Another issue has been in the question of employment queues. It is presumed that men are the bread winners and primary earners of the family. The fact that women are often totally responsible for domestic work from which they have not found an escape creates a presumption that they are primarily domestic workers and secondarily economic or income earners. However, detailed statistics reveal that women are often the sole supporters and prime bread winners.

FEMALE-HEADED HOUSEHOLDS

Another issue is the female-headed household. Census data usually gives the percentage of such households as around 10 per cent and the primary cause of their occurrence as widowhood. However, a study of this data by region, class and other characteristics reveals that:

1. There are more female-headed households among the poorest (up to 35 per cent) and the reasons are not only widowhood but also male migration and abandonment;

2. That male out-migration is an increasingly important cause; and

3. That even though households (including those which have matrimonial cultural roots) have female heads, decision-making is strongly in men's hands. There is, thus, no great difference between utilisation of development benefits between male and female-headed households. However, when women are sole supporters or are alone in the household, the destitution is acute. In all the IRDPs in the 1980s, there has been a directive to specially reach these households. Some States even have a pension scheme for single women above the age of 40, below the poverty line and living alone.

Tribal women have special problems linked to their culture. They generally hold forest-based occupations. Deforestation and forest use by industrialists, as well as forest preservation by Acts, have all added to their economic stress. Actually, forestry can provide them with a massive source of employment in occupations like nursery cultivation, fuel and fodder and cattle-rearing.

Another problem is the difference between male and female labour. One of the reasons for the inadequate attention to women's employment is that the difference in characteristics between male and female labour has not been taken note of. Various cultural and traditional factors have led to the clear demarcation of economic roles between men and women. The labour market is not neutral. Males are considered for certain jobs while females for others. For example, in construction work, men do the skilled job of bricklaying while women mix the mortar; women carry earth while men do the digging. In rice cultivation, it is common to find only women transplanting paddy. Weeding, vegetable plucking and bundling of harvest produce are usually done by women.

Another difference between male and female labour is that women's work is evaluated according to traditional perceptions. Most employers see the contribution of women as being less in value than that of men.

FUTURE STRATEGIES

From the viewpoint of policy and also programme support, women's employment can be categorised in terms of:

1. Existing employment in traditional industries/occupations; and

2. New employment avenues.

There is considerable evidence that women's employment in existing occupations has been affected seriously by technological *laissez-faire*. Growth of a competing mechanised sector with huge resources and influence at its command has grown within the same industries in which women are employed in large numbers such as handlooms, woollen and cotton industries. The mechanised sector has snatched away both raw material and market from women producers who are unorganised and resourceless.

The emerging situation has led the Government to adopt a new Ten-Point Technology Policy to set right the prevalent *laissez-faire*. The policy announced on January 3, 1983, promises to protect employment of women and the weaker sections engaged in the traditional industries; provide maximum employment to women and weaker sections; use traditional skills and capabilities making them commercially competitive; ensure the correct mix between mass production technologies and production by the masses and ensure maximum development with minimum capital outlay.

It is a measure of the Government's seriousness in implementing this policy that a Technology Policy Implementation Cell (TPIC) was established in the Cabinet Secretariat. The problems facing the country on the employment front and the need for adoption of appropriate technology which optimises employment have been aptly summed up by the Cell, which has emphasised the gravity of the unemployment situation.

At the end of 1983-1984, there was an estimated backlog of about 20 million unemployed persons in the country; at least five to six million people were being added to the employment market each year and the organised sector of industry was hardly in a position to absorb one to 1.2 million persons a year. The main choices available to alleviate this situation appear to be:

1. To plan for a substantial increase in employment in the primary sector, namely, agriculture and rural employment, as the bulk of the unemployed persons reside in rural areas;

2. To increase employment opportunities in the tertiary sector, for example, services, trade and banking where the additional investment required to create new workplaces is comparatively low; and

3. To encourage the use of employment-intensive technologies in all, or at least selected sectors of the economy, especially in the case of agro-based small scale handlooms, handicrafts and cottage industries.

There are apparent conflicts among the objectives of maximisation of growth rate, output and employment in a developing country. However, it is quite clear that greater direct and indirect employment opportunities for a given investment ought to be preferred, unless there are exceptional circumstances warranting a departure from this rule. And here, the choice may not merely be between an indigenous technology and an imported one, but it could also be among several competing imported technologies or indigenous ones themselves.

The question of choice could also pertain to futuristic technologies, that is, those which should be developed or acquired by the country from outside for the future.

RE-ORIENTATION OF POLICIES

Given the freedom of choice and necessary capital, most entrepreneurs would prefer to deploy costlier machines than employ more workers, not only for reasons of profitability but also because:

1. Machine management appears to be inherently simpler than men management; and

2. The problem of labour management seems to grow more and more acute with the increase in the number of workers employed under one roof. The tendency would need to be countered if the utilisation of 'appropriate' technologies is to be promoted seriously.

   For this purpose, the credit, licensing, wage and labour management policies will need to be re-oriented suitably so that they not only prefer the establishment of smaller industrial units or units based on 'appropriate' technologies but also keep the demands for premature wage increases effectively under check..

Another measure necessary to encourage employment and labour-intensive techniques which are of significance to women's employment is the need to pursue the concept of Common Production Programmes as suggested by the Karve Committee. This would include:

1. Reservation of spheres of production;

2. Non-expansion of the capacity of a large-scale industry;

3. Arrangements for the supply of raw materials; and

4. Co-ordination for research, training, etc.

The inadequacy of the institutional arrangements for the implementation of various public policies supporting employment in existing traditional industries is evident. The success of decentralised production depends on efficient institutional arrangements for supply of essential inputs, cheap credit, constant upgradation of both techniques of production and skills, consumer-oriented responsive marketing strategies and, above all, more personalised service.

NEW EMPLOYMENT OPPORTUNITIES

The potential with regard to new employment opportunities is not so limited as is generally believed. One reason why the potential for creating additional jobs is considered to be limited is the inability of the organised industry to register any significant increase in employment in the previous decades. Employment in the organised sector during the decade 1972 to 1982 increased nominally by 55 lakh (employing scarcely one of every 10 new entrants to the labour force during the period). And here, too, community and social services which include educational and health institutions provided substantial employment. The manufacturing activity in the public and private sectors combined absorbed only 14 lakh additional persons (or a quarter of the total of 55 lakh) during the decade despite substantial investment during successive Plans. The limits of the organised sector in providing any significant relief to the economy on the employment front is thus easily recognised.

However, the potential in sectors other than the organised sector is not so restricted. The following have been identified as some of the potential areas:

1. Development of agriculture in dry-farming areas through soil and moisture conservation, afforestation, land-shaping and adoption of crop technologies appropriate for rainfed areas.
2. Expansion of traditional labour-intensive industry through protection and promotional resources.
3. Extraction of larger employment from the organised industry through vigorous scrutiny of the technology/employment alternatives by the industrial licensing authority.

The actualisation of these employment opportunities would also help to put purchasing power in the hands of larger numbers than at present and that, in turn, will stimulate demand for goods and services other than the elementary requirements of food grains.

It is in the same perspective that the simultaneous and cumulative pursuit of programmes such as the IRDP, NREP, MNP, Special Area Programmes, development of agricultural output and productivity in dry-farming areas assume great significance. If purchasing power is generated in the hands of the poor through work and in a dispersed manner in vast areas, conditions would be created for strengthening employment and income for the weaker sections, including women.

Construction work which has been quite lively offers a potential as does the provision of infrastructure services. For example, one of the aims of the Five Year Plans is to provide social infrastructure in the form of schools, hospitals, recreational centres, etc. This requires building and is what is called the Minimum Needs or Basic Needs Provision Programme. It is a very critical input in women's well being. Thus, women can benefit from the inputs of the programme in terms of labour; and from the output of this programme in terms of health and educational services.

Expansion of schooling and primary health centres, extending to intensification of child care services which can further expand into provision of nutritious meals, provides enormous scope for female employment on a mass scale. Primary schools usually employ almost 50 per cent female teachers. Nurses and extension workers taking care of creches and pre-school nurseries are women. As shown in the example of the free mid-day meal programme in Tamil Nadu, more than 164,000 women have been employed to manage the cooking and feeding of children, which gets recycled into relief for women from the responsibility of cooking the mid-day meal, apart from the relief from the expense. It has also been found that free food prevents the unequal nutritional status between males and females in India. Such discrimination in favour of the males is usually associated with scarce-resource households. Thus, the potential for employment of women in terms of numbers lies in the area of provision of social infrastructure and basic amenities.

ACTION FOR THE FUTURE

Scanning the employment scene, especially the numbers that need attention (whether it is to safeguard employment or to provide a better wage), it becomes apparent that the main avenues for women's employment in the future as in the past will continue to be in this order:

(i) agriculture; (ii) non-farm employment in rural areas (handloom, handicrafts, agro-processing, services); and (iii) construction (of buildings, roads, irrigation work). This will be the source of income for the masses.

Intensification of agriculture, whether through expanding or cultivating or providing inputs such as water to increase the number of crops per year and so on, can provide an opportunity to women workers. However, it has been found that the expansion of opportunities depends on whether activities are mechanised and crops are changed—a linked point.

If women have to be part of the mainstream of future development, new avenues will have to be thrown open to them. There will have to be an upgradation of skills. Technical, financial and marketing support will have to be extended to them. There would not only have to be a large investment in their training but the training itself would have to be far more innovative and diverse in character. For instance, women who now migrate long distances in search of earning opportunities need to be trained in work which they could get nearer home. Thus, the demand pull sectors of production would have to be identified and training organised.

Further, women in rural areas participating in agriculture, such as the growing of crops, cannot be trained only in new technologies but also in related activities such as fertiliser feeding into the fields, spraying of pesticides, treatment of seed, repair of pumpsets, etc. Training of farm women in prevention of grain loss and food processing is useful but not necessarily an income-earning activity.

In the non-farm sector, there are many new demands in the rural areas in the field of extension which provide other areas for training. Rural industry is dominated by women in the cottage-based sector. Yet training institutions do not have the facilities to absorb women, nor is it part of the over-all design of rural industrialisation.

Vocational training institutes still tend to concentrate their curriculum for women in activities such as cutting and sewing, secretarial services and beauty care. Organisations working with the poorest women have pointed out how the majority of rural and urban women prefer to be trained in more demand-oriented skills like watch repair, plumbing and light engineering.

An evaluation of the functioning of the National and Regional Vocational Training Institutes for Women revealed that about 52 per cent of the ex-trainees in a sample size of 35 per cent of total ex-trainees had been unable to find suitable employment on the strength of the training received by them. Those who had secured jobs found the training beneficial. Only seven per cent reported themselves as self-employed. Some basic changes are apparently needed in the selection of students and in the courses offered, since there seems to be a mismatch between courses offered and employment available. The trainees are also not in a position to start self-employment ventures because of lack of mental orientation, encouragement from the institutes and guidance and support in the form of infrastructure and credit.

CREDIT FACILITIES FOR WOMEN

Studies conducted on access to credit facilities for low income earning women bring out one central problem faced by them—that they have no security to offer. The problems faced in extending credit to women are socio-economic. Attitudes to women do not allow them to take up independent ventures. Further, women are largely unaware of existing credit facilities or are physically unable to reach banks, particularly in the rural areas. Where there are banking institutions, women, again especially in rural areas, are reluctant to approach them because they are unfamiliar with their policies and cumbersome procedures. Another obstacle, which is now sought to be changed, is the tendency of banks to finance large enterprises rather than small ones. This is a disadvantage to women as they tend to be involved in small enterprises.

Existing development programmes that provide credit to women for self-employment are IRDP and Ministry of Social Welfare programmes. The IRDP is especially focused on the target group comprising agricultural labourers and rural artisans whose economic advancement is essential for rural development. IRDP loans are given through local lending banks and one-third of each loan is subsidised. During 1980-1983, about 9.9 million families were subsidised and loans amounting to Rs. 2,121 crore sanctioned. Except for approximately 30 per cent, the beneficiaries were all below the poverty line. Women beneficiaries were seven per cent of the total in 20 States and Union Territories.

Schemes that come under IRDP are agriculture, animal husbandry, horticulture, fisheries, sericulture, co-operation and small industries. IRDP consists of both credit-linked and non-credit linked subsidy schemes. The method of identification is the survey of income and land-holding of each home in a chosen cluster of villages. Families earning below Rs. 3,600 per month are identified as potential beneficiaries. There are usually 600 beneficiaries from each cluster. To reach credit to women under IRDP, loans of up to Rs. 5,000 do not require a guarantor. Women beneficiaries are, however, few. For instance, in two districts of Karnataka, the following ratio was recorded of male and female IRDP beneficiaries: in Udipi, males 14 and females 11; in Gulbarga, males 143 and females only seven.

The Ministry of Social Welfare also provides credit to individual women through Mahila Mandals. Loans are given to buy sewing machines, milch animals and to set up poultry units, kitchen gardens, etc. There are also non-government organisations that see credit facilities as the primary need for women, especially for women in the unorganised sector. Some organisations have aimed at the development of self-employed and landless women through such methods as making institutional credit and subsidies reach the target group. In 1974, one such organisation started a women's bank, which is a kind of intermediary organisation between the women members and the nationalised banks. It submits loan applications to banks and pays out money to the women.

ORGANISING WOMEN WORKERS

Most of the studies on the issue of women's employment have pinpointed the importance of organising women workers. It has also been found that trade unions have not taken much interest in the unionisation of women workers and when they have, it is usually still dominated by men.

Yet those who have successfully organised women workers have found that this has not only strengthened and increased women's income though wage struggles and by the provision of backward and forward linkages, but has also provided forums for opinion formation. These forums have been effective on many issues such as:

1. Resistance against changes in technology which could create loss of employment;
2. Appeals for improving legal services to safeguard women's rights; and
3. Reduction of occupational and health hazards.

Thus, organisations of women workers built around occupational and other entry points is a critical need. From the above analysis, it is evident that the attention of the Government is being directed towards the following:

1. Strengthening and developing NREP to absorb a larger number of unemployed women;
2. Building social inputs (like easy accessibility to water and fuel; and provision of nutrition) into the development programmes;
3. Strengthening MNP;
4. Training women for employment in the service sector;
5. Providing social security coverage such as the provision of child care, maternity benefits, health and life insurance;
6. Organising the unorganised women's work force;
7. Facilitating credit and access to banking facilities for self-employed women; and
8. Creating a Maternity Relief Plan.

There is clear evidence that social support for women is sadly lacking and despite the many attempts at women's empowerment, there is still a lot of hostility towards women attempting to climb up the social ladder. It may therefore be said that social support is required to make woman a viable, economic unit; and providing infrastructure becomes important once the role of the household is recognised as a 'releaser' and 'inhibitor' of female labour supply. The household contains within it characteristics that provide much of the impetus or inhibition towards female labour participation or to the emergence of the female into the labour force. Those policies which unlock the household would automatically provide the key to female entry into the labour market.

While demand pull expressed in employment opportunities, training and raising of awareness are vital factors, they are not in themselves sufficient to bring about the kind of responses from female labour that is noticed among male labour. Yet poverty presses them into unaccounted productive work, free collection of goods for themselves or for wage employment—irregular, underpaid, physically strenuous. The fact that households with zero or no resources put their females into the labour market, whatever the cost, whatever the type of work, makes it essential to analyse the labour force participation and the need for employment in class terms. If the labour force is analysed against the class stratification of the educated/uneducated; rural/urban; agricultural labour/non-agricultural labour and self-employed, it will be found that all the poor are working. The poor cannot survive unless they bring into their households some returns each day.

It is imperative that the poorest should be engaged in economic activity leading to bread. The question is: what kind of employment generation will absorb this critical mass of unemployed women who are in the deepest crisis? The large public work programmes, food-for-work programmes as well as the employment aspect of supply of basic needs are potential sources of employment for these women. Policies and programmes should be so designed as to accommodate women specifically in these programmes and to add the additional package of services required by women because of their reproductive and maternal roles.

WELFARE OF RURAL WOMEN

The bulk of India's population lives in villages, depending mainly on agriculture, and most village women work in the fields as part of the family unit. Even those village women who are engaged as hired labour in agriculture are generally paid in produce and are usually exploited. Agriculturists, seeking to enhance their social status, do not allow their women family members to work as it is regarded as demeaning and the payment is meagre. Many village women migrating to towns seek employment as cooks, kitchen helpers and children's nurses in middle class families. There being no law regulating the conditions of this kind of labour, they are generally at the mercy of their masters.

The basic structure of the female labour force in India is, thus, mainly traditional. According to the 2001 Census, out of 242 million workers, 152 million were male and 90 million female. Of the total female labour force in the rural areas, 87 per cent were engaged in agriculture, 3.6 per cent in household industries and 3.4 per cent in other services. In the urban areas (in small towns), 22 per cent of the female workers were engaged in agriculture, 28 per cent in the service sector, 10 per cent in household industries and 13 per cent in manufacturing concerns.

Consequent to rapid urbanisation during the last few decades, the manufacturing and service sectors are expanding in the urban areas, offering more openings to women in these sectors. Indian women are slowly but steadily joining the 'wheel of labour' and hence their status as housewives and mothers is bound to undergo a change along with the changing social pattern. There has been an increasing tendency among urban educated women of the middle classes to take up paid employment on account of an ideological change in social values that is partly due to the increasing economic pressure on the urban middle class families. Further, the thousands of women receiving education need to be guided into lucrative professions so that their tremendous potential motivates village women. It is necessary to evolve a scheme to provide adequate incentives to educated women to enter various professions and social activities. The paucity of kindergartens and crèches often creates a conflict between a woman's job and her family tasks.

In view of the seemingly irreconcilable dual role of women in employment as well as at home, a majority of married women now aspire for a full time job at the beginning of their married life. Thereafter, for a few years, they take time out to raising a family and resume employment when their children are sufficiently grown up not to need full time attention. In actual practice, it is difficult to live this dual life without damaging the interests of one or the other. Rural working women as well as those of the urban poorer sections still live traditional lives. In the absence of a mechanism to ensure that agricultural and construction labour, as well as artisans, are fully protected by law, they are exposed to ruthless exploitation by middlemen. Thus, landless peasant women working in cottage industries or engaged in domestic service lead an unhappy life and have to live in slums.

When labour legislation commenced in India, there was a substantial number of women workers in industry (jute and textiles), mines and plantations, etc. After independence, in the Constitution of India, welfare of women workers was incorporated in the Directive Principles of State Policy. Article 39(a) provides that all citizens, men and women, have the right to an adequate means of livelihood. Further, Article 42 enjoins upon the State to make provision for securing just and humane conditions of work including maternity relief. Article 46 provides that the State shall promote with special care the education and economic interests of the weaker sections of the people, which includes women, who have been exposed to centuries of exploitation. Above all, Article 15(3) provides the State with the necessary protection enabling it to make special provision for women and children within the framework of the Fundamental Rights.

In conformity with these provisions, various legislative measures have been taken to provide for protection and welfare of women workers in shops, commercial establishments, plantations, mines, factories and in various services and provisions. Special welfare measures for women in organised industry are maternity benefits and provision of crèches in all institutions employing 50 or more women.

As far as working conditions of women are concerned, it can be said with justification that they continue to occupy the role of 'marginal workers' in the economic life of the country. Actually, the socio-psychological factors coupled with certain traditional concepts of the woman's role in society have inhibited their integration as a permanent and distinctive part of the work force in India. This is partly because a large majority of Indian women take to work mainly on personal, family or community compulsions and withdraw from employment as soon as such compulsions cease to exist.

Although about 78 per cent of the women at work are still those engaged in agriculture and allied activities, there has been an increase in the number in employment in the non-agriculture organised sector. This was mainly in the urban areas.

One of the important factors contributing to this unsatisfactory state of affairs is the lack of adequate facilities for education and vocational training, particularly because of continued social prejudice against the working woman. Adding to the problem, is the large number of untrained women displaced from the industrial sector on account of modern structural and technological changes .

NON-UTILISATION OF EDUCATED WOMEN'S FORCE

The benefit of education has so far been mainly confined to the urban middle class families that have a rather restrictive attitude to women working outside the home. This is partly due to the traditional concept that the status and prestige of a family is diminished if the women of the family seek outside employment. This attitude is, however, changing rapidly in line with the emerging social scene. It is rather a paradox that although illiteracy is the greatest impediment in expanding employment for women, education itself does not necessarily lead to their employment. While lack of literacy and vocational training of rural women make them unsuited to meet the requirement of modern industry and trade, educated women of the urban middle classes are impeded by tradition.

Another problem is the inability of the present economy to absorb all the available labour force, and the fact that no consideration is given to women's role as housewives and mothers which is a vocation in itself. Apart from presenting an idealised image of women as housewives and mothers (supported by references in ancient scriptures) hardly any attempt has been made to appraise the role of woman as a housewife *vis-à-vis* employment.

It has also been observed that some educated women who hold jobs before marriage, leave their jobs after marriage or soon after marriage and devote their time to their homes and husbands. Thus, a large number of urban women, well educated and well trained for different professions, are reduced to a state of idle, drawing room decoration pieces.

Our society is passing through a stage of transition where many traditional concepts are breaking down as they do not conform to present day conditions. The spread of education and the development of industry, demarcation of jobs between men and women based on sex, caste and creed is being strongly challenged. The educated women's force needs to be assigned a positive role to accelerate the process of national development and modernisation. They must be involved in spreading education and social consciousness among the masses and in the uplift of women. This unutilised force can help greatly in eradicating illiteracy in the poorer sections of society and bringing them into the mainstream of productive life.

It is the enlightened woman who has to set free her less unfortunate sisters from the bonds of tradition, ignorance and superstition. These educated women must be aroused to an awareness of the undignified existence of large numbers of women in the present social structure.

WOMEN IN EDUCATION

There has been much debate and controversy about suitable professions for women. In the traditional Hindu society, the majority of women look for employment in the field of education where they hold leading positions. Other professions to which they have taken in substantial numbers are medicine, law and secretarial or administrative service.

Teaching is by far the predominant area providing employment to as much as three fourths of all educated and trained women. Within the profession, the largest group is primary school teachers. Women have been extremely successful in this profession and are now indispensable at certain stages of education. It is normally claimed that women can teach almost by instinct and that they have a natural gift for educating and moulding the character of young children. Women are not restricted to teaching only in the educational field. They also hold high level posts as professors, principals of schools and colleges and directors and ministers of education in the State and Central governments.

The concentration of women professionals in the teaching and medical professions is mainly due to the respectability attached to these spheres. In Indian society, the teacher has always been held in high esteem. After education, the next important profession for women, in quantitative terms is medicine and nursing. Women have always dominated nursing as they are better able to empathise with patients. However, society did not always look upon nursing as a noble profession. Even as recently as five decades ago, a girl had to display courage and determination if she wanted to take up nursing as a profession. The scenario is now changing. Education and changing societal norms have seen a large and steady increase in the number of women entering nursing not only for economic reasons but also for their personal satisfaction. As far as the medical profession is concerned, there is still a great shortage of women doctors in the country. The long and arduous training and the heavy fees involved discourage women from becoming doctors. A number of women who have completed their medical training often do not pursue the profession as it makes large inroads in the time available to them for looking after their children.

—oo(O)oo—

26

SCIENCE AND TECHNOLOGY FOR WOMEN

IT is now well accepted that science and technology are powerful forces for economic, social and cultural development. As long ago as 1958, the Government of India in its Scientific Policy Resolution emphasised that "the key to national prosperity, apart from the spirit of the people, lies in the modern age in the effective combination of three factors, technology, raw material and capital, of which the first is perhaps the most important." In today's world the imprint of science and technology is clearly visible everywhere. The benefits that the developed countries were able to derive through the application of science and technology have made them reach where they are now. It became possible for them to improve the standards of living. This experience gives credence to the premise that in the less developed parts of the world, science and technology can be employed to bring about improvements in the quality and standards of living. Science and technology, therefore, represent an approach and a means whereby the human capital of the country can transform the available natural resources into valuable human products.

Nearly half the available human capital is women. If their involvement in science and technology is not looked after, national development will be unbalanced and limited. However, due to historical reasons, the bulk of Indian women have remained socially and economically backward. In recent times, the independence movement and the contribution of Mahatma Gandhi has seen a larger number of women coming out of their homes to acquire greater social awareness. Indian women today have made entry into several fields hitherto considered as men's preserves. According to an estimate, more than 500,000 teachers, nearly 40,000 medical doctors, 18,000 qualified scientists and a couple of thousand lawyers are women. According to a survey conducted in 1981, among the total scientific personnel, 14.4 per cent are women out of whom 86 per cent qualified in science, 11 per cent in medicine and three per cent in engineering/technology. In each of these three fields the percentage of women comes to 20.4 per cent, 17.8 per cent and 1.4 per cent, respectively.

Among the post-graduates, two-thirds of the women Science and Technology personnel are engaged in teaching jobs and 10 per cent in research.

The Department of Science and Technology initiated a scheme entitled "Science and Technology for Women" in the Sixth Plan. The scheme recognises the need for application of science and technology to improve the life and status of women by reducing the drudgery of women especially in rural areas, providing them with opportunities for income generation, improving their health, sanitation and environmental conditions and finding ways of protecting them from occupational hazards. An important objective of this took off in 1981 and many projects have been sponsored which cover programmes on research and development, surveys, field trials and demonstration of technologies relevant for women, training programme and programmes for disseminating information on technologies through publications, exhibitions, preparation of audio-visual aids, etc.

One of the priority tasks under the scheme was the preparation of a compendium of technologies relevant to women especially in rural areas entitled "Science and Technology for Women." This report lists the names and addresses of women's welfare organisations in all the States of India. The report has since been translated into Hindi and widely circulated amongst scientific institutions, voluntary agencies, etc. so that these technologies could be tried out and demonstrated. Recently, the compendium has been revised and updated.

An all India "Co-ordinated Project on Fuel and Cooking Systems" was initiated in 1982 to reduce the drudgery of rural women who have to cover long distances for collection of fuel wood. Effective utilisation of solar energy, bio-gas and bio-mass are the main strategies. More than 12 institutions including voluntary agencies are participating in the project, and several models of the smokeless *chulas* are being tried out in various parts of the country. Feed-back received from various areas resulted in improvements being made in the design of these *chulas*. The programme also covers training of women in construction, repair and maintenance of these *chulas* and also in teaching women how to grow fuel trees. The drudgery of kitchen work is decreased considerably by working in a smoke-free environment. Similarly, the propagation of solar cookers has been very successful under this scheme, especially in rice-eating areas. There are, however, some drawbacks such as high cost of solar cookers, the breakability of the mirrors, etc. which require remedial action. The scheme also covers bio-gas plants, energy plantations and improvements in water purification, etc. In all the programmes undertaken, an effort is always made to ensure a tie-up between the voluntary agencies and the scientific institutions.

The National Research Development Corporation of India, which is a Central Government enterprise, has been serving as a bridge between research and industry over the last four decades of its existence. It is responsible for utilising the results of indigenous R & D with a view to accelerate economic development and technological self-reliance. As part of its activities, the Corporation is engaged in the development and promotion of appropriate technologies and transferring the same to rural areas for improving the quality of life of the weaker sections of the population. It has successfully taken up projects on agro-waste compaction machines for converting agricultural waste into fuel briquettes, mini milk/fish preservation, chilling plants using bio-gas, blue-green algae production, etc. Some proven technologies like leaf-cup making machines for utilisation of tree leaves, improved bullock carts for rural transportation and chlorine tablets for safe drinking water are already available with the NRDC. Most of the NRDC technologies are simple and do not require large investments.

Conscious of its obligations towards women, the NRDC has been promoting technologies which are appropriate for women in general and women entrepreneurs in particular. The Corporation has brought out a book entitled "Appropriate Technologies for Women from NRDC of India." This publication lists about 66 technologies specially identified as suitable for women entrepreneurs. These technologies have been classified as follows:

a. Food and allied areas;

b. Chemicals, drugs and pharmaceuticals;

c. Machinery and equipment;

d. Energy and fuel;

e. Building material; and

f. General.

As part of its appropriate technology promotion programme, the NRDC has taken up the task of setting up a network of Rural Technology Demonstration-cum-Training (RTDCT) centres at selected focal points all over the country. The emphasis here is on technologies for fulfilment of the minimum needs of the people so as to bring about significant improvement in the quality of life. Such centres have already been put up. Many of the technologies put up at these centres are quite appropriate for women entrepreneurs.

The NRDC has the necessary expertise to undertake preparation of project reports and feasibility studies on nominal charges for selected technologies. It can also finance development of specific technologies appropriate for women. The NRDC works closely with all major government funded R & D agencies in the country and overviews both government and industrial activities, covering a wide range of technologies. And as such, women entrepreneurs and organisations concerned with programmes relating to women can draw upon the expertise and resources available with the NRDC for promoting their objectives.

As a result of indigenous research and development, a large number of technologies are now available for women entrepreneurs to take advantage of. These technologies give added value to farm products and place essential household goods and services at the disposal of the consumer by providing easy low investment self-employment to women. Such technologies for low-cost industries can be adopted by women even at the household backyard level.

Prominent among the areas where such technologies are available are food and food products, post-harvest technologies, Ayurvedic medicines and drugs, chemicals and pharmaceuticals, household machinery and equipment, minimum needs for people such as domestic aids for pure drinking water, literacy aids, educational toys, low cost latrines, energy and fuel-saving appliances, improved *chulas*, better hurricane lanterns, fruit and food-packaging artefacts.

Some typical examples of the technologies are chakli mix (a composite mix for crispy snacks); coffee and tea whiteners based on casein, garlic powder, instant mixes for *rasam* and *sambhar*, fruit bars, papad machines, infant foods, etc.

The socio-economic conditions of women in India compel them to take up occupations which are often hazardous. One of the main objectives of the scheme 'Science and Technology for Women' is to effect an improvement in the health and environmental conditions of women through the application of science and technology. Some of the occupations employing women in large numbers are cashewnut processing, retting of coir and jute, textiles, handlooms, dyeing, printing, glazing of pottery, rubber tapping, cotton and tea plucking, hospital and laboratory work. Women engaged in these occupations are exposed to physical stresses and chemical toxicants leading to health problems which are further aggravated due to malnutrition, anaemia, parasitic infections, frequent child birth, longer working hours, etc. The harmful effects of toxic substances vary in males and females. It is a part of the Science and Technology policy to identify occupational and environmental health problems of Indian women, assess the degree and magnitude of toxicity and suggest measures to solve this problem. The Department of Science and Technology has brought out a publication titled 'Occupational and Environmental Health Problems of Indian Women' which is a state-of-the-art report. The report has recommended that studies on certain occupations involving large numbers of female workers with potential risks be taken up on priority. These include industries such as retting of coir and jute, electric and electronic industry, mining and coiring, ceramics, construction industry, food products, cashew industry, chikan-embroidery, etc. Non-occupational exposure such as those caused by domestic pollution, detergents, cosmetics, food adulterants, tobacco, etc. are also areas needing detailed study. The report has recommended that in order to assess the health risk of Indian women workers and safeguard their health against occupational and environmental hazards, an all-India Co-ordinated Project is desirable. A five-year project, with initial mid-term and final review through interaction among the collaborating scientists is envisaged. National level institutes in the fields of health, environmental engineering, nutrition, etc. are proposed to be involved.

In India, since Independence, major efforts have been made to create a scientific and technological infrastructure covering a broad spectrum of disciplines. In order to make the fullest use of the human capital resource of the country, the effort is now to involve women in all major socio-economic activities and to ensure that science and technology is an integral part of these developmental programmes of the country. In the Seventh Five Year Plan period, all major scientific departments and agencies have been asked to ensure that there will be fullest involvement of women in scientific and technological activities. There would be special programmes on application of science and technology for women both in rural and urban areas and it would be ensured that this capital resource would be optimally and meaningfully utilised for overall national development.

A step taken by the UGC has been to enhance by 10 years the eligibility age of women scientists to receive research scholarships.

As stated in the Technology Policy Statement:

> "Above all, the entire population must be imbued with self-confidence and pride in national capacity.
>
> Indian Science and Technology must unlock the creative potential of our people and help in building the India of our dreams."

For this to happen, Science and Technology must unlock the creative abilities of the women folk of our country and give priority to programmes to improve the lives of this half of our population.

—oo(O)oo—

27

INTERNATIONAL WOMEN'S DECADE

THE International Women's Decade in India witnessed unprecedented efforts from various sectors to reassess the roles of women, to enlarge the information base, to search for alternative strategies for women's equality and development and to develop policies and programmes addressed to women's specific problems and needs. The Committee on the Status of Women in India (CSWI) had been appointed by the Government in 1971 to undertake a "comprehensive examination of all the questions relating to the rights and status of women" in the context of "changing social and economic conditions in the country and new problems relating to the advancement of women". The Committee made the first major attempt to comprehend the trend of changes in women's status in the light of the Constitutional guarantees to Justice—social, economic and political; Liberty—of thought, expression, belief, faith and worship; Equality—of status and of opportunity; and Fraternity—assuring the dignity of the individual and the unity of the nation, when it submitted its report titled 'Towards Equality' to the Government at the beginning of the Decade. Apart from reviewing the impact of various legal and administrative provisions for women's advance and their current situation in all sectors, the Committee had been asked to suggest further measures "which would enable women to play their full and proper role in the building up of the nation".

The CSWI did not need to debate the need and value of gender equality, as this principle had been accepted in India more than half a century earlier, through the fundamental rights resolution of the Indian National Congress in 1931, and then built into the Constitution of the Indian Republic. The Committee's focus was on diagnosis of social trends and response to the principle of equality, with a view to identifying more effective strategies for its realisation. In the process, the Report raised some fundamental questions regarding the contradictions that appear when policies aimed at achieving gender equality have to be pursued within social structures which rest on unequal power and resource bases. The hierarchical structure of Indian society, with its diverse and complex socio-economic institutions, organisational patterns and cultural values that sanctify such institutions/patterns, makes it difficult for uniform strategies to be equally effective with different groups. Thus legal reform, education and political rights—the three instruments designed by free India to realise women's right to equality—had failed to benefit the large masses of women affected by problems of poverty, powerlessness, over-work and illiteracy.

DYNAMICS OF SOCIAL CHANGE

Identifying a linkage between the demographic trends of declining sex ratio (number of women per thousand men in the population), lower life expectancy, higher infant and maternal mortality with declining work participation, illiteracy and rising migration rates among women from the poorer sections of society, the Report stressed that the dynamics of social change and development had adversely affected a large section of women, particularly among the poor and had created new imbalances and disparities.

While the national debate on the women's question ended with the acceptance of Constitutional equality, the Report identified many areas where continued ambiguity and ambivalence in the general understanding of the need and implications of women's equality had resulted in inadequate or contradictory measures for women's advancement.

The history of discussions on women's rights in India indicated sharp variance in social response to this concept. In the Constituent Assembly, not a single dissenting voice challenged the 'historic decision' on equality, but the very first attempt by the Government to translate this abstract principle into some operational legally viable terms faced considerable resistance. In the CSWI's view, Equality is an article of faith in our Constitution, and is necessary, not merely on the grounds of social justice, but as a basic condition for the social, economic and political development of the nation. Disabilities and inequalities imposed on women have to be seen in the total context of society where large sections of the population—male and female, adults and children—suffer under the oppression of an exploitative system. It is not possible to remove these inequalities for women only. Any policy or movement for emancipation and development of women has to form part of a total movement for removal of inequalities and oppressive social institutions, if the benefits and privileges won by such action are to be shared by the entire women population and not be monopolised by a small minority. The Report also stressed the need for 'special temporary measures to transform *de jure* into *de facto* equality'.

The investigation and the recommendations of the CSWI and the guidelines provided by the World Plan of Action at Mexico have provided the basis for most of the debates on strategies, instrumentality and other policy measures to operationalise women's equality. After a full day's debate on the Report of the CSWI, Parliament adopted a unanimous resolution urging the Prime Minister to "initiate a comprehensive programme of legislative and administrative measures aimed at removing as far as possible the economic and social injustices, disabilities and discrimination to which Indian women continue to be subjected."

CONSCIOUS PARTICIPATION

Certain significant outcomes of these policy debates are a—shift in recognition—from viewing women as targets of welfare policies in the social sector to their emergence as critical groups for development. This recognition is reflected in the Sixth Five Year Plan (1980-1985) which contains, for the first time in India's planning history, a chapter on Women and Development. This shift represents reassertion of the principle of women's equality of rights—to participate effectively in the process of development, ensuring thereby movement in the direction of the Constitutional goals. It is also a reassertion of an ideology enunciated by the Father of the Nation that the future India cannot be built without the willing and conscious participation of one half of its population—women, and his own belief that it is only through such participation that women could overcome the resistance and barriers to their own equality and that the community as a whole could transform its own institutions. It is therefore a matter of satisfaction that Indian women today have entered many fields earlier considered to be only men's preserves—many of them have taken to various professions and have become scientists, lawyers, doctors, engineers, ministers, administrators, entrepreneurs, managers, etc.

A second significant development is the recognition of women as a group adversely affected by the process of economic transformation. In this case, the Constitution's guarantee of equality would be meaningless and unrealisable unless their economic status and their rights to economic independence and recognition as a contributor to the family and the national economy is improved. This is a major departure from development thinking of the past few decades, which places women squarely in the centre of policies for reduction in economic inequalities and eradication or alleviation of poverty. The Sixth Five Year Plan emphasises three strategies as essential for women's development:

a. Economic independence;

b. Educational advance; and

c. Access to health care and family planning.

The fact that economic independence is linked with access to resources is recognised in the following statements:

1. The main drawbacks in women's development have thus been mainly preoccupation with repeated pregnancies without respite, in physical work load, lack of education—formal and informal—and a preponderance of social prejudices along with lack of independent economic generation activity or independent assets. The strategy thus has to be threefold—of education, employment and health. They are inter-dependent and dependent on the total development process. In addition, the voluntary

adoption of the small family norm has to be promoted among all couples; and

2. Economic independence would accelerate the improvement of the status of women. The government would endeavour to give joint titles to husbands and wives in all developmental activities involving transfer of assets. This would be taken up for implementation to start with in programmes like distribution of land and house sites and beneficiary-oriented economic units.

This shift in terminology from welfare to development and the extension of women's areas of concern from the social services sector of education, health and welfare to the critical areas of economic development—agriculture, rural development, land rights, forest policy and access to training and investment resources for their fuller participation in independent economic activities—represents a major gain of the Decade. The first Working Group appointed by the Planning Commission on women's affairs was the Working Group on Employment of Women (1977-1978) and the first cell on women to be established was in the Ministry of Labour and Employment (1975). The first legislation on women introduced during the Decade was the ordinance promulgated in 1975 on Equal Remuneration for Men and Women, later converted into the Equal Remuneration Act, 1976.

INFORMATION EXPLOSION

Another significant development of the Decade is the explosion of information about women hitherto 'invisible' to planners and social analysts. The CSWI had pointed out that the stock of information regarding women workers was limited to the six per cent who were employed in the organised sector of the economy and left out the overwhelming majority who were occupied in agriculture and other unorganised occupations. The Indian Council of Social Science Research (ICSSR) which had assisted the CSWI's investigation by organising several studies, responded to the Committee's plea for sustained effort in this direction by sponsoring a research programme on women under the direction of a committee of eminent social scientists drawn from various social disciplines, including law. The Programme of Women's

Studies gave first priority to research on changes in occupational and employment patterns, particularly of women in the unorganised sector. The lead taken by the ICSSR was followed by a growing body of researchers around the country, bringing to light a massive amount of information regarding these 'invisible' women who were supporting their families and themselves in various types of occupations in the primary, secondary and tertiary sectors.

Recognising the need for improving the data base on women, the National Sample Survey (NSS) was directed by the Planning Commission to obtain better information on women's work in its 32nd round, which has been used in the exercises undertaken for the Sixth Five Year Plan. The Census of India, which had been criticised for its narrow definition of workers in the 1971 Census that successfully excluded a large body of women from recognition as workers, introduced a new category of 'marginal workers' in the 1981 Census. The results of this have helped to substantiate the view of the CSWI and social scientists investigating women's economic conditions that an overwhelming majority of poor women are victims of unemployment, under-employment and irregular marginal employment. Women now constitute a majority of the category of marginal workers.

The most significant development that has marked this Decade is the revival of the social debate on the women's question. The CSWI had lamented the fading out of the women's question from the public arena from the mid-Fifties. The Government has all along been aware that success in translating the Constitutional goal of gender equality would be impossible without the co-operation of public opinion and active participation by women themselves. One of the objectives of the ICSSR's research programme was to revive the social debate on women's role in society, which had developed side by side and as an integral part of the freedom struggle, "but had faded out of public memory in the decades after Independence."

ORGANISED ARTICULATION

A heartening development of the last 38 years of democracy is the growth of organised articulation of women's problems by social organisations and the support that they have been able to enlist of the

Press and some other sections of the media, and the academic and legal communities. There has been a rapid growth in women's organisations to protest against crimes of violence against women, against the institution of dowry, against discrimination in employment and economic status, and demanding better attention from the Government in women's development needs. Older, more established organisations have also become more active in these matters. All these organisations have displayed a new capacity to harness the results of academic research, the presence of sympathetic individuals in the media, in political parties, in law, academia, the bureaucracy and other professions to promote a process of consultation and dialogue between the Government specialised development agencies created by the Government and non-governmental organisations.

These consultative dialogues represent a feature of the Indian political system, developed immediately after Independence. They have been more prominent in areas that represent a national consensus. On the issues of women's equality and development, they have emerged as significant phenomena during this Decade. The CSWI was a committee of non-officials appointed by the Government. After the mandate from Parliament on the report of the CSWI, the Government framed a National Plan of Action (NPA) for Women based on the CSWI's recommendations and guidelines provided by the UN's World Plan of Action. Simultaneously, an inter-ministerial Empowered Committee examined the recommendations of the CSWI to formulate the Government's decisions thereon. These ministries were consulted while drawing up the NPA which was endorsed by the National Committee of leading women under the chairmanship of the late Prime Minister Indira Gandhi, appointed to advise on appropriate ways of celebrating the International Women's Year.

The National Committee on Women was constituted in September 1976 under the chairmanship of Prime Minister Indira Gandhi to ensure "a fair deal for women" and as an alternative to the National Commission recommended by the CSWI and the UN World Plan of Action. A Women's Welfare and Development Bureau was established in the Ministry of Social Welfare to service the National Committee and act as the nodal point within the Government to co-ordinate policies and programmes and initiate measures for women's development. The

Bureau was expected to serve as a clearing house of information on matters connected with women's development and to collaborate with other ministries for programme planning, implementation, monitoring and evaluation. To operationalise its co-ordinating role, the Bureau was backed by an inter-ministerial standing committee. Special cells for women were also established in the ministries of Labour and Employment and Rural Development, as they have a critical role to play in promoting and strengthening women's economic participation.

During 1977-1978, when exercises began for the Sixth Five Year Plan, the Planning Commission appointed the Working Group on Employment of Women and also encouraged the ministries of Agriculture and Rural Development to review their programmes and policies so that women's needs and aspirations were incorporated within their development activities planned for the rural areas. Two exercises were undertaken subsequently by the ministries of Agriculture and Rural Development:

a. Report of the Working Group on Development of Village Level Organisations of Rural Women;

b. Report of the National Committee to review the Role and Participation of Women in Agriculture and Rural Development.

Simultaneously, the Ministry of Education, then engaged in promoting a National Adult Education Programme (NAEP), recognised that women constituted the majority among adult illiterates and appointed a special committee to advise on Adult Education Programmes for women. The Ministry of Industrial Development also appointed a working group on Self-Employment for Women. All these groups included researchers and representatives of women's organisations as well as government representatives.

In 1977, the Advisory Committee on Women's Studies of the ICSSR addressed a memorandum to the Government of India titled "Critical Issues on the Status of Women, Employment, Health, Education—Priorities for Action." The memorandum represented the considered views of this group of social scientists on needed policy changes to arrest the process by which women were becoming "dispensable—economically and demographically." This preceded the appointment of the various working groups mentioned above.

NATIONAL CONFERENCE

During 1978-1979, as preparatory action for the Mid-Decade review, the Government promoted a series of State-level conferences, involving various non-official organisations, researchers, women legislators and representatives of concerned departments. These culminated in the National Conference on Women and Development sponsored by the Ministry of Social Welfare in Delhi in May 1979. The National Conference made specific recommendations in the fields of employment, health, education and political participation. The Government also assisted voluntary organisations to organise seminars and conferences on knotty issues like dowry that could help promote public opinion against such practices. Recognising the value of research and teaching on women's issues and concerns to bring about needed changes in people's ways of thinking and social values, various agencies of the Government assisted in the organisation of the First National Conference on Women's Studies in 1981. The conference resulted in the formation of the Indian Association for Women's Studies, whose primary objective is to promote the incorporation of women's issues into teaching and research activities of educational institutions and to provide a common forum for increasing interaction between academics and persons engaged in action programmes for women's development. The Association organised a Second National Conference on Women's Studies, which too received substantial support from the national and State governments and other specialised agencies.

In 1980, a group of national women's organisations and institutions specialising in research on women submitted another memorandum to the Government entitled "Indian Women in the Eighties: Development Imperatives", containing their recommendations for urgent action in the fields of employment, health, education, legislation and the establishment of national mechanisms for better attention to women's development. The memorandum was the outcome of an apprehension on the part of the signatories because the draft Sixth Five Year Plan Framework had not indicated clearly any specific measures for women's development. This began a dialogue between the Planning Commission, representatives of women's organisations, researchers and other women activists, resulting finally in the inclusion of Chapter XXVII on Women and Development in the Sixth Five Year Plan.

Another outcome of these consultations in the Planning Commission in 1980 was the involvement of the Council of Scientific and Industrial Research (CSIR) and the Department of Science and Technology (DST) in efforts to promote women's access to science and technology. While the DST developed a programme for this purpose another working group was appointed under the chairmanship of the vice-president, Council of Scientific and Industrial Research (CSIR), to examine personnel policies for bringing about a greater involvement of women in science and technology. The Group made a number of recommendations to reduce the constraints on women scientists to enhance their professional participation. On the basis of the Group's recommendation, the University Grants Commission (UGC) relaxed the age limit for women scientists who wanted to take up research.

Attempts to institutionalise these consultations may be seen in the establishment of advisory committees under the Equal Remuneration Act for the Central Statistical Organisation (CSO), the holding of one-day consultations by the Planning Commission while reviewing the achievements during the Sixth Five Year Plan, and the establishment of new working groups for the Seventh Five Year Plan. On the side of non-official groups also there is a trend towards consolidation, institutionalisation and co-operation. The CSWI had commented on women's organisations getting fragmented after independence, which had affected their representative character and solidarity. Another criticism levelled by the CSWI was of the inadequate attention paid by women's organisations (whose membership was primarily drawn from urban middle class educated women) to the problems of poor working women, particularly those in rural areas.

During the Decade, there has been an increasing trend of women's organisations taking up development activities among rural women and poor women in urban areas. In contrast to the past, such activities now focus more on employment generation rather than exclusively on health, welfare and educational efforts. Organisations have received assistance for such activities from government agencies such as the Central Social

Welfare Board (CSWB) whose socio-economic programme for generating employment for women has expanded greatly during the Decade. The Department of Science and Technology and the Ministry of Rural Development, as well as new institutions created by various State governments—Women's Development Corporations and international agencies like the ILO, UNICEF and the UN Voluntary Fund for the Women's Decade. Some bilateral assistance from various developed countries have also been utilised for this purpose.

Government programmes in the welfare sector, like ICDS, MCH, the Midday Meals programme, *balwadis,* creches, etc. have greatly helped in generating vast employment opportunities for women.

COMMON FORUMS

Women's organisations which have multiplied substantially during these 10 years display several other characteristics. The first is an increased degree of concern and protest against the rising incidence of crimes of violence against women. Organisations have joined hands in common forums to demand improvement in laws for the protection of women against rape, harassment and dowry, against discrimination in employment, and against the exclusion of women's issues and concerns from the curricula of educational institutions. Typical examples of such joint forums are the Dahej Virodhi Chetana Manch (forum to combat the dowry menace), the Forum against Oppression of Women, the Indian Association for Women's Studies and the National Movement for the Eradication of Women's Illiteracy.

A second significant feature of the new women's movement is the emergence of new militant and articulate organisations of poor working women which see development activities not as ends in themselves but as a means to improve women's overall status in the family, the neighbourhood and the political system. Outstanding examples of this type of organisation are the Self Employed Women's Association in Ahmedabad (SEWA) and the Working Women's Forum in Chennai. These organisations, each of which now has a membership of around 20,000, have been responsible for articulating the problem of poor self-employed women in unorganised occupations, who do not enjoy the benefits of any legislative protection, trade unions or recognition from the community. The efforts of these organisations have resulted in due recognition being given to the major role played by poor self-employed women in the survival of their families and in contributing to the national economy. The organisations have also demonstrated the positive role that sympathetic credit institutions can play in promoting low-cost economic activity by setting up their own co-operative banks. They have created new functions for credit institutions. The banks not only provide cheap loans to their members, but also organise training, productivity building, improving market outlets and providing technological support. They have also taken over bulk purchase of raw material to protect women from exploitation by wholesalers. The leadership provided by these credit institutions has helped to influence the development and activities of some of the government-sponsored Women's Development Corporations.

The use of development activities to empower women to fight for their rights has also helped to inspire other women's and people's organisations which have begun to work at grass-root levels. There is a new trend among these groups—a shift from doing things for needy women to doing things *with* them—that is, a move from the charitable to the participatory approach. These groups have attracted a small number of young, highly educated, professional women—as observers, mobilising field cadres, or trainers—in contrast to the earlier tradition among women's organisations that depended primarily on voluntary effort of middle-class women who did not need to earn a living and could engage in social work.

PARTICIPATORY DEVELOPMENT

The new organisations attach a lot of importance to the ideology of participatory development, and of women's rights to equality, dignity and social justice—and the training of their own cadres as well as members of the target group in decision making. Debates among these groups have led to the emergence of a new concept of '*intermediaries*' like educational institutions, research agencies and voluntary organisations at State and national levels which act as support groups between women's organisations at the grassroots level and the agencies responsible for development whose out-reach seldom comes near the women who need their assistance. The intermediaries are trying to use their own assets—of education, information and capacity to pull development support from various sources for the benefit of their client groups, without developing a patron-client relationship.

Recognising the valuable role that these intermediaries could play in extending the Government's own capacity to reach women at the grassroots, the Ministry of Social Welfare initiated in 1983, an experimental programme for establishing Women's Development Centres in selected women's colleges in Delhi. While reliance on voluntary organisations for women's development activities is an old tradition in India, this is a new trend of attempting to harness educational institutions for even non-educational development activities for women who will never reach the portals of such institutions in ordinary circumstances. It also represents an effort to utilise the enormous asset that India has—a large number of educational institutions catering exclusively to women—for the benefit of the 75 per cent of the women population who still remain outside the reach of the educational process. This experiment follows a series of previous attempts to involve educational institutions in national development activities like the National Social Service Programme and the National Adult Education Programme.

The first half of the Decade was a period of research, review and rethinking with attempts to establish needed administrative mechanisms within the Government to make women's issues visible to development planners and administrators. The policy debates were characterised by a note of urgency in response to the bleak findings of the CSWI.

NEW ISSUES IDENTIFIED

As the Decade advanced, however, new issues have been identified that make women's equality and development a far more complex goal than had been understood before. The rising incidence of crimes against women, the resistance to women's development displayed by localised power groups and the limitations of a complex bureaucracy to design or deliver appropriate programmes to women at the grassroots have led to an increasing realisation that women's development cannot be a one-way process—of benefits flowing from the Government to improve women's conditions. It has to be a combination of strategies that empower women to articulate their needs and aspirations and provide opportunities to enhance their participation in the shaping of development decisions.

The CSWI had commented on the failure of an earlier policy to induct women into local government bodies—panchayats (village councils) and municipalities—through a system of reservation of a few seats. Describing the existing provision of a few seats for women to be filled through election, co-option or nomination as a form of 'tokenism', the CSWI noted that the greatest obstacle to women's participation in such bodies came from "the general apathy and indifference of these local bodies to women's development and to change of status, particularly in rural areas." The CSWI therefore recommended the establishment of statutory women's panchayats at the village level to ensure greater participation by women in the political process "as a transitional measure to break through the traditional attitudes in rural society." The need for establishing and strengthening grassroot level organisations of women, particularly in rural areas—both as channels for development assistance and as a forum for women's participation in development decisions—has now been acknowledged.

Another knotty issue that has characterised the policy debates is the choice between special programmes for women and ensuring a fair share within general programmes. Women activists have criticised the lack of understanding, neglect of and apathy to women's issues in the general administration of all development activities. On the other hand, social scientists involved in evaluating women's programmes have criticised the marginalisation of women through special women's programmes that are ill-equipped in terms of personnel, resources and decision-making powers. They have also argued that special programmes tend to degenerate into welfarist activities and perpetuate the problem of women's invisibility in the wider development process. Sensitising individuals within the planning agencies, they claim, is not an adequate substitute for incorporating and institutionalising women's claims within all development activities.

One strategy that was tried during the Sixth Five Year Plan was to reserve a minimum quota for women in beneficiary-oriented programmes like the Training of Rural Youth for Self-Employment (TRYSEM). Another device that was discussed is the earmarking of a share of sectoral allocations (or a special component approach) in all major development activities with a view to ensuring adequate administrative and resource support. A third device recommended by various groups was a system of annual reporting by all concerned departments or ministries at both the State and national levels which could improve monitoring as well as enforce a recognition of women as a responsibility on different levels of government personnel.

ROLE OF OTHER INSTITUTIONS

National and international development strategies emphasise the role of government and women's organisations in achieving the goals of the Decade. The developments in India during the Decade have identified the important role that other institutions can play in this effort. Research and teaching institutions, financing agencies, trade unions and political parties, legal and other professions, the media and institutions that train professionals for these fields, all have a role to play in this effort. People's organisations have been a valuable source of innovative ideas and experiments. The growing economic crisis drew several responses from different groups—peasants, workers and voluntary action groups—which differ in terms of quality of intervention, organisational structures and ideological perspectives. Some of the women's action groups have thrown up interesting experiences in combining situation and group specific strategies with a collective struggle against oppression and exploitation of women.

These experiments provide a better understanding of the processes that marginalise women and earn for them the reputation of being passive, backward and apathetic to change. They have demonstrated that these characteristics, which for generations have been believed to be peculiar to women, are the results of situational constraints emanating from their unequal positions in society, and not from their psyche. The success of strategies for women's advance lies ultimately in the removal of these constraints through supportive measures, empowering women to assert their own views and demands on the development process. No doubt this is what the Father of the Nation had in mind when he invoked the time "when women will begin to affect the political deliberations of the nation."

—oo(O)oo—

28

DEMOGRAPHIC PERSPECTIVE

A study of the demographic perspective must necessarily start with the data provided ˙y the Census of India. The decennial Census of India is the largest single source of statistical information on the population of India. The last such census was conducted in 2001. As of today, a set of key population statistics based on 5 per cent sample data of the 2001 Census have been released by the Office of the Registrar-General. The brief analysis presented here is based on these key tables.

GROWTH OF FEMALE POPULATION

Unlike in most Western countries, the number of males exceeds the number of females in India. According to the 2001 Census, the male population was 531,277,078 and the female population was 495,738,169, adding up to a total of 1027,015,247 on March 1, 2001. A simple index which gives a comparative picture of the growth of male and female population is the sex ratio which is defined in the Indian Census as the number of females per one thousand males. In India, the sex ratio was 933 females per one thousand males in 1981 as compared to 930 in 1971. In 2001, it was 933 whereas in 1999, it was 927.

There has been a continuous decline in the sex ratio ever since 1901. For example, the sex ratio in 1901 was 972; it declined to 946 in 1951, 941 in 1961 and 930 in 1971. For the first time in the history of

Sex Ratio 1901-2001

Census Year	Sex Ratio (Females per 1000 Males)
1901	972
1911	964
1921	955
1931	950
1941	945
1951	946
1961	941
1971	930
1981	934
1991	927
2001	933

Source: *Census of India*, Final Population Totals, 2001.

post-independent India, the sex ratio *increased* during the decade 1971-1981. Further, a detailed study of the sex ratio in different States of India shows that the increase has not been uniform. There are States where the sex ratio had gone down between 1971 and 1981. To give a few examples, in Gujarat, the sex ratio increased from 934 to 942 during 1971-1981, while in Bihar it decreased from 954 to 946 during the same period.

In the absence of adequate and reliable data going back into the past, it is not possible to arrive at any firm conclusion on the causes of the decline in the sex ratio and the differential improvement in health conditions of males and females. The hypothesis most of ten put forward by scholars in this field suggests that the neglect of women in India is a persistent phenomenon. The 1981 Census data however raised hopes and gave cause for optimism, insofar as the long-term trend towards the decline in the sex ratio had been stemmed. The hypothesis which has been advanced to explain the slight increase in the sex ratio is that the special measures taken by the Government in the field of maternal and child care have started bearing fruit and the female survival rates

Sex Ratio (Statewise) 2001

State	Sex Ratio
Andhra Pradesh	978
Arunachal	Not available
Assam	932
Bihar	921
Chhattisgarh	Not available
Goa	960
Gujarat	921
Haryana	861
Himachal Pradesh	970
Jammu and Kashmir	900
Jharkhand	941
Karnataka	964
Kerala	1058
Madhya Pradesh	920
Maharashtra	922
Manipur	978
Meghalaya	975
Mizoram	938
Nagaland	909
Orissa	972
Punjab	874
Rajasthan	922
Sikkim	875
Tamilnadu	986
Tripura	950
Uttaranchal	964
Uttar Pradesh	898
West Bengal	934
National Capital Territory (Delhi)	821
Union Territories	
Andaman and Nicobar Islands	846
Chandigarh	773
Dadra and Nagar Haveli	811
Daman and Diu	709
Lakshadweep	947
Pondicherry	1001

are now higher. This hypothesis does seem to be plausible but cannot be fully substantiated in the absence of detailed data on various aspects of maternal and child health care, immunisation, nutrition, etc. Nevertheless, the Census figures on 1951 onwards do indicate that only in 1971-1981, the growth rate of the female population was higher than that of the male population, unlike the situation in the earlier decades.

LITERACY

The 2001 Census presents literacy figures by sex for the overall population and also for ages above 5, 10, 15 and 35. In spite of the fact that the percentage of literates as compared to the total population increased from 52.51 in 1991 to 65.38 in 2001, the overall figure of literacy is low. It was 75 per cent for males and 54 per cent for females. This means that three-fourths of the male population is literate. This brings down the gap in male-female literacy rates from 28.84 in 1991 to 21.70 in 2001. At the national level, 95.6 million females turned literate in the decade 1991-2001 while the total number of female illiterates came down to 190 million. In female literacy, Chhatisgarh occupies the first place with an increase of 24.87 during the decade ended 2001 followed by Rajasthan, Uttaranchal and Orissa which have narrowed the gap in the literacy rate and moved up in female literacy. An interesting finding is increase in female literacy is at a faster rate than the male literacy rate in all the States and Union Territories except Dadra and Nagar Haveli.

Out of 242 universities, five are women's universities. Of 11,089 colleges, 1,260 are for women.

EDUCATION FOR WOMEN'S EQUALITY

The Government of India is committed to bring about a basic change in the status of women through education. Presently, the scheme is in operation in 7,335 villages in 51 districts spread over eight States—Andhra Pradesh, Assam, Bihar, Gujarat, Karnataka, Kerala, Madhya Pradesh and Uttar Pradesh.

Of the total number of 2.97 lakh Non Formal Education (NFE) centres, 1.17 lakh are exclusively for girls. In 1999, of the 272 lakh

Literacy (Statewise) 2001

State	Literacy
Andhra Pradesh	51.17
Arunachal	44.24
Assam	56.03
Bihar	33.57
Chhattisgarh	52.40
Goa	75.51
Gujarat	58.60
Haryana	56.31
Himachal Pradesh	68.08
Jammu and Kashmir	41.82
Jharkhand	39.38
Karnataka	57.45
Kerala	87.86
Madhya Pradesh	50.28
Maharashtra	67.51
Manipur	59.70
Meghalaya	60.41
Mizoram	86.13
Nagaland	61.92
Orissa	50.97
Punjab	63.55
Rajasthan	44.34
Sikkim	61.46
Tamilnadu	64.55
Tripura	65.41
Uttaranchal	60.26
Uttar Pradesh	42.98
West Bengal	60.22
National Capital Territory (Delhi)	75.00
Union Territories	
Andaman and Nicobar Islands	75.29
Chandigarh	76.25
Dadra and Nagar Haveli	42.99
Daman and Diu	70.37
Lakshadweep	81.56
Pondicherry	74.13

enrolment in secondary and senior secondary institutions, 101 lakh were girls. Since the inception of the National Literacy Mission (in 1988), 57.96 million persons have been made literate and approximately 60 per cent of the learners under the programme are women. Emphasis has been laid on enrolment and retention of the girl-child in formal schooling and non-formal education (NFE), recruitment of rural women as teachers and removal of gender bias in the curriculum. Perhaps a more sensitive index of literacy is the female literacy rate in rural areas in contrast to urban areas. In 1981, the female literacy rate was 18.0 per cent in rural areas and 47.8 per cent in urban areas. It will be seen that there is a narrowing down of the rural-urban ratio in regard to the female literacy rate. This is indicative of the spread of female education in rural areas.

Another way of looking at the literacy figure is to compare the male and female literacy rates. In 1971, the overall male literacy rate was 39.5 per cent as compared to the female literacy rate of 18.7 per cent. In 1981, the overall male literacy rate was 46.9 per cent as compared to the female literacy rate of 24.8 per cent. In 2001, it was 75 per cent for males and 54 per cent for females. Here also, there is a narrowing down of the ratio of the male and female literacy rates. This is also true of the rural and urban literacy rates by sex.

In a country like India, there is marked demographic diversity. The State-wise variations in the literacy rate are indeed striking. For example, in Kerala, the female literacy rate was 87.86 per cent in 2001. In Rajasthan, the female literacy rate was 44.34 per cent.

SCHOOL ENROLMENT

The 1981 Census introduced a new question which is extremely valuable in understanding the state of education in the country. A direct question in regard to persons attending school or college was asked at this Census and the data were tabulated separately for males and females for the age groups 5 to 9 years and 10 to 14 years.

In the rural areas as a whole, only 25.8 per cent of the girls in the age group 5 to 9 were going to schools as compared to 55.6 in urban areas (the overall figure was 32.2 per cent). In the age group 10 to 14 years, in the rural areas as a whole, 44.3 per cent were going to schools as compared to 65.6 per cent in the urban areas (the overall figure was

50.4 per cent). The inter-State differences are striking. In Kerala 83.1 per cent of the girls in the age group 10 to 14 in rural areas were attending school, compared to only 10.4 per cent in Rajasthan. The overall school enrolment ratio for girls was less than the all-India figures (37.5 per cent) in the States of Andhra Pradesh, Bihar, Haryana, Madhya Pradesh, Orissa, Rajasthan and Uttar Pradesh. In other words, both in regard to the overall literacy rate and the literacy rate in the younger age groups of 5 to 9 years and 10 to 14 years, large tracts of India need special attention and massive programmes for schooling. In 1999, out of 272 lakh enrolment in secondary and senior secondary institutions, 101 lakh were girls.

AGE AT MARRIAGE

Despite the progress of education and social reforms, there has been, during the past several decades, a slow rise in the average at marriage in India. That the low age at marriage has many undesirable consequences for the health of mother and child has been recognised for a long time. Efforts to enforce the Child Marriage Restraint Act which stipulated a minimum age of 15 years, have not always succeeded. In 1978, this Act was further amended and the minimum age at marriage was raised to 18 years for girls and 21 for boys. An encouraging feature of the 1981 Census was that for the first time, the female age at marriage in 1981 was higher than the minimum age prescribed by law. It was 18.3 years in 1981 as compared to 17.2 years in 1971.

Raising the age at marriage has been an important contributory cause to the decline in fertility in several States and also in Kerala. A better insight into the mechanism of marriage and family can be had by considering the marital distribution of the female population. The 1981 Census figures show a sharp decline (compared to 1971) in the proportion of married females in the age group 15 to 19 years; though this is not true of the age group 20 to 24 years. For example, in 1971, in India (excluding Assam), 55.4 per cent of the females in the age group 15 to 19 were married. This figure declined to 43.5 per cent in 1981. In the case of the age group 20 to 24, married females accounted for 88.8 per cent of the total females in this age group in 1971; and 84.4 per cent in 1981. The decline is marginal in this age group.

Kerala has the lowest infant mortality rate, the lowest overall mortality rate, the highest expectation of life at birth, the highest average age at marriage and the lowest birth rate. The impact of comparatively late marriages from the point of view of mother and child care, and fertility and mortality are evident from the case of Kerala. In contrast, Rajasthan is marked by high infant mortality rate, high overall mortality rate, low expectation of life at birth, low average age at marriage and a high birth rate.

FAMILY PLANNING

There is no doubt that the high rate of population growth affects not only the health of the mother and child but the health of the economy as well. Ever since the first Five Year Plan of India was launched in 1951, family planning has become an integral part of development planning, particularly in the context of health. However, the progress on the family planning front has been far from spectacular, primarily because of widespread illiteracy in the rural areas. However, in the last decade, there has been considerable progress in regard to the practice of family planning through modern contraceptive methods.

It has been estimated by the Department of Family Welfare that in 1982-1983, over 34 million couples were protected through family planning methods (from the risk of pregnancy) compared to 13 million in 1971-1972. To quote another figure, in 1971-1972, only 12.4 per cent of the couples were effectively protected while in 1982-1983, the comparable figure was 25.9 per cent. In spite of this progress, there is a long way to go before the much cherished goal of population stabilisation is attained. The couple protection rate (CPR) was 46.2 per cent or 74.2 million persons in 2001.

One of the disquieting features of the demographic scene is the higher infant and child mortality rates of females compared to those of males. The same is true of the expectation of life at birth which is higher for males than for females. An encouraging feature, however, is the gradual narrowing of the gap between the male and the female infant mortality rates. For example, according to the Sample Registration Data of the Registrar-General, the infant mortality rate for *rural males* was 141 and for *rural females* 161 in 1972. In 1978, the comparable figures were 132 for males and 143 for females. In the urban areas, the male and female infant mortality rates are more or less the same. The overall situation in 1978 was as follows: 123 for males, 131 for females and 127 for the total population.

LIFE EXPECTATION AT BIRTH

A fairly good measure of the state of health is the expectation of life at birth. According to the Registrar-General's estimates, during 1941-1951, the expectation of life at birth was 32.5 years for males and 31.7 years for females. In the next decade, that is, 1951-1961, the figures were 41.9 for males and 40.6 for females. During 1960-1971, the expectation of life at birth for males was 46.5 while it was 44.7 for females. The decade 1971-1981 showed some encouraging signs of a somewhat higher expectation of life for females. In 2001, it was 62.3 years overall. But no firm conclusion can be drawn because of the statistical problems involved in the calculation(s) of expectation of life at birth according to different methods and various sources of data. In any case, it can reasonably be hoped that in view of the greater emphasis on maternal and child health programmes, female life expectancy would soon overtake male life expectancy as is true in all developed countries of the world.

NATIONAL HEALTH POLICY GOALS

The Government of India issued a statement on the National Health Policy in 1982, which was approved by Parliament in 1983. This Health Policy recognised the deficiencies in the existing health infrastructure, particularly in the rural areas and formulated a comprehensive policy in the field of primary health care with special emphasis on the preventive, promotive and rehabilitative aspects. The Policy identified the following priority areas as requiring urgent attention:

1. Nutrition,
2. Prevention of food adulteration and maintenance of quality drugs,
3. Water supply and sanitation,

4. Environmental protection,
5. Immunisation programme,
6. Maternal and child health services,
7. School health programme, and
8. Occupational health services.

The Health Policy also put forward the goal of net reproduction rate of one (NRR=1) by the year 2000 in order to pave the way for stabilisation of population. This was not achieved. Of particular interest is the emphasis laid on the reduction of infant mortality, pre-school child mortality, and maternal morality. A set of goals was put forward. To give a few examples:

It was expected that the infant mortality rate would be brought down from the level of 125 per thousand in 1978 to 60 per thousand by the year 2000. However, in 2001, the infant mortality rate was 70 per 1000 live births. Children dying before the age of five were 98 per 1000. The crude death rate was expected to come down from 14 to 9 by 2000 AD and the crude birth rate from 35 to 21 per thousand during the period. In 2001, the crude death rate was nine per 1000 and the crude birth rate was 26.4 per 1000.

In conclusion, it may be stated that among the priorities which deserve attention are: the need for attaining 100 per cent school enrolment among girls in the age group 5 to 9 and 10 to 14; giving opportunities for skill formation, training and employment to girls, particularly in the age group 12 to 20; and for inculcating the small family norm in the younger generation. The rapid decline in infant mortality is necessary not only from the point of view of the health programme but also for the success of the family planning programme.

—oo(O)oo—

29

INSTITUTIONAL CHANGES

REMOVAL of poverty and attainment of self-reliance were the two major objectives that the country set out to accomplish through the successive Plans. As necessary corollaries, higher growth and better distribution of incomes and a very significant step up in the domestic rate of saving were to be achieved.

The Plans have made removal of poverty as the foremost objective. It was, however, recognised that given the magnitude of the task, the removal of poverty could not be accomplished in a short period. The Plans also stressed:

- Improving the quality of life of the people in general with special reference, through a Minimum Needs Programme (MNP) whose coverage is so designed as to ensure that all parts of the country attain, within a prescribed period, nationally-acceptable standards;
- Strengthening the redistributive bias of public policies and services in favour of the poor, contributing to a reduction in inequalities of income and wealth; and
- Promoting the active involvement of all sections of the people in the process of development through appropriate education, communication and institutional strategies.

The total resources deployed for development registered a phenomenal rise. The plan investment in all sectors of the economy increased by 3.6 times during the first half of the decade over the previous five years and by 6.7 times in the second half of the women's decade. It is noteworthy that, except at the margins, all the resources for development in India are from the country's own public and private resources.

Most significant has been the shift in the pattern of investment in favour of programmes of poverty alleviation, minimum needs, social services (education, health, family planning and housing). They have received proportionately much higher and unprecedented plan allocations. There was also a record increase in investment in irrigation which aimed at improving productivity and employment in the agricultural sector which is India's principal economic sector.

The full force of these increases was, however, offset to a considerable extent by substantial increases in *prices* and *population* during this period. The prices at the wholesale and consumer level as also for urban non-manual employment, nearly doubled between 1973-74 and 1982-83. The population increased from 54.82 million to 68.52 million between 1971 and 1981 and to 1,127,015,247 in 2001. One aspect of the population increase was that it was much higher than anticipated by the planners which implied revision of plan estimates/ investment on minimum needs and additional jobs.

IMPLEMENTATION

Experience has shown that increased plan allocations are necessary but not a sufficient condition for reaching out the intended benefits to either the poverty population in general or women in particular.

The National Committee on Backward Areas and the Expert Group on Poverty Alleviation Programmes of the Planning Commission have pointed out that only a small proportion of the Plan funds are actually reaching poor households or backward areas.

Addressing itself to the problems and style of implementation, the Fifth Plan stressed the need for "improving the apex implementation machinery of the Government of the Centre and the States...to spearhead the reform of the implementation process at lower levels.." The Fifth Plan had argued that, in the past, public participation and commitment could not be actualised "because development tasks regarding public involvement were not carefully assigned to various representative institutions and voluntary organisations along with the concomitant resources and adequate motivation could not be created (for local and Panchayat Raj bodies) because schemes at the national and State level did not contain any provision for the exercise of initiative either for introducing the modification or for the taking up of supplemental activities to suit local conditions." The Sixth Plan reiterated these suggestions but with no significant improvement in results.

A paper on 'Choices of Implementing Agencies' which analyses the main continuous causes for poor implementation has argued for a more durable and reliable institutional base embodying real decentralisation in the form of a District Government, in short, to devolve development functions to representative bodies at the district level with constitutional backing. The Central Government, too, has initiated consultations with the State governments for effective ways of decentralisation of development planning administration.

SOME ASPECTS OF PLAN ALLOCATIONS

While the pattern of plan investment has gradually shown greater accommodation for sensitive programmes like the Minimum Needs Programme, some imbalances in allocation of resources deserve notice in order that correctives could be undertaken.

Elementary education is fundamental to human development. India's Constitution makers had made it obligatory for all children until they completed the age of 14 years. But even the Sixth Plan expected to enrol only 50.3 per cent of the 6-11 years age group, two-thirds of the non-enrolled children being girls. If universalisation of elementary education is to be achieved, nearly 50 million additional children (6-11 years of age) will have to be covered. Efforts to meet this challenge have to be mounted.

The accessibility of schools continues to be particularly difficult for girl students as also for boys and girls from poor households. The hours observed by the schools, the inadequacy (also indifferent attendance) of teachers, buildings, equipment along with the very thin (and irrelevant) content of education have been acknowledged as major impediments. Attempts at non-formal education to supplement the school system have been too feeble, if not ineffectual. These shortcomings need to be overcome.

Poor Plan allocations are stated to be one of the important factors of these problems besetting elementary education. The allocations are poor both with regard to the needs of elementary education as well as in relation to other sectors. Even with the MNP, for example, allocation for elementary education during the Fourth Plan was only Rs. 226 crore as compared with nearly twice that sum for rural electrification at Rs. 427 crore. In the Fifth Plan, the allocation for elementary education, though raised to Rs. 452 crore, was still below the provision made for rural roads at Rs. 498 crore. Again, during the Sixth Plan, rural roads were allocated Rs. 1,165 crore compared with Rs. 919 crore for elementary education. Even at Rs. 919 crore, the sum is so inadequate that (as pointed out by the Steering Group on Elementary Education for the Seventh Plan), nearly 95 per cent of it goes only towards teachers' salaries leaving little for educational equipment or activities let alone syllabus innovations.

Another area neglected hitherto is village and cottage industries. These are highly important for generating non-farm employment which matters most to weaker sections and women and in backward areas in particular.

INSTITUTIONAL CREDIT

Direct Plan allocations are supplemented by institutional credit. Institutional credit has two objectives:

1. To release the poor from excruciating indebtedness to private moneylenders; and

2. To enable the poor—especially the self-employed which includes a large proportion of women—to acquire productive assets for economic progress.

There has been a manifold increase in recent years in the availability of institutional credit to what the policy-makers rightly recognise as the 'neglected sectors.' However, within this group, the bulk of the resources has gone to the relatively stronger elements such as the modern small-scale industry, bigger farmers for agricultural mechanisation (tractors, etc.); government corporations for holding community stocks ("indirect finance"); for purchase of taxis and scooters and to the retail trade. The self-employed, including professionals, accounted for less than 0.8 per cent and even within this group, the bottom categories of the self-employed barely figured.

The wider implications of inadequate allocations for elementary education and rural health in particular can be appreciated against the findings of a study of the Centre for Development Studies, Kerala; that the widespread availability of rural health care facilities and high literacy rate in Kerala were cumulatively responsible for the remarkable decline in the Kerala birth rate.

Population is frequently mentioned as the foremost issue in India's development, but the strategy which can effectively deflate the population growth has not received due attention even after the findings of the Kerala Study in the mid-Seventies. Of the total resources investment in development during the Sixth Plan, elementary education and rural health combined received only 0.8 per cent of the total investment.

It is, therefore, not sufficient that the gross investment in the economy should be increasing. It is even more important that it flows adequately where it is most critically needed. From the woman's point of view, the two sectors, namely, elementary education and rural health, are of paramount importance. The past neglect of girls' education has to be remedied. The special health care needs of women have to be met.

It is equally important to provide adequate wherewithal for economic activities of the poor and the self-employed by way of Plan support and institutional credit.

POSITION OF WOMEN IN DEVELOPMENT

One of the issues that comes up in the discussion of the methodology for safeguarding the interests of women in the development process in developing countries is: how far is there justification for women-focused investment and women-uplifting strategies.

Broadly describing the less-developed countries (LDCs) as those which find themselves in a situation where large sections of the population are poor or deprived in terms of basic necessities like food, health, education, housing; where there is also inequality in the dispersal of these facilities and finally, where there is a shortage of currently-available material resources for setting the situation right as rapidly as possible, it becomes clear why there could be this doubt about justification.

Entire populations—not only of women, but men and children—require all the attention and strengthening that can be mobilised. Thus there is the question why women in particular, from this equally deprived or otherwise oppressed population, need to have their interests safeguarded.

It is also true that in such societies there is a built-in gender specific format within the society—what can be called the place of women—which is not strongly identified or articulated and often cannot be identified due to the overall pressures for survival, especially survival with dignity.

Various forms of overall political and economic environment such as racism and militarism apart from colonialism, appear as priority, as clouds which have to be dissolved before individualisation based on gender can be legitimised. Thus we see the women's movement in these countries moving between the gender specific concerns with a fluidity.

In fact, it can be said that there is a continuous attempt by the women's movement and those who articulate on its behalf to find the right chord to strike in such a situation. This kind of doubt or concern or position is not only limited to the perspective of women (leadership) in India but is part of the perspective of those engaged in this field all over the world.

The kind of perspective thus influences both the nature and style and quantum of development which could be called specifically women-focused. Thus it is necessary to see how women appear or disappear in the overall development focus and method.

Research has exposed the differential impact of development of men and women. The analysis of this phenomena has revealed the basis of this differential impact, namely, specification of women in a society, and in the household. While this specification and its rigidity often gets resolved or diffused within sections of societies or social and economic categories of society which have access to resources including knowledge, the differential not only persists but tends to increase in no resource and zero resource families and households and sections of the population.

Women are known to be still engaged in cooking, cleaning, child care, often water and fuel-fetching much more predominantly and regularly than men all over the world. They perform these roles along with the earning of income especially amongst the low-resource households since they are regularly responsible for the domestic and household zone. Programmes meant to improve household income do not necessarily improve women's well-being.

NEW PROBLEM AREAS

The same reasons create a difference in the needs of women and capability to absorb certain kinds of development. The neglect of this differential impact has often revealed new problem areas as a result of a development programme. For example, a programme of improving rice cultivation may have had extension services directed to men, while women in fact are the main transplanters of rice seedlings.

Hence, production does not move in the anticipated direction or speed. Although it is now widely recognised that women make important contributions to agriculture, little has been done to make women productive through extension and input supply services."

In another situation, intensification of production could add to the hardship of women in terms of the work burden.

In a third, intensification of production could displace women from earning opportunities due to the introduction of a technology which does not continue to use their earlier contributions, for example, hand spinning of wool to machine spinning, hand rolling of cigarettes to machine rolling, etc. A study of the modernisation of the traditional handloom weaving industry of Kashmir reveals that women are displaced as the new looms use only mill-made yarn; thus hundreds of women hand spinners lose their livelihood. Furthermore, new looms are not an addition but are replacing the old ones.

A similar situation in agriculture can be seen in Rajasthan and West Bengal. In these areas a majority of women of the working-force age-group earn a steady income from the weeding of fields; improved agriculture with inputs like chemical fertilisers remove the weeds and take away a source of income for rural female labour.

Women's need for fuel has shown that their ability to absorb new research on alternative sources of energy has been much greater than that of men. The movement in the Himalayas has highlighted the differences in articulated needs between men and women. For example, in an area, men wanted to plant fruit trees to earn cash incomes, and women wanted fuel and fodder trees. For some time to come this allocation of responsibility will continue and development will have to take notice of it.

Looking at this from another perspective, women have begun to move towards the direction of capitalising on this difference rather than lamenting it.

SURVIVAL STRATEGIES

Responding to the current economic and cultural crisis in the globe today, a meeting of women researchers from five continents held in India affirmed that it was women's survival strategies in the face of crises that could provide the model for survival-development strategies for the Third World. It was suggested that global, economic and political crises which were squeezing many countries into poverty, into accepting new colonialism and dependence, could only be withstood and overcome if the methods followed by poor women for survival in the larger context of exploitation and crisis can be used as a model.

The model was to strengthen the small-scale, decentralised and less dependent, more self-reliant forms of organisation, not only of production but of society. Local level function-based organisations were identified as being more effective, more flexible, more adaptable in comparison to men's highly politicised impersonal forms of organisations. Described below are some specific aspects of women's development in India in recent years.

In the programme-wise outlays and expenditure for women's welfare in the social welfare section under Central and Centrally-sponsored schemes, statistics on the promotion of grassroots level women's organisations are a new feature. There is however an obvious discrimination in allocations for this section despite its being a new programme and thus requiring greater initial expenditure. But the *real* area for planning and development to relate itself to women, especially amongst the poor, is in the economic sectors: agriculture, industry and construction as well as in basic needs.

Programmes like NREP, IRDP, Dairy Development, Sericulture Development, Handloom, Handicrafts and Village Industry Development, provide a large economic base to women workers who form 50 per cent and more of the labour of these sectors. However, the fact that women are present in equal numbers, if not predominantly, is not taken notice of in investment or project design. Their biological and domestic needs are ignored, that is, no social amenities are built into the project, and secondly, neither extension nor training is tuned towards them. In some cases, the new investment might even disengage them unintentionally because of ignorance of their existence in the occupation.

Areas of critical importance to women, namely, health, drinking water, education, are less than one per cent of the planned expenditure. Roads take more than two-and-a-half times the expenditure on health. Yet any articulation by women reveals health to be a priority over roads.

Further analysis of development expenditure affirms the view that where poverty is pervasive, the perception of needs and priorities by planners is a male or patriarchal perception. Thus, even here, whether in village or district or higher level bodies which pick up the signals, design and implement development, the voice/opinion of women will be different from that of men in choice of priority, even for the community. Hence it is now clear that even in such societies women have to be consulted and vehicles for expression of their opinion created.

METHODOLOGIES TO INTEGRATE WOMEN IN DEVELOPMENT

There are many structures instituted at the governmental and non-governmental level for the advancement of women and for delivery of development services to them.

As early as 1953, in order that the extensive voluntary effort generated by the freedom movement should not be dissipated, the Central Social Welfare Board (CSWB) was created as the first government structure to foster systematically voluntary effort in social welfare. The CSWB had a very special status in that though set up and funded by the government, it had a large measure of autonomy and flexibility in the utilisation of funds.

Headed by a chairperson, always a woman, the 39 members of its central body were drawn from amongst voluntary social workers, non-government organisations, representatives of State governments, representatives of Parliament and of the ministries of the Government of India connected with social welfare programmes.

The programmes of the CSWB that are particularly aimed at improving the delivery of development services to women are the socio-economic programmes, Mahila Mandals, and Training of Rural Women in Public Cooperation.

The CSWB is a national body that is involved in women's development at three levels—policy, programmes and implementation. The Board generates policy at the central level through its linkages with voluntary women's organisations, formulates its own development programmes for women on the basis of funds given by the government and implements programmes through its Welfare Extension Projects which reach remote areas of the country.

The major government structures for implementing development programmes for women at the Centre are the ministries of Education, Social Welfare, Health and Family Planning and Labour.

In 1963-1964, the Government established the Department of Social Welfare which was later made into a full-fledged ministry in charge of policy, planning and implementation. The Ministry of Social Welfare remains the nodal government agency for women's development in India.

In 1971, the Government of India decided to initiate a comprehensive review of women in India and appointed the Committee on the Status of Women in India. The Committee's report was receivedby the Government in 1975 and emphasised the need for a national machinery to co-ordinate and intensify the efforts and measures needed for women's development. In response to this recommendation, the National Plan of Action for Women was drawn up. The NPA, like the World Plan of Action, stressed the need of a national machinery for women.

NATIONAL MACHINERY

The national machinery set up in 1975 consists of

a. a national committee;

b. a steering committee for the national committee;

c. an inter-departmental co-ordination committee; and

d. a women's welfare and development bureau.

The National Committee functions on the policy as well as programme implementation level. It advises the Central and State governments on the legislative and administrative measures necessary for removing, as far as possible, economic and social injustices, disabilities and discrimination against Indian women. It also reviews the progress and implementation of programmes designed for this purpose. The steering committee identifies fundamental questions and demarcates the roles of government, political parties and women's organisations. The official level inter-departmental committee, constituted on the recommendation of the steering committee provides analysis of the bureaucratic framework in terms of women's development programmes and their implementation.

The primary function of the women's bureau is to plan financial and physical targets for the implementation of the NPA. This also necessitates the collection and analysis of data, the co-ordination of development programmes for women in different sectors and through State governments.

In the Planning Commission, the Social Planning Division has been delegated to frame and evaluate a policy with respect to women.

The women's bureau provides programme guidelines to the Commission based on what they conceive as the felt needs of different groups of women in the country. Since the planning process began, the focus for women's development has been largely in the areas of health, education and welfare. This remained largely unchanged till the Fourth Five Year Plan. The Fifth and Sixth Plans which correspond to the Women's Decade have emphasised the need to provide training for women, functional literacy, nutrition and child care. Employment has been another priority area, along with training in marketing and management.

Various Central ministries formulate their own programmes either specifically for women or which include women in them. These run concurrently with the schemes of the Ministry of Social Welfare and the Social Planning Division. They include health programmes of the Ministry of Health and Family Welfare and State health departments, education programmes of the Central Department of Education and its State counterparts, and vocational training programmes. The Ministry of Agriculture and Irrigation also has women's programmes, conducted by its Department of Rural Development and the Extension Directorate in the Department of Agriculture.

NATIONAL CORPORATIONS AND BOARDS

There are many national corporations and boards in India which are autonomous but government-supported. They are associated with products such as milk, handicrafts, handlooms, coir, silk, etc. They provide institutional support in terms of finance, training and marketing. However, here it is pertinent to discuss the National Dairy Development Board (NDDB)—which is in charge of a massive programme to increase the production of milk—and the Khadi and Village Industries Commission (KVIC).

The relevance of this project here is that the programme is based on cooperativisation of the milk producers, a pre-condition to receiving either inputs like animal fodder or veterinary services or market support through the milk collection centres. This project has helped to strengthen, to make remunerative and provide a regular income from small-scale dairying and ownership of even one milch animal for thousands of peasant households across the country. Its basic strategy is infrastructure support on a collective basis for individual, self-employed, dispersed rural households, a valuable model for the promotion of any production on a decentralised scale be it milk, fish, eggs, coir, handicrafts, etc. especially for women who in many of these villages prefer home-based work.

Amongst the dairy households, research revealed that though women were the main workers, not more than 10 per cent were in the co-operatives. This is gradually being rectified. It was also found that their health was deteriorating due to overburdening of work. A health and child care and food activity centre has been set up to take care of this.

In the national economy, women's participation is low. But in the case of the KVIC programmes, women's participation is approximately 45 per cent. The activities of the KVIC focus on self-employment schemes which assist individual artisans in various trades. Besides financial assistance, individual artisans are given support in the form of co-operatives and institutions.

The principle objective of the science and technology programme of the KVIC is upgradation and transfer of technology which makes the tasks of artisans, particularly women, less onerous by lessening the drudgery in their work. Technologies so developed are simple and not capital intensive.

The University Grants Commission (UGC) showed a concern in developing programmes relating to women's studies in Indian universities. Research units on women's studies were established in State Universities. In the Ministry of Labour and in the Department of Rural Development, which play a critical and vital role in women's development, special cells for women's programmes have been set up.

TRAINING INSTITUTES FOR WOMEN

Institutional training is provided by different ministries, primarily the Ministry of Labour and Rehabilitation and the Ministry of Social Welfare. These vocational training institutes provide instructor training, basic training and advanced training in selected trades suitable for women. The National Vocational Training Institute at Delhi, and two regional vocational training institutes in Mumbai and Bangalore were set up by the Ministry of Labour in 1977 in response to changing patterns in women's employment in the labour market.

The pattern of women's employment is monitored by employment exchanges which have provided valuable data on job availability in the organised sector. It is seen that the number of women job seekers rose two-and-a-half times from 1971 to 2001.

Given the federal structure of the country and the well-defined roles and responsibilities of the Central and State governments, machinery at the State level for co-ordinated measures for women's development is a critical need. Earlier, there were no separate cells for women's development planning at the State level. However, urged by the Central Government many States have set up directorates of women's welfare and also women's economic development corporations.

The Women's Development Corporations set up in 1975 by the Andhra Pradesh and Maharashtra governments were meant as one-stop agencies for women's development, but in fact undertake only a part of the necessary functions. The Punjab Women and Children's Development and Welfare Corporation, set up in 1979, follows a model similar to those of Andhra Pradesh and Maharashtra. The Andhra Pradesh and Punjab organisations are essentially co-operative financial bodies which identify activities suitable for women and provide credit and an institutional framework conducive to self-employment. The Maharashtra Women's Development Corporation is a marketing organisation functioning through mahila mandals to promote employment.

RURAL WOMEN'S ORGANISATIONS

The Department of Rural Development and the Central Social Welfare Board have a permanent network of extension personnel at the block and village level. This infrastructure is used by all departments to implement the women's component of their programmes. These two agencies together maintain almost 50,000 rural women's clubs or mahila mandals, sponsored by the States, all over India. Three or four women staff each mahila mandal to conduct the regular activities of craft training, creche and balwadi (a nursery for pre-school children) services.

Considering the critical need of economic participation by women and of women's organisations at the grassroots level, the Working Group on the Development of Village Level Organisations for Rural Women was set up by the Ministry of Agriculture in 1977. The objectives of rural women's organisations, as stated in the working group, was that new programmes should focus on drawing a majority of rural women into the mainstream of development and enable them to function as instruments of social change.

The Working Group further recommended that a single type of organisation like mahila mandals cannot meet all the needs of the various groups of women in a community. Hence the need to encourage several types of women's grassroots organisations like co-operatives and trade unions.

Initiatives and responses of non-government organisations to the challenge deserve notice. Non-government activity in India has received an impetus both through the support of policy and programmes at the national level as well as through the initiative of voluntary women's organisations.

There has been a variety in the growth of non-government women's organisations in India, all varying widely in their ideology, size, focus and financial status. Including village level institutions, there are approximately 50,000 women's organisations in India.

A categorisation of these organisations is possible according to the size and nature of their coverage, the focus of their programmes and objectives and by the methodology which they adopt for reaching women. During the 1950s, organisations which fought for social reform established national networks with branches at State and district level, and focused on the emancipation of women in the field of education, health and social reform through social legislation. Through extensive training programmes, they created links with rural village women's groups for extension welfare projects.

Women's wings of political parties became the platform not only for political participation by women but also for large-scale agitations on social issues. Political participation of women was also carried out through student bodies, trade unions, kisan sabhas and professional organisations. We have also seen the growth of 'intermediary organisations' which compound research, training, and consultancy—feeding the women's movement, the academic areas of curriculum and text books, as well as the government at the policy, programme and implementation level. They bridge the usual divide between research and action.

These are usually funded by the Indian Council for Social Science Research (ICSSR), the various sectoral ministries as well as development and UN agencies for specific activities like documentation, seminars and consultancy projects. Their role has been close to women's organisations but different. They have attracted the attention of those concerned with the subject sufficiently to be referred to in the report on Women and Development Working Group set up to prepare a chapter for the Seventh Five Year Plan. This type of intermediary organisation-mediating between policy makers, researchers, women's organisations and grassroots activism, is now being spread through the universities—as women's study centres as well as a women's project within the National Service Scheme which is a requirement of students.

At the grassroots level, there are agencies engaged in organising rural women and also engaged in developmental activity with the poor. This generally has the same focus as government programmes such as agriculture, animal and dairy development, rural industries and social services. Community works include relief and rehabilitation work. These agencies have professionalised voluntarism but have adopted and experimented with different strategies for achieving development objectives. With the objectives of the women's development redefined, the focus of voluntary efforts and the focus of government effort has been enlarged from a purely welfare approach to women's need to a recognition of the need not only to integrate women in development but also to redefine women's needs from a feminist and participatory perspective. The growth and contribution of voluntary agencies has been in a new direction and in new activities apart from the traditionally identified social welfare activities.

NON-GOVERNMENT ORGANISATIONS

The non-government organisations (NGOs) have provided support to women's development through forums for articulation of the needs of poor women and the recognition and integration of these in macro-level planning.

For instance, the whole issue and debate on self-employment and on the integration of the unorganised sector of whom over six per cent are women, was generated by the growth and activities of organisations like SEWA. SEWA is a trade union for poor, unorganised women workers who supply essential goods and services to city dwellers. Women activities and voluntary workers have focused on the rights of this category of women workers, hitherto classified as non-workers due to errors in data collection method. The growth of such trade unions of the self-employed have received recognition and support from government departments, especially the Ministry of Social Welfare and the Ministry of Labour.

The SEWA methodology, namely, survey, identification of occupational clusters of women and identification of their priorities has been made the basis of the new programme for the Development of Women and Children in Rural Areas (DWCRA). This programme is implemented in India by the Ministry of Rural Development with financial support from the UNICEF. At the action level, the SEWA methodology has been replicated by other non-government organisations. There are now seven SEWAS in India forming an unified body—Sewa Bharat.

Similarly, the realisation of the impact on women of environmental denudation and the need for a national conservation policy was recognised by the efforts of the Dashdi Gram Swarajya Sangh (DGSS). The year 1974 was the beginning of the Chipko movement ('hug' the trees so as to save them), initiated by this organisation, a voluntary group dedicated to styles of hill development which would safeguard local interests. As development priorities for the hill people, the Government of India set up a commission to investigate the issues in hill development. The Commission declared the entire catchment area as protected and recommended the involvement of government in massive afforestation programmes. Financial aid to the DGSS has been channelled through appropriate State government departments and voluntary agencies co-opted on an Advisory Committee of the Planning Commission on Hill Development.

In 1980, public action by women's groups on the rape issue resulted in a great deal of feminist activity in India. The anti-rape movement became the first major issue on the action front around which women began to get together and protest collectively at several places in the country. The Forum Against Rape subsequently became the Forum Against Repression of Women.

Similar action has been taken by women's organisations on the issue of portrayal of women in the media. A committee of voluntary workers was formed in 1979 to safeguard, articulate and protest and mobilise public opinion against the media's vested interest in the portrayal of women.

On the research level, the growing awareness of the lack of accurate data on women and the consequent obstacles in integrating women into development, led research organisations to create associations and forums for the advancement of women's studies. The Economists Interested in Women's Issue Groups (EIWIG) formed in 1981-1982, provides a network for strengthening non-government effort in research and articulation on behalf of women in the field of economics and statistics.

The Association has organised several national level seminars on women's issues, and has been an important focus for changing curriculum, identifying resource persons and sponsoring national level research projects.

A national network of the Kasturba Gandhi National Memorial Trust has called for the eradication of female illiteracy in India. A national committee of voluntary organisations with the promised support of the Ministry of Education has been formed with the idea of strengthening government's efforts in this direction using all available resources and methodologies.

INTERACTION WITH NGOS

There has been continuing emphasis on the part of the government that given the extent of poverty, and the magnitude of the task of development, both government and non-government organisations must complement each other. This interaction is reflected on three levels—policy, programmes, and the micro-level.

The Committee on Employment has recommended that already existing programmes like the NREP and MNP could be developed to absorb a large number of unemployed women. The working group on Women and Development also stresses the need for social security and health insurance programmes specifically for women.

SEWA was represented on this committee and this has brought greater recognition of the needs of self-employed women in the unorganised sector.

The process used by the Ministry of Labour in setting up the committee on employment greatly facilitated interaction between the civil servant in charge of the cell and the Minister and in addition had a woman officer in the Cell to act as a secretary.

The Voluntary Action Bureau, set up by the CSWB in 1982 to investigate reported cases of dowry violence and atrocities against women and children was an experiment in collaboration between the Board and voluntary organisations. An advisory committee made up of representatives of both government and voluntary agencies was set up to guide the activities of the Bureau.

Apart from attending to actual cases, the Committee was to promote co-ordination between the CSWB and various voluntary agencies, and to educate and mobilise public opinion against social crimes.

The Development of Women and Children in Rural Areas (DWCRA) programme, initiated in 1982, is another such experiment in co-ordination between the government and voluntary agencies. The DWCRA was conceived as a joint venture at the planning stage itself, as identification of women's needs and participation and the block plans for women were entrusted to six women's voluntary agencies, including research institutions working in urban and rural areas. Women's organisations have been co-opted to prepare block level plans for the first time to provide a data base for the programme. It was hoped that in the process of conducting surveys and group meetings for the plan, these organisations would establish rapport with the community. Training of functionaries was also to be done by the voluntary agencies.

Several initiatives were taken by the Government to build forums for discussion on women's issues and strengthen interaction at the micro-level. The Committee for Implementation of Legal Aid Schemes (CILAS), set up in 1982-1983 which serves the purpose of assisting activist groups in public litigation and safeguarding people's interests are officials of the government who work in close contact with non-government social action groups.

A second such forum is the People's Action for Development, India (PADI), through which voluntary agencies express their views to the government. PADI also channelises funds to voluntary agencies and in turn promotes efforts for implementing development programmes.

Mobile Creches for Working Mothers' Children is another voluntary organisation which is aimed specifically at reaching women workers in construction activity with support services like creches, nutrition, health and adult education.

To facilitate voluntary agencies implementing development programmes at the micro-level, the Ministry of Social Welfare and the CSWB give grants-in-aid to voluntary organisations.

Thus we see that co-option by government and voluntary effort in women's development is occurring at every level—both institutionally and informally.

Problems of government and non-government agencies for women's development however are manifold. The Government faces bureaucratic bottlenecks, functionaries are not oriented towards women's issues and other implementation procedures which, given the scale of development necessary, hamper programmes from reaching the target group.

On the other hand, voluntary agencies lack sufficient resources, trained personnel and management abilities. Furthermore, NGOs are often centred around a personality and this reduces their staying power. It is these problems that reduce the effectiveness of institutions for women's development. The roles, objectives and implementation procedures of an institution used to be the focal point when setting up agencies; the formation of institutions cannot in itself bring change.

Strategies which can improve the implementation process for government agencies are simplification of procedures (for example, people unable to read or write need to fill in a form to procure government loans), and training functionaries to orient them to a women's perspective. Voluntary agencies could improve their effectiveness by being less dependent on a personality in its activities, and not over-extending themselves as this causes breaks in linkages and interaction with other NGOs and government agencies.

ROLE OF INSTITUTIONAL ARRANGEMENTS—OBSTACLES AND PROSPECTS

There certainly has been a visible impact on a wide range of institutions and agencies in terms at least of making them aware that there is a women's component or a woman issue

The range would include:

1. Political parties where the women's wing has been given far greater importance in terms of allocations for meetings and other activities since 1975. These groups have joined forces with non-political women's organisations and research institutions at national, regional and local levels on national issues such as dowry, action against atrocities and on economic policies, such as resisting technological change which displaces women. In other words, political parties have strengthened their own women's wing and are aware that there is a women's voice/vote which might be linked to women's needs;

2. National research and development organisations, whether dealing with social areas such as education and pollution control or economic areas such as rural development and nutrition for separate programme areas dealing with women; and

3. Ground level development effort such as district level planning and credit for poverty households which are also providing a women's component.

Thus, it can be suggested that whether it is at the policy level, programme level, research area or training area, national institutions and autonomous bodies as well as those linked to government now are at least linked to women's interests.

Yet the issue remains whether the institutional support which has so far been provided is adequate. One of the strong suggestions implemented was to have a separate Commission for Women and a separate executive authority for women. Such an idea was tried out for another group of disadvantaged people, namely Scheduled Castes and Tribes. For the Scheduled Caste and Tribal population, there is a Commission which is mainly an evaluating and reporting body with no budget for expenditure.

There is a component plan, and also a sub-plan within the national plan specially oriented to development in areas which are intensely populated by these categories.

However, this three-pronged approach has not been found satisfactory. The Commission which observes, evaluates and reports has found that even with these arrangements there has been no difference in the inequity faced by these groups. This analysis pinpoints the weaknesses of the system of both designing the programme as well as disbursing the funds and development impulses towards these disadvantaged, less visible groups.

NEED FOR CHANGE IN PROCESS

This concern is similar to the concern expressed by women that in order to participate and benefit from development, what is needed is not only institutional arrangements such as having a women's organisation in a village which would also get a share of the development budget, but a change in the *process*; development design, development aim and development content.

The NREP became a regular part of the Sixth Five Year Plan from April 1981. Under this programme, the generation of additional employment to the extent of 300-400 million man-days per year for the unemployed and under-employed in the rural areas was envisaged. The programme generated 1,157 million man-days of employment in the three-year period. Some crucial constraints in implementation have been the supply of foodgrains as part of the wages; difficulties of local resources mobilisation; works implemented through the NREP are often not co-ordinated and integrated with the requirements of the families identified for assistance under the IRDP.

Works selected under NREP are not being decided as was expected through popular participation and consultation with village panchayats and gram sabhas. The tendency is to go in for building construction with high material components counter to the basic objectives of the programme, and with a low female participation rate.

The biggest problems faced in the implementation of the ICDS schemes begun in 1974-1975 are those of co-ordination between the department/agencies involved in the delivery of the package. These are Education, Public Health, Block, CARE and UNICEF. Often two block areas are included in one project and the Block Development Officer (BDO) has no hand in the selection of the anganwadi workers. The Health Department feels that most of the programmes in the schemes, namely health check ups, immunisation and referral services, are in their area, and they should have control over the scheme.

Cooperation and support from the people is lacking; there is no substantial participation at the village level. Anganwadis are often situated in such locations that one or the other section of the village community will not be able to participate. If anganwadis are situated in the Scheduled Caste areas, then mothers of other castes do not participate in the programmes and vice versa. Such communal feelings which seriously affect the implementation of a programme can only be removed if the co-operation of the village leaders is obtained. Where moves *have* to been made to form district and project level co-ordination committees, they are ineffective because functionaries like the BDO and DC take little interest in its affairs.

Lastly, the 'beneficiaries' are not well-informed of the benefits to be derived from the various programmes.

The programme evaluation organisation of the Planning Commission points out several deficiencies in MEGS. The fundamental premises of the scheme is that works undertaken should provide gainful and productive employment, gainful to the individual and productive for the economy, for unskilled persons in rural areas who are prepared to do manual work, but cannot find such jobs. The scheme is meant to continue for several years and has its own administrative machinery, research and development unit.

LACK OF COMPLEMENTARY INVESTMENT

In most completed works, however, the necessary complementary investment has not been made. The areas where this is lacking is well construction, land-levelling, application of fertilisers and other essential inputs. This has resulted in the sub-optimal use of the potential created. No specific agency seems to have been assigned responsibility for the follow-up. Furthermore, the physical condition of the works have deteriorated with time due to lack of maintenance which was the responsibility of departments executing the works of zila parishads.

The scheme, though it employed a large percentage of women, has not taken any note of this fact either in conception, design, implementation or personnel, nor even in evaluation of impact. The only item relevant to women workers' participation in the scheme is that creches should be provided. However, creches are rarely established and where they are, they are no more than flimsy shacks with minimal facilities. Women are also inhibited from participating because of the male/female labour mix requirement for construction work—women often cannot mobilise men to join their gang. Yet, more males register than report for work, while more females report than register. There has been no investigation of this pattern. It is probably that men register and then send women to work on the sites.

A system must be devised by which a community's self-identification in terms of strength and weakness should precede the next step where the community articulates the development that it prefers which then is translated into a response in terms of money and technical and human services. Ultimately, a reform of such magnitude and high purpose can progress significantly only with the most active involvement of the people themselves (particularly the Scheduled Castes and Scheduled Tribes).

This was brought out very clearly in an exercise for looking at development utilisation amongst poverty households in response to the Plan endeavours. The main findings of this study have been summarised below:

1. Where additional employment opportunities are available, they are attributable to programmes and projects which being gender neutral tend to be better utilised by men. Men have used training programmes better; their title to property is usually adequate to make them eligible for loans and grants under IRDP and such other programmes, whereas women have often to provide co-guarantors; men are more aware of opportunities and possible benefits whereas women usually get to know about only those schemes which the men of the household care to pass on to them, except when there are active mahila mandals or other non-governmental agencies devoted to the welfare of women. In consequence, the extent of benefit derived by women as wage earners is not commensurate with their felt needs.

2. The government machinery has proliferated and spread out to villages in many forms, but this has not been reflected in a corresponding increase in its reach of the poor, more especially of poor women. Even allowing for the many, there is little doubt that they generally tend to approach their tasks mechanically in terms of set procedures and targets which may not always be relevant to the individual beneficiary. Local caste and power groups often limit their interest and activity. Actual beneficiaries of programmes have many times turned out to be not the neediest or the most eligible on objective grounds., but those who were economically better off and socially or politically better connected.

3. In general, women beneficiaries found it easier to deal with women functionaries such as ANM, LHV and anganwadi workers and agricultural extension workers when available. Efforts by women to organise co-operative

societies of their own, as by fisherwomen in the Udipi area, found the going hard, due to the cumbersome procedures but mostly due to lack of official and technical support. It was the commonly expressed view that with more women functionaries at all levels of government departments, they would find it much easier to deal with the administrative system and would be better able to utilise opportunities for economic and social improvement.

4. Mahila mandals, where they existed, were not very impressive. They were, for the most part, confined to upper caste women, often reflecting the power structure in the village. Apart from providing some opportunity for women to learn tailoring, embroidery or such craft, they had little impact on the overall work situation for women. The mahila mandals were set up as delivery mechanisms for services and this became an end in itself. They have not really empowered village women to participate effectively in development, that is, decide financial allocations and priorities as women.

5. Planning, as now conceived and practised, benefits women only incidentally and residually rather than as equal claimants with men. Their special requirement and problems are virtually bypassed by the planning process.

Looking to the future, it is recognised that "women, who constitute half of the workforce in rural areas have to be given much greater recognition than hitherto and equipped with and trained for skills to operate their own and household incomes."

The Plan stresses that rural development programmes must be implemented in an integrated manner using a decentralised framework with participation at the grassroots level through panchayats and zila parishads. The approach to the Seventh Plan is an added impetus to concepts and efforts initiated for the development of women. The basic approach towards women's development is to be one of attitudinal change of women towards themselves and of society in general. "For propagating these concepts and creating the right types of awareness, important instruments that may be used are radio, television, educational institutions, mahila mandals and voluntary agencies." Voluntary organisations will have to be encouraged and fully utilised in taking the programmes to the masses. The grant-in-aid rules would be simplified so as to enable deserving voluntary agencies to obtain help from ministries.

It is proposed to prepare a document on the role of voluntary agencies in development and give them due recognition. It may be necessary now to specifically demarcate the kind of roles and functions that non-government organisations can perform in implementing the objectives of women's development meaningfully and find strategies to support and strengthen these organisations. There is scope within the Indian political system, bulwarked by the long tradition of social welfare and voluntarism for a variety of styles, approaches and alternatives to reach poor women with anti-poverty programmes.

VOLUNTARY AGENCIES

By virtue of their close contact at the grassroots and micro level functioning, voluntary agencies are in a better position to develop human resources and create a framework for their participation. Women are not only to be reached by the welfare model but as part of other subsets such as farmers, landless labour, bonded labour, artisans, etc. Voluntary agencies are eminently suited to experiment with the most effective strategies for reaching them, not being limited by the inflexibility of a bureaucratic structure and its rules and regulations.

The Government is ready to build on the expertise and experience of the NGOs and facilitate their use in areas they are best equipped to handle. In turn, voluntary agencies can function as monitors of government programmes and feed back information from the field to the government. Co-ordination between the government and voluntary agencies is considerably hampered at the procedural level. To change this situation, the administrative structure needs to be further streamlined and this may be achieved by delegating chosen voluntary agencies to disburse financial aid to others at the district and block level. They can also provide a new kind of orientation to government functionaries by undertaking training programmes for civil servants and familiarising them with women's perspectives on their need for development. This is already being done informally. The government could also help to upgrade the skills of voluntary agencies personnel, especially in areas such as financial management and project design.

Lastly, the government and voluntary organisations need to co-operate in stressing the need in the future for an accurate and up-to-date picture of the various problems of women based on community-wide surveys which are now virtually non-existent. They will help to better identify target groups; the information and experience gathered can be incorporated into local planning, regional, State planning and national planning.

The issue now in the Indian context is one of methodology; the integration of women into a development process by a participatory delivery of programmes on the one side and, on the other, the strengthening of women's organisations, articulation and their capacity to absorb development inputs and become a part of the process. For this, the next few years, it is hoped, will see the growth of a systematic decentralisation process and a streamlining of linkages of government delivery and implementation by NGOs, which will speed up the process of women's development.

—oo(O)oo—

SECTION IV

The New Millennium: Stark Contrasts

30

Matrimonial Advertisements

A feature almost unique to Indian society is the matrimonial advertisement seeking suitable matches for boys and girls. In India, these advertisements run to countless pages each day in various newspapers of the country. A foreigner would be puzzled to think of a reason for this spate of newspaper advertisements unless, of course, he knew something of the traditions and culture of India.

During the post-independence period, rapid urbanisation and the disintegration of the old caste *panchayats* (organisations of particular communities) despite the strong tradition of exogamous and endogamous rules for marriages in India, parents looking for suitable matches for their children were finding it difficult to find partners who complied with these rules. It was then that they took recourse to newspapers that served to publicise their needs in a very wide area. In each matrimonial advertisement, the caste of the person seeking a suitable match is almost always mentioned. A random survey of these advertisements revealed some interesting features. In cities, the average age of boys wanting brides was between 23 and 28, while in the case of girls it was between 20 and 25. Of these advertisers, 66 per cent of the boys were within the age group 26 to 28 and an almost equal percentage of girls fell in the age group 23 to 25.

It was further observed that most of the advertisements were from the upper middle classes. Further, a majority of them related to persons who were highly educated, had well established social and economic standing or belonged to prosperous business families.

A majority of the boys specified employed girls, preferably teachers. Doctors preferred to marry doctors. Educated parents of girls sought doctors and engineers or other professionals while business families looked for boys from the business community.

Apart from these newspaper advertisements, caste organisations and marriage bureaux have come into existence. In the West, these bureaux matched those couples who, individually, had been unsuccessful in finding a suitable mate. In India, however, the advertisements are an attempt to fill the gap created by the disintegration of the old caste *panchayats* that had enabled them to find a match in caste, creed, education, money, social status, etc. These advertisements are followed up with an exchange of letters between the parents and a meeting is arranged at the girl's house. If the parties are satisfied, the marriage is agreed upon.

Despite expansion of education among the youth and criticism of the old tradition of arranged marriages based on caste and economic considerations, there is still a gulf between ideas and practice even among the most sophisticated classes. There was a tendency among the young people, mostly college students, to follow Western forms of behaviour. Dating and petting has become common in India. However, when it comes to marriage, a majority of the young people follow their parents' wishes in choosing a suitable partner. In effect, while it was all right to go around with a boy or a girl, and even indulge in pre-marital sex sometimes, the youth were reluctant to marry people who indulged in such activities.

Thirty years ago, the optimum age was 20, or just below--the age at which beauty queens get selected. With emerging demand for brides with higher education and specialisation, the same has moved up by a few years. But anyone pushing 30 has to do some explaining, such as "looking younger than she is". That is the irony. Young men and women climbing up the career ladder through their late twenties face an altogether different prospect; while some men keep on notching gains, women start losing heavily in the marriage market.

Beauty is the common denominator, as for as well as offered--some offers with epithets like 'exceptionally' or 'ravishingly' beautiful.

There is almost an obsessive concern with height. With the ideal around 158 cm or 5 ft., 3 in, many girls are still failing to make it—better nutrition has yet to make its due impact on height.

It is rather intriguing why slimness is so much in demand. Perhaps the term is popular because 'slim' is such a nice-sounding word. After all, who can vouchsafe that today's slim will not be tomorrow's plump? An obese condition that is apt to attract unwelcome attention is euphemistically described as 'healthy'.

In our colour-conscious setting, the skin pigment is paramount. The ads give umpteen gradations of fair: very fair, most fair, extremely fair, milky white. On the other hand 'wheatish' alone is there to accommodate all shades of the less fair. It is a pity, the Queen's English is not inclined to incorporate this picturesque word.

It is still a sexist world where a girl's physical attributes are under far closer scrutiny than that of the boy. Any female infirmity, such as stammering or squint, or even spectacles, has to be listed out bravely while boys rarely bother to mention their bodily 'imperfections'. And this is when males, on average, are heir to more body disorders than females.

However, one significant development has occurred. Instead of keeping mostly mum over the boy's personality, his looks increasingly find a mention. But mostly remains confined to the word 'handsome' or 'very handsome'. Indeed, if what is advertised in 'boys' and 'girls' turns out to be true, we should rate ourselves as the most beautiful people on the planet.

The most popular epithet used for girls is 'homely', both offered and demanded. Surely, there are other descriptions of her good nature, such as amiable, affectionate, simple-natured, sweet-natured, soft-spoken, cooperative, cheerful or perfect. Yet the adjective 'homely' takes the cake. 'Homely' in the Concise Oxford Dictionary, means simple, primitive, unpretentious. Americans are far more harsher; the New Webster defines it as plain in appearance, unattractive.

Yet, to us, the word 'homely' (taken as home-loving) symbolises the very quintessence of what an Indian male and his family would want of the new bride; at the minimum it denotes a good homemaker, a devoted housewife, an obedient daughter-in-law, and would be doting mother—in short, a giver and not a taker. And the homely part is not to be pared down, irrespective of her being engaged in out-of-home work.

Close on the heels of beauty comes education; the higher, the better, preferably professional or technical with its better potential for earning. Yet the 'open sesame' is still convent education—popularly associated with the ease of speaking English and a flair for social mixing. Many bride seekers specify it as eminently desirable whereas some others make it an obligatory requirement. Similarly, on the girl's side, such education is invariably highlighted. Even a brief spell of convent schooling could qualify for being 'convented; some have started putting forth phrases like 'throughout convent education'.

There was a time when a bride wanting to work outside met with family resistance, even hostility. The wheel has come full circle in the last 2-3 decades. Working wives are now preferred, often actively sought after.

At certain levels, a girl's job and salary become as crucial to her marriage prospects as her looks and family. Of course, some people are seeking career women as wives for more equal partnership—let alone women themselves finding work satisfaction as the prime consideration in a double income. With the growing consumer culture and inflation, the attractions of a double income are obvious.

What strikes one most while reading today's matrimonial ads is the growth thrust on money power. Parents of girls enumerate their wealth. And so do the parents of boys. At one time, the only child was thought to be somewhat unfortunate, having missed the fun of having siblings. Now the fact of someone being the only child is boldly advertised for its property potential.

The groom's side seems to have an easier job in ads. You list your requirements of the bride and then mainly concentrate on detailing the groom's income—often mentioned in terms of five figures or six figures or seven figures--and the family property, more so if it includes a house in South Delhi. Age, height, looks, and family do play a part but it is primarily his capacity as a solid provider that matters.

Grooms do not have to spell that they are caring or that they would be a help at home. At best, it is made out on their behalf that they have 'clean habits'.

Composing a concise matrimonial ad for a near one is not such a simple affair. You have to compress a complex human equation in some 50 words--loquacity costs money. To pack maximum meaning into minimum words, a sort of telegraphic language has emerged that calls for some skill in deciphering. 'Decent marriage', for one, is a meaning-laden term.

In our matrimonial ads (increasingly backed by technology advances like e-mail) while the concept of an ideal husband has remained largely unchanged over the years, the concept of an ideal wife has undergone a sea change in the last few decades. Besides being young, beautiful, slim, tall, fair, homely, well-educated and hailing from an acceptable family, she should be an actual or potential working mate. The Indian woman's role in marriage as evidenced from these ads, has been changing rather radically as compared to the Indian man's.

—oo(O)oo—

31

DOWRY

THE solemnisation of a marriage is an important social function all over the world. In Indian society, it has more significance because, as stated elsewhere, it creates a bond not only between two individuals but also between two families. Among almost all the patrilineal communities in India, the transfer of the bride to the groom's family is accompanied by dowry. Among certain communities, the dowry is given as a bride price to the girl's parents. This bride price is paid in cash or kind depending on the region and the tribe. This practice was also prevalent among certain lower castes, but they are now slowly converting bride price for dowry.

The sex ratio in a community has an important bearing on the institution of dowry especially where the marriage is controlled by strict rules of endogamy and exogamy. Besides bride price, another custom that is disappearing is that of child marriage because of the efforts of social reformers and legislative measures. Unfortunately the evil of dowry remains.

The prevalence of dowry and bride price must be considered as they reflect on the status of women. The idea behind the payment of a bride price is based on the consideration for the loss of a productive worker in the girl's family to the boy's family. Among communities where the custom of bride price prevails, the girl enjoys a good status, as she involves no burden to her parents. However, girls for whom a bride price is paid are always conscious that, in their husbands' families, they are considered as having been bought. Among some tribes and poorer sections of society, the bride price took a heavy toll on the parents of the boy and in some cases, the debt incurred by the parents had to be paid off in life-long servitude to landowners and rich castes. Thus, the custom of bride price is fundamentally based on the concept of women being property, and their exchange involves payment. To end this indignity to women, a provision was made in the Dowry Prohibition Act, 1961, against the payment of bride price.

The term 'dowry' signifies a payment (in cash or in kind) made to the son-in-law or to his parents. Dowry also includes enormous wasteful expenses incurred on entertaining the bridegroom's marriage party. Dowry giving families are obliged to continue giving gifts on festive and ceremonial occasions and on child birth, marriage, etc. This practice goes on for a few years and is usually considered to cover inadequate dowry at the time of marriage.

Dowry is linked with many social and cultural elements that justify and perpetuate the practice. Among Hindus and Muslims, the notion of dowry is the pre-*mortem* realisation of the daughter's right of inheritance to parental property, as she has to leave her natal family to join that of her husband's.

As stated earlier, parents gave huge dowries on the marriage of girls to ensure economic security of the couple. In course of time, this developed into a major consideration and virtually assumed the form of the price of the bridegroom. Because of the prevalence of endogamous marriages in Hindu society, this resulted in a kind of competition and the boy's parents began demanding dowry based on their social and economic status. This tradition resulted in much social malpractice.

Among the various movements of social reform initiated during the last century, the one for eradicating dowry has been in the forefront. Almost all reformers and thinkers as well as social organisations have raised their voice against it. During the post-independence period, this reform campaign gained momentum and even legislative measures were taken imposing limits on the amount of dowry and imposing fine and imprisonment for their violation. However, the custom of dowry still holds strongly in Indian society with people evolving new methods of evading legal prohibition and social disapproval. Dowry has become the main item of discussion in the negotiations for marriage. Before legal restrictions were put in place, dowry was openly exhibited as it was felt that the higher the dowry the higher the status of the contracting families.

The failure of social and legal sanctions against dowry calls for an analysis as to whether there are defects in the legal provisions or the tradition is so deep-rooted that it calls for a more radical approach. To do this, we must consider what dowry consists of, why it is asked for and why it is paid. In common parlance, dowry is that amount of money or goods that is given by the bride's parents to the bridegroom's parents. However, in practice, all that one party receives from the other is termed dowry. Dowry is usually paid by the parents of the girl although in certain castes and communities, it is the other way around. This has been discussed earlier. The background and circumstances on which dowry is based can be briefly stated as under.

Historically, the most important psychological reason for the payment of dowry is the natural desire of every parent to ensure that his daughter is not considered a slave in the family that she marries into. As a token of affection and support they send presents in the form of money or goods to convey that the bride is not helpless but the beloved daughter of a prosperous family and should be treated accordingly. In course of time, this practice degenerated into the present evil tradition of dowry.

In earlier times, women and property were treated at par. Apart from certain ruling classes, the lot of women among the masses was extremely hard and their humiliation was considered normal. This motivated parents of girls to ensure decent treatment to their daughters in their husband's house by giving dowry at the time of marriage and sending presents to the husband's family throughout her life. To some extent, this practice continues in Hindu society.

Thus, dowry or gifts to the husband's family were regarded as the cost of ensuring that the girl was properly treated. In certain forms of marriage, there was an explicit condition that in case of ill treatment of the bride or divorce, the dowry was to be restored to the bride or her parents. The '*mehr*' ceremony among Muslims whereby each Muslim husband assumes the responsibility of paying an amount of money to the wife in the case of divorce testifies to this.

The practice of dowry has now assumed another aspect. Today, dowry is not merely a guarantee against possible ill-treatment of the bride, but is tantamount to purchasing certain comforts and economic security for it. Among the higher and upper middle classes, women are economically dependent on their husbands. In other words, they are considered to be an economic burden on their husbands and to alleviate this burden the bride's parents have to give a dowry consistent with the financial standing or potential of the bridegroom and his family. Dowry can be termed as the price paid to purchase comfort and luxuries for the bride. It is significant that the practice of dowry is more prevalent among the upper and higher middle classes, whereas in the lower classes it is not significant because, among them, women participate equally in productive labour and other activities and, thus, are not a burden on their husbands. On the contrary, the bride adds to the income of the family.

The practice of dowry cannot be eradicated by legal and social sanctions, as they do not touch even the fringe of the problem. During the last quarter of a century, dowry has assumed another aspect. Now the amount is influenced by the educational qualifications or economic standing of the bridegroom and is decided before giving consent to the alliance.

Negotiations for dowry are commercial transactions with more or less well defined slabs for different professions among different caste groups, for example, men in higher administrative, engineering and medical services receive the highest dowries. Thus, the tradition of giving gifts to the bride when she went to her husband's home assumed the form of a commercial transaction. The justification for dowry usually presented by parents of the boys are:

1. They have spent huge amounts on their son's education which they have to recover on the occasion of his marriage;
2. They have to give dowry for their daughter's marriage, which means they have to receive dowry for the son's marriage.

It is clear from this that the problem of dowry is too complicated a social problem and the expansion of education has failed to liberate the minds of the people from the influence of this tradition. On the contrary, today the highly educated boys with lucrative incomes expect a much higher dowry. The girl's parents, wishing their daughter to join a prosperous family, have no option but to pay the dowry demanded of them. Education among girls has also proved to be of little help in solving this problem, as they aspire to marry men who are more highly educated than they are and which requires payment of higher dowry.

Material considerations, that is, financial position and professional opportunities have always been an important criterion for deciding the marriage, even in the West where marriage is said to be mainly based on mutual attraction. What is deplorable is not the practice of dowry itself but the fact that it is compulsive.

Section 3 of the Dowry Prohibition Act of 1961 prescribes a penalty for giving or taking dowry with a fine of up to Rs. 5,000 and/or imprisonment up to six months. However, the Act has failed to curb this practice and, in spite of the huge growth of this evil custom, there are very few cases reported under this Act. A well phased programme to transform the standard of values and behaviour and radical reform at the attitudinal level are required to re-establish the dignity of women. This can best be done by arousing social consciousness in this regard.

DOWRY IN THE WEST

Before industrialisation of the West, when land was the only potential source of income, parents exercised great influence on their children's choice of a spouse through their control over the inheritance. Rural youth had to obtain their parents' permission for marriage, unless they were sure of acquiring land through their own effort. The dowry system was, therefore, prevalent in a major part of Europe and girls had little scope to marry according to their own choice. A survey conducted in 1952 revealed that 65 per cent of German women contacted in that sample said they had brought a dowry with them [Elizabeth Noelle and Erich Peter Neumann (Eds.). *Jorbuch der Offentichen Meinung 1947-1955.* (*Altensbach am Bodenses*)].

Till quite recently, dowry was prevalent in southern Italy. Banfield comments, "without a dowry, a Montenegro girl cannot make a satisfactory marriage." (Edward C. Banfield. *The Moral Basis of a Backward Society.* New York: The Free Press of Glencoe, 1958).

In a survey in Belgium, the answer to the question: "Do young people take account of the material difficulties that they would encounter after marriage?" supported the fact of parental control concerning choice of a spouse. Thirty-nine per cent agreed that young people did not pay attention to the material consideration while the remaining 61 per cent replied that young people gave weight to it even if the parents did not intervene in the choice of a spouse (Clare Le Plae, *Les Financialles.* Louvain Institute de Recherches Economiques et Sociales, 1947). In the early stage of a courtship, parents sometimes did not intervene simply because they did not know what was going on.

The change in the custom of dowry in the West can be attributed to many factors. Land is no more the primary source of wealth and parents have less control over the occupations of their sons and daughters. The growing tendency among young people to decide for themselves and the relative instability of the marriage which often ends in divorce, force parents not to make substantial expenditure on the marriage of their children. In this connection, Shelsky commented: "Formerly, one could not marry except on the condition that he had already a good situation (an essential factor for security) while now one marries in order to construct an existence together, to create a certain security (*La Sociologie Compare e de la Famille Contempraine*, Paris Centre Nationale de la Recherche Scientifique, 1955).

Dowry has disappeared from Europe, except among certain higher social strata where, strictly speaking, it is not dowry. Similarly, Indian society has been undergoing a change, especially after independence, and new values and standards of behaviour are developing. This is the only silver lining to the cloud of dowry that covers Indian society. Also increasing male-female promiscuity in colleges and professions and court marriages when parents object to their choice, may contribute to the elimination of dowry in India.

—oo(O)oo—

32

THE PURDAH SYSTEM

DOUBLE standards of morality enjoining strictest chastity on unmarried girls and marital fidelity on wives while granting unrestricted freedom to men, led to the introduction of the *purdah* system among many African and Asian societies which prohibited women, including girls approaching puberty, from letting themselves be seen by any man apart from the male members of their immediate family. When outside the house, women had to veil their faces.

On the development of the *purdah* system, Qurratulain Hyder states: "During the eighth century A. D., the Arab ruling classes under Ommayad Caliph Walid II acquired a taste for opulence and licentiousness of Roman proportions. As courtesans and local and foreign dancing girls flocked to Baghdad, respectable people began to segregate their women." [Devaki Jain (Ed.) *Indian Women*. New Delhi: Government of India, Publications Division, 1975).

This was subsequently systemised and respectable housewives were required to veil their faces in public as a matter of course. The *Quran* also emphasised modesty, decorum and chastity and women were advised not to display their ornaments and features to outsiders. Traditional values evolved on the behaviour pattern of the upper classes of society and adopted by other sections of society in a bid to enhance their status in the social hierarchy. This explains the spread of the *purdah* system.

Historians agree that the *purdah* system did not exist in India until the advent of the Muslims. The participation of women in religious ceremonies as well as social functions during the *Vedic* period testifies to unrestricted association of women among men. However, by the time of the epics (c. 100 B.C.) the possessive attitude of the ruling nobility resulted in seclusion of the women of the royal and aristocratic families, but the system of *purdah* as such did not exist in early Hindu society.

As is evident from sculptural panels in Buddhist and Hindu monuments the urban women did not lead a life of seclusion. They are often depicted on the balconies of their houses watching festive processions. The only exception was the community of Namboodiri Brahmin women of Kerala who covered their faces with palm leaves when they left the house. Their freedom was so restricted that even in their own wedding ceremonies, the Namboodiri bride was substituted by a Nair girl in those ceremonies which required the bride to leave the women's section of the household.

During the Muslim rule in India, the fusion of the two cultures resulted in the introduction of this custom in Hindu society in the 15th century, especially in the villages, where it persists to some extent. The introduction of the *purdah* system in Hindu society was perhaps motivated by way of imitation of the practice of Muslim rulers and also as protection for the women. Some contemporary lawgivers have justified the *purdah* system on account of its being based on the old Vedic injunction to keep a close watch on women.

The Indian family still consists of members of three generations along with collateral relatives, in which men and women form separate groups with little inter-personal contact. Women's activities are restricted to the house while the men take care of outside activities. There is little common interest between men and women and sex constitutes almost the sole tie between husband and wife.

The *purdah* system in rural Hindu society is less rigid than among the Muslims and *purdah* is observed only in the presence of elderly male members as a token of respect. Among Indian Muslims, the custom of a woman coming out of the house wearing a veil or in fully covered vehicles was started by the ruling nobility, from where it extended to other sections of society including rural areas. Today, however, the *purdah* system is observed only in a few families and the vestiges are fast disappearing as education spreads among women and the objective of equal rights for women gains grounds. This has led to certain basic structural changes within the value system and behavioural norms.

—oo(O)oo—

SECTION V

Empowerment at Work

33

Empowering Women

THE Sixth Five Year Plan (1980-1985) is a landmark in the women's cause because it introduces the concept of Women and Development. No more piecemeal strategies, but an integrated, realistic and *regenerative* development effort; the pyramid, so long wobbling unsteadily on its axis, is at last set right. The target is now clearly visualised in terms of economic independence for women as well as educational advancement and access to comprehensive health care systems. All are inter-related, all part of one basic dynamic.

It was long recognised that any genuine developmental effort must aim at improving the quality of life of women in society, which only a multi-faceted approach can achieve; isolated statistics are rarely a satisfactory index. Development is possible only when it is a people's movement, and therefore, our planners, from the outset, recognised the value of working with motivated groups, women's organisations and other non-governmental agencies. Women are playing a seminal role in development projects, both as participants and as beneficiaries. Working together with committed groups, there is a determination to effect fundamental and far-reaching changes at the grassroots level where all development begins. Welfare is not a trickle of water sprinkled over parched earth, but a determination to restore to earth her vital, creative life-giving power.

Literacy is one of the most fundamental of our freedoms, essential for a healthy, independent and fulfilled life. The Government has been working closely with voluntary organisations in many projects for adult and vocational education, and special schemes for giving assistance to children of pre-school age.

Programmes of vocational education pay rich dividends. Take the case of Pratima, a young lovely, spirited girl, always doubling over with laughter, able to hold her own with anyone. She would marry a man of her own choice, it was sure. But appearances can be deceptive; she was yet another victim of dowry, discarded within four months of marriage. In spite of this harrowing experience, she retained her zest for life; her determination was intact. A condensed education programme enabled her spirit of independence to have a material base; she became a midwife, able to help the suffering as well as to live a life of dignity.

Ironic though this sounds (and terribly sad). Pratima was one of the lucky ones, so many like her get burnt. Yet the Condensed Education Courses (for women between the ages of 18-30 years) have gone a long way towards enabling women to stand squarely on their own feet; and in asserting their own independence as they move one step closer to the national goal.

Pratima is not alone; her sisters in Orissa and Maharashtra and Sikkim and every corner of the country are participating and benefiting from the Condensed Courses of Education. Many of these are conducted by non-governmental organisations and registered voluntary women's organisations (provided they have at least three years' operational experience in conducting educational programmes), by educational institutions, and other bodies. The Government, through the Central Social Welfare Board, provides grants to cover expenses on maintenance of students, stipends, salaries for instructors, equipment, accommodation, and other necessary expenditure. Because of this co-ordinated effort, thousands of women are providing valuable service to the community. As *dais*, nurses and primary school teachers, they also spread ideas about nutrition, hygiene and family planning. By living and working *within* village, local or tribal communities, they are able, by their own example, to make great inroads into local habits and customs that normally resist change, especially when it comes from the outside world. Most important, these women, by earning their own living, establish that a woman can be independent, and thus hold a torch up to others.

The three-fold targets of economic independence, educational advancement and health care for women have be articulated in policy planning documents, but several organisations, government and voluntary, have recognised and been working towards this goal from the very beginning.

Some vocational training schemes have assisted urban women. At some places, training is given to women in radio and television maintenance; the world of electronics, a new and exciting field with tremendous possibilities, is opening out to women. Most of the women who have completed such courses are absorbed by the local electronics industry. One such successful person recounted how her brothers, loving and supportive though they were, just refused to believe that a woman could handle such difficult and sensitive work. One simply cannot overestimate the positive impact of schemes of this sort; women get a tremendous sense of confidence, as well as the material satisfaction of supplementing a meagre family income. Social mores, sexist attitudes, popular prejudice; all are undermined. This woman and her brothers are as close as ever; family ties have not been weakened but bonded with mutual respect.

In fact, it is really remarkable—and encouraging—how widely an educational programme diffuses, and in turn promotes, further development. And success is much more obvious when literacy is coupled with other broad-based developmental programmes. This is what voluntary organisations are always working towards.

Women are being taught such a range of skills to enable them to earn a living. There is a whole gamut of socio-economic programmes that extend to women who require assistance. Grants of up to Rs. 3 lakh are available to voluntary organisations, depending upon the nature of the scheme. Many production units, training-cum production units ancillary to large industries, handloom, handicraft or self-employment units have benefited from these programmes, as have agro-based units such as dairy, goatery, piggery, sheep breeding and poultry farms.

As women break new ground, and in increasing numbers, so many new inputs are necessary. Fine work is being done by the Mahila Mandals all over the country. They are provided assistance, particularly in rural areas, to benefit village women and children. Another exciting programme is Training of Rural Women in Public Co-operation. Training camps are organised all over the country to encourage women to participate in the developmental process at the grassroots level. The Government provides resources to voluntary groups to conduct field surveys, hold short-term training camps and pursue follow-up action for up to half a year. Thus every attempt is being made to ensure that more and more women participate in the vital decision making process of the community; decisions affecting women are so often taken in fora where their voice is strangely silent. The training camps aim to counteract this; to educate women and also to motivate them to play a greater, more meaningful role in their own lives.

For urban women, striking out in new directions can be a painful and tortuous experience, as the existing infrastructure is far from adequate. This is particularly true in the case of unmarried women, which underscores the need for many more hostels for working women. The Government provides assistance for setting up hostels for women from low income groups.

For the most part, schemes for the development of women filter through the whole family; and often beyond it as well. Health camps held in Sikkim, for example, to reach women of remote areas to motivate them on child immunisation and family planning, have attracted large numbers of villagers; and modern ideas on hygiene, nutrition and proper cooking methods have captured the popular imagination. The medical services offered by these camps have benefited not only women and their families, but entire villages; and even reached lamas in secluded mountain monasteries.

As brave new winds of change sweep across the land, we have to ensure that children (the most vulnerable and the most precious part of any society) are at the receiving end of beneficial schemes; without this no other developmental effort really adds up to much. To help the child is to help the mother, and when the mother is employed or otherwise unable to bring up her infant, a creche provides a safe and simple answer. Children up to the age of five are cared for by specially trained attendants, given supplementary nutrition, taught basic education and personal hygiene and given regular medical check-ups. The Central Social Welfare Board launched its own Creche Programme in 1977 (earlier this was handled by the Department of Social Welfare). Children of low income group families are eligible for assistance; the creche programme initially urban in character and specifically for uncared-for children of migrant labour, has not extended to rural and tribal areas. The Board gives grants towards recurring expenses per unit of 25 children, and also some additional help towards equipment. Institutions that participate are required to match the grant by 10 per cent (except on salary). The persistent demand for more and more creches from all over the country testifies to the popularity of this scheme; as also to the fact that we have touched only the tip of the iceberg where child-welfare is concerned.

Other programmes for child welfare and development where the Government gives resources to voluntary bodies include a Supplementary Nutrition Programme designed to benefit children (of the age group 3-5 years) of families of low income groups. Grants include assistance towards staff salaries as well as providing food supplements. Family counselling centres provide a wide range of services to benefit women and children who are victims of violence and exploitation. Legal aid, counselling, medical treatment, vocational training and shelters are all provided within this scheme. The grant given to the organisation wishing to establish such a centre is up to 80 per cent of approved expenditure per centre (subject to a maximum amount) per year. A bride harassed by her in-laws for bringing insufficient dowry, another escaping from exploitation, maybe forced prostitution, can all find shelter and sanctuary in homes devoted to helping women; and also the hope of a new life, a new tomorrow.

In 1958, a scheme for holiday camps for children was initiated. Recreation being regarded as essential for the healthy development of one's personality, it was realised that this was so often denied to children of deprived families. Many voluntary agencies came forward, sharing the commitment to bring some moments of undistilled joy into a child's life.

By and large, this programme focuses on children between the ages of 10-16 years, from families whose income is below a certain level and which does not allow for much to be spent on recreation. For about two weeks, a group of about 50 children live, laugh and play together; learning how to function as a group, and enjoying the experience of community participation. This scheme was extended to benefit handicapped children too. Grants are given to different types of camps, including those for handicapped children. These grants cover different kinds of expenses and are aimed at making children feel that they are part of a larger community, and can participate meaningfully in it.

The handicapped, of course, require special care and love if they are to develop a sense of self-reliance and confidence. Various voluntary groups are working constantly to provide shelter and comfort to those who cannot look after themselves. In Mangalore, good work is being done teaching inmates of a home spinning, doll making, even poultry farming; young physically handicapped girls can also enjoy the work experience by making jute bags, or painting; work and self reliance alone bring dignity to life. And looking at the joy on faces, young and old, the frustrations, the hurdles, the struggles, acquire a new meaning.

The Constitution guarantees equality to all; and in working to fully realise this, everyone has a role to play; the State, voluntary organisations, motivated individuals, everyone. Development of women, welfare of children, these terms are synonymous with the development and enrichment of society.

Standing as we are today, at the beginning of a new millenium, it is time to take stock of what has been achieved, and to chart out targets for the future. Much has been achieved in some crucial sectors; in others, a valuable beginning has been made. More and more women are coming forward, often against all odds, to take their rightful place in the building of a society of which we are all a part. Even deep-rooted social bias is beginning to give way before determined assault. The progress of any society is primarily dependent on the role women play in the community. We must work to ensure that woman is born free and bold, capable of immense strength and boundless compassion; a true custodian of all that we cherish; woman inspired, women empowered.

—oo(O)oo—

34

WOMEN TODAY

WHEN a woman presses her way into the bazaar in the textile city of Ahmedabad, she alternately smiles and glowers. Redesigned used garments are piled on her head, and she smiles at prospective customers, advertising her inventory. But whenever a bazaar hoodlum crosses her path, symbolising the obstructions she has faced in the past as an unaided poor working woman, she glowers. The last decades have flung some slender but serviceable bridges to women to begin the journey from a limited unfulfilled existence to a life of purpose and dignity. And this woman is on the bridge.

Women themselves have chiselled the tools that are now heaving them out of the inner spaces of society where they were confined. Their strength has found expression in the exploding grid of women's organisations. The stirrings of strength have arisen from deep country, from mud-walled huts, from exhausted fields, from steep hillsides, from cratered valleys. Women have responded to the combined pressures of depleting resources, modernisation, inflation and acted 'spontaneously' to seek stable income and some dignity. An infinitesimal percentage has succeeded, ruled as Prime Minister, climbed Everest. But the beginning is substantial.

Shift scene. A young tribal woman in Bihar's central plateau. The Grand Trunk railway line has changed her life. Twice a week, she and other women board a second-class compartment, often ticketless, with an assortment of forest products—twigs for cleaning teeth, fuelwood, leaf plates. Eager customers on the train and platform purchase their wares. The train travels to major cities in the green Ganges basin, where the women buy salt, lentils, kerosene, soap, readymade garments, nylon ribbons and travel back on the homeward journey two nights after they had left the village. The trip means money, essential goods and freedom. As women are more adept at sales, the men stay behind in the village. Women are on the move.

In distant Kerala, the southern State famous for its indices of high female literacy and low population growth, a woman farms her one-fifth hectare plot in the Periyar river catchment in the multi-cropping mode. Dadap trees fringe the plot, and around their trunks are twined black pepper vines. Coffee bushes thrive in the shade, and in turn provide a canopy to cardamom plants. A few rubber trees stand gashed for the daily collection of latex. Until a few years ago, the woman helped her husband with paddy cultivation on this plot. Then he left for the Gulf, and she turned to ecologically balanced plantation crops. Now her land has a mosaic of agricultural activities at any time of the year, and her cash income has trebled.

In nearby Andhra Pradesh, a woman's throat dries in the hot winds that scoop fine soil from the family's one-hectare field. Here, as in well over half of the cropped area in the country, dryland conditions impose a stark lifestyle on farming households such as hers. For three months in the year, the family scrapes the scalped land for a poor foodgrains crop, defenceless against drought years. During the other months, the men might migrate to construction sites or cities for work, and women stay behind to coax a living out of animals, poultry, petty trade. Yet a revolution is underfoot and dryland women farmers will be at its pulsating core. The Government's research programmes of scientific rainfed farming promise to raise outputs manifold and to develop 'dry' high yielding varieties of seeds.

Marigold flowers crest the hair of a landless agricultural wage labourer in Maharashtra. Here is a genealogy of manual workers. The pursuit of wage labour comes naturally to her and the family. But work is available fitfully, and at below-subsistence wages. Now the Employment Guarantee Scheme provides a minimum fortification against want. She complains of the long hours, the contractor's wiles, the lack of civic facilities at camp sites but proudly asserts that the EGS has given life a backbone. It has shown that work is her birthright.

For the landless and subsistence farmers, a country-wide subsidy-cum-loan scheme has been implemented. These households are assisted to acquire a productive asset to augment their income. Women too have taken loans, often for cattle and goats.

When the cow is sick, the vet instructs the husband on how to treat it. While the woman listens in an inner room. Almost all the work of tending animals is done by women. Her skill at animal husbandry in Karnataka is common to countless other women across the country. This provides the basis for a phenomenon described as the White Revolution, under which India has emerged as the world's third largest milk producer. Income from milk has invested village homes with gleaming brass vessels, new clothes, nourishment, more education, but perhaps not enough status gain for the woman.

There are these sisters who graduated in architecture and hotel management, respectively. One works with a busy firm of architects in Chandigarh, the other is an executive in a Mumbai hotel. Life has a limitless promise—Life is not only marriage for them.

As a research associate in Astro Physics, a woman from Jammu and Kashmir observes galaxies. But her head is not in the clouds. She is equally interested in solar cookers and smokeless chulhas (mud ovens) which will reduce women's involuntary inhalation of kitchen smoke, save time and provide higher calorific energy directly to the vessels.

A young married woman who works in a Mumbai bank dreams of new clothes, movies, festive occasions and leisure. After a ritzy, extravagant wedding, she moved into her husband's joint family home. Today, her dreams are vulnerable to the reality of the 'double day'; work at the office and at home, all of which must be executed with a disarming smile. However, she has declined to hand over her salary to her mother-in-law, defying a fairly common convention.

Professional women are pursuing careers in a vast range of modern sectors. They include scientists, doctors, engineers, lawyers, administrative and police officials, diplomats, teachers, media experts and airline pilots.

But women's work is a statistical paradox. Official statistics recognise only one-seventh of the country's women as gainfully employed, while the rest are presumably non-gainfully engaged. This raises the question of the valuation of women's work. Consider this woman's work-day. Before the chilly dawn in the Uttar Pradesh hills, she has swept the dwelling, chopped the fodder and fed the buffalo, collected the animal dung and started the fire for the children's morning snack before they leave for school. The daylight hours are claimed by the terraced farm-holding, some walnut and apple trees, the mountain spring, inclined pastures, hearth and animals. Twilight and night are for the children and a husband who is on leave from a job in the plains, or has abandoned himself to a lethargic life.

Yet this woman would occur in the national accounting statistics as chronically underemployed. As in other parts of the world, the question of evaluation of women's work engages attention, but defies solution. Modernising society assesses workers via the index of cash earnings. Women work predominantly in the non-valorised, unorganised and household sectors, where transactions are not monetised. And women's contribution to family life is without a price tag. A woman in Bangalore tends an ailing father-in-law; another visits her son's school to talk to his teacher. Another woman in Orissa prays for her family's prosperity while one in Manipur wipes a child's tear. Women weave the tapestry of life with wisdom, resourcefulness and extremes of self-effacement.

And women everywhere reproduce beauty which nourishes the eye—on walls adorned with earth plaster, mirrors, seeds; in auspicious floor and wall drawings daubed with fresh colours of turmeric and banyan leaves; in vivid textures; in the rhythm of dance. Their music is creased into the life cycle, lilting, sonorous.

A woman is her children; without them she is nothing, observe many women in towns and villages. Women derive their status from their husbands, and power from their sons. But alternative views are emerging.

Unfettered fertility is a by-product of the patriarchal social system, and equally of a habitual casualness to child production. The informal economy has a phenomenal capacity to assimilate, and the populace has banked on its elasticity. But now more and more women are making the link between boundless child-bearing and the quality of life. In less than ten years, tubectomies have increased five-fold; today tubectomies outnumber vasectomies by 6 to 1. The Government aids family planning by providing a high-density delivery service for contraception and sterilisation. The primary question is that of stimulating demand for these services and women have proved to be motivated clients.

Primary health care has undergone a change in outlook. The health infrastructure, whose hardware reaches almost all large villages, has been complemented by village women trained in mother-child health, family planing, control of blindness, tuberculosis, leprosy, malaria eradication and sanitation. Reports from several parts of the country indicate that in three years, Community Health Guides have reduced infant mortality sharply, achieved 90 per cent family planning practice by eligible couples, introduced sanitary soak-pits in villages and secured bank loans for women's supplementary income generation.

Meet a Community Health Guide who has initiated a movement of community health care and community afforestation in a village in Maharashtra. Window sill nurseries festoon the dwellings, the saplings awaiting transfer to eroded field boundaries. Women's links with trees and plants have been celebrated in ancient texts. Exclaims a goddess: "I shall support the whole world with the life-giving vegetables which I shall grow out of my body." To our forebears, trees were not only the abode of female deities, but also contained their essence and divinity. Women represented the deified vegetation energies. And today, this Community Health Guide mingles health and forestry, spearheading a movement for ecological restoration at the village level.

A 12-year-old girl draws neat diagrams assigned to her as homework. She is unmindful of the crowded ambience of her Kolkata tenement home. There is love and literacy in her family. She tries to understand Tagore and Vivekananda. She hopes to go to medical college and if, there is money, she is confident her parents will encourage her. Her sister married by choice and she is sure that her parents will not insist on an arranged marriage for her.

In a village in Uttar Pradesh, primary school students gambol and roll in the mud outside the schoolroom. The teacher is not present.

There is only one girl amongst the frolicking students. There are many girls on enrolment day, but then their parents withdraw them to look after the babies, and to help with the housework. Mid-day meal programmes introduced in some States have increased school attendance, especially by girl students who sling their siblings on the hip, and attend classes.

Girls are known to be industrious and diligent students. Today, in the age group 5-19 years, female literacy is significantly higher than 20 years ago. Education up to higher secondary level is free for girls. University education is heavily subsidised.

In contrast, however, the programme of adult education for women has not succeeded and women lapse into illiteracy soon after the short-term courses are over. Yet, vocation-related literacy programmes have proved effective.

Women understand that their vote is important. Candidates to village panchayats, multi-purpose co-operatives, the State Assembly and the national Parliament woo women at election time. But they do not vote regularly. Indian women have participated with unreserved enthusiasm in the electoral process on issues of national concern. Their participation during the national struggle for freedom moved Gandhiji to observe: "The awakening of our women has helped mightily to awaken India. We cannot achieve freedom without them."

Historic changes have taken place in law as it relates to women. The judiciary has taken an enlightened stand and dismantled the legal framework for the exercise of some archaic practices. For instance, it is no longer possible to petition for the restitution of conjugal rights, or to alienate women from coparcenary rights to dwellings.

In 1964, Nagamani filed a petition in the high court for the restoration of the custody of her children, aged 3 and 5 years, who were forcibly separated from her when she left home on her husband's unlawful second marriage. But the high court allowed her access to the children only on the ground that after the divorce, she had married again. Today, a mother is almost guaranteed the custody of her children as the courts have ruled that a mother has a more 'onerous' role in the upbringing and well-being of a child.

Deep concerns animate women's lives. They do not have resources and skills for permanent, well-paid jobs. They are investing disproportionate time and energy into firewood collection and fetching of drinking water. Women do not yet determine their own fertility and tend to be poor in health. Their children lack opportunities for a life of joy and achievement. Society subjects women to acts of physical violence. Women are themselves thoughtless practitioners of infructuous social practices that have to be shunned. Women seek status in the family. They seek dignity in society.

Five thousand years ago, an artist sculpted the leitmotif of Indian women's strength and authority. A girl, whose lean limbs show the grace of running through forest glades and climbing trees in the Harappan era, stands with an easy assurance, one hand on her waist. The body is proud in a stance of power and youthful promise.

Gradually, we begin to see the new woman arising out of past tradition and current imperatives. There is a transformation, but not, it seems, complete rejection of social values. The women's movement is assisting society to create space for the new Indian woman—a significant being who is poised to conduct India in the new millennium.

And nobody is asking if the accompanying social revolution is feminine or masculine, because they know that it is human.

—oo(O)oo—

BIBLIOGRAPHY

Agarwal, V. S. *India, as Known to Panini.* Lucknow, India: 1953.

Aiyangar, K. V. R. *Aspects of the Social and Political System of Manusmriti.* Lucknow, India: 1949.

Aiyangar, K. V. R. *Some Aspects of the Hindu View of Life According to Dharmasastra.* Vadodra, India: 1932.

Aiyappan, A. *Nair Polyandry*, 1932.

Allen, J. *et al. Women in Top Jobs—Four Studies in Achievements.* London, U.K.: George Allen and Unwin, 1946.

Altekar, A. S. *The Position of Women in Hindu Civilisation.* Varanasi, India: Motilal Banarsidas, 1956.

Angell, Robert Cooley. *The Family Encounters the Depression.* New York, U.S.A.: Scribners, 1936.

Anonymous. *Adi Parva.* Critical Edition. Pune, India: Bhandarkar Oriental Research Institute, 1933.

Anonymous. *Brahma Purana,* Anandashrama Sanskrit Series, 1895.

Anonymous. *Census of India, 2001.* New Delhi, India: Government of India, 2002.

Anonymous. *Education in the States. Statistical Surveys for 1970-71 and 1971-72.* New Delhi, India: Ministry of Education.

Anonymous. *Social Welfare in India.* New Delhi, India: Planning Commission, Government of India, 1975.

Anonymous. *Women's Employment in Asian Countries.* Geneva, Switzerland: International Labour Organisation (ILO), 1953.

Appadorai, Angodipuram (Ed.). *Status of Women in South Asia.* Mumbai, India: UNESCO, 1954.

Baber, Roy E. *Marriage and the Family.* New York, U.S.A.: McGraw Hill, 1939.

Bader, Clarisse. *Women in Ancient India: Moral and Literary Studies.* (Translated by Mary E. R. Martin). London, U.K.: 1925.

Baig, Tara Ali. *Women of India.* New Delhi, India: 1958.

Basham, A. L. *The Wonder That Was India.* London, U.K.: 1954.

Beard, Mary R. *Woman as a Force in History: A Study in Traditions and Realities.* New York, U.S.A.: Macmillan, 1946.

Bhandarkar, R. G. *Vaishnavism, Saivism and Minor Religious Systems.* Strasbourg, Germany: 1913.

Buehler, G. *Laws of Manu.* London, U.K.: 1886.

Buehler, G. (Ed.). *Apastambha Dharmashastra.* Mumbai, India: 1932.

Burgess, E. W. and Locke, H. J. *The Family: From Institution to Companionship.* New York, U.S.A.: American Book Company, 1945.

Chakravarty, B. M. Patterns of Family Living and Marriage in 100 Middle Class Families. Ph.D. Thesis. Delhi School of Social Work (Unpublished).

Chakladar, H. C. *Social Life in Ancient India—Studies in Vatsyayana's Kamasutra,* 1929.

Chandrakant, L. S. *Polytechnic Education in India.* Mumbai, India: B. D. Taraporewala and Sons, 1971.

Chandrakant, L. S. *Technical Education in India.* New Delhi, India: Ministry of Scientific Research and Cultural Affairs, Government of India, 1962.

Chatterjee, M. *Feminism and Women's Human Rights* (two volumes). Jaipur, India: Aavishkar Publishers, Distributors, 2004.

Chaudhuri, Nirad C. *The Continent of Circe: An Essay on the Peoples of India.* London, U.K.: Chatto and Windus, 1965; New York, U.S.A.: Oxford University Press, 1966.

Chaudhuri, Nirad, C. *The Autobiography of an Unknown Indian.* London, U.K.: Macmillan and Co., 1951; Mumbai, India: Jaico Publishing House, 1973.

Childe, V. Gordon. *New Light on the Most Ancient East.* London, U.K.: 1934.

Coombs, Philip H. *The World Educational Crisis.* Indian Reprint. Allahabad, India: A. H. Wheeler, 1970.

Cormack, Margaret. *The Hindu Woman.* Mumbai, India: Asia Publishing House, 1961.

Das, Saragadhar. *Purdah: the Status of Indian Women.* New York, U.S.A.: Vanguard, 1932.

de Bary, Theodore, W. M. *Sources of Indian Tradition.* Indian Reprint. Delhi, India: Motilal Banarsidas, 1958.

De Rougemont, Denis. *Love in the Western World.* (Translated by Montogomery Belgian). New York, U.S.A.: Harcourt Brace, 1940.

Desai, Neera. *Women in Modern India.* Mumbai, 1957.

Deshpande, S. R. *Economic and Social Status of Women Workers in India.* New Delhi, India: Ministry of Labour, Government of India, 1963.

Devi, S. *Tradition and Modernity Among Indian Women.* Jaipur, India: Pointer Publishers, 1998.

Devi, S. *Women's Status and Social Change.* Jaipur, India: Pointer Publishers, 1999.

Dollard, John *et al.* *Frustration and Aggression.* New Haven, U.S.A.: Yale University Press, 1939.

Dubois, J. A. *Hindu Manners, Customs and Ceremonies.* Oxford, U. K.: Oxford University Press, 1906.

Dutt, M. N. *Agni Purana.* (2 volumes). (Ed.). Panchanan. Kolkata, India: Tarkaratna, 1882.

Exner, Max J. *The Sexual Side of Marriage.* New York, U.S.A.: Norton, 1932.

Fyzee, Asaf A. A. *Outlines of Muhammadan Law.* Oxford, U.K.: Oxford University Press, 1952.

Griffin, Willis and Pareek, Udai. *The Process of Planned Change in Education.* Mumbai, India: Somaiya Publications, 1970.

Hiremath, R. C. *Women in the Changing World.* Jaipur, India: Pointer Publishers, 2002.

Holt, Arthur E. *The Fate of the Family in the Modern World.* Chicago, U.S.A.: Willet Clark, 1936.

Hultzsch, E. (Ed.). *Baudhayana Dharmasastra.* Leipzig, Germany: 1884; Kashi Sanskrit Series, 1995.

Jolly, J. *Hindu Law and Customs.* (Translated from the German edition of 1896). Kolkata, 1936.

Kane, P. V. *History of Dharmasastra, Ancient and Medieval Religions and Civil Law.* Pune, India: Bhandarkar Oriental Research Institute, 1930-1953.

Kapadia, K. M. *Marriage and Family in India.* Mumbai, India: Oxford University Press, 1963.

Kapur, Promilla. *Changing Status of the Working Women in India.*

Kapur, Promilla. *Marriage and the Working Women in India.* Delhi, India: Vikas Publications, 1970.

Karve, J. *Kinship Organisation in India,* 1953.

Kaushik, V. *Women's Movements and Human Rights.* Jaipur, India: Pointer Publishers, 1997.

Kothari, D. S. *Educational Science and National Development.* Mumbai, India: Asia Publishing House, 1970.

Law, Bimala Charan. *Women in Buddhist Literature.* Srilanka: 1927.

Majumdar, D. N. 'Family and marriage in a polyandrous society'. *Eastern Anthropologist,* volume 10, 1955.

Mees, G. H. *Dharma and Society.* The Hague, 1935.

Montague, Ashley. *The Natural Superiority of Women.* London, U.K.: George Allen and Unwin Ltd., 1954.

Myrdal, Gunnar. *Asian Drama: An Enquiry into the Poverty of Nations.* London, U.K. Penguin, 1968.

Nehru, Jawaharlal. *Autobiography.* London, U.K.: 1936.

Nurrulah and Naik. *A Student's History of Education in India.* Kolkata, India: Macmillan and Co., 1962.

Pinkham, Mildreth Worth. *Women in Sacred Scriptures of Hinduism.* New York, U.S.A.: 1941.

Prabhu, P. H. *Hindu Social Organisations.* Mumbai, India: 1954.

Pruthi, R. *History, Society & Culture in Ancient India* (two volumes). Jaipur, India: Pointer Publishers, 1999.

Pruthi, R. *Vedic Traditions and Rituals.* Jaipur, India: Pointer Publishers, 2000.

Rajkumar. *Women & and the Indian Freedom Struggle.* (Seven volumes). Jaipur, India: Pointer Publishers, 1999.

Ramabai, Pandita Saraswati. *The High Caste Hindu Women.* Philadelphia, U.S.A.: 1888.

Ross, A. D. *The Hindu Family in Urban Setting.* Toronto, Canada: 1961.

Sengupta, Padmini. *Women Workers of India.* New York, U.S.A.: 1960.

Sahu, A. *Women's Liberation and Human Rights.* Jaipur, India: Pointer Publishers, 2000.

Shastri, Shakuntala Rao. *Women in Sacred Laws.* Mumbai, India: 1960.

Shastri, Shakuntala Rao. *Women in the Vedic Age.* Mumbai, India: 1954.

Singh, Khushwant. *The Sikhs*. London, U.K.: 1953.

Stanley, Eugene. *Planning Occupational Education and Training for Development*. New Delhi, India: Orient Longman, 1970.

Thomas, P. *Women and Marriage in India*. London, U.K.: 1939.

Verrier, Elwin. *The Aboriginals*. Mumbai, India: Oxford Pamphlets on Indian Affairs, 1944.

Verrier, Elwin. *The Muria and their Ghotul*. Mumbai, India: Oxford University Press, 1947.

Verrier, Elwin. *Tribal Myths of Orissa*. London, U.K.: 1954.

Vora, Dhairyabala. *Evolution of Morals in the Epics*. Mumbai, India: 1959.

Wasi, Muriel. *Transition*. Delhi, India: Atma Ram and Sons, Ltd., 1971.

Watts, Allan, W. *Nature, Man and Woman: A New Approach to Sexual Experience*. London, U.K.: Thames and Hudson, 1958.

Woodsmall, Ruth Frances. *Women and the New East*. Washington, U.S.A.: 1960.

—oo(O)oo—

INDEX

R

S

T

U

V

W

—oo(O)oo—